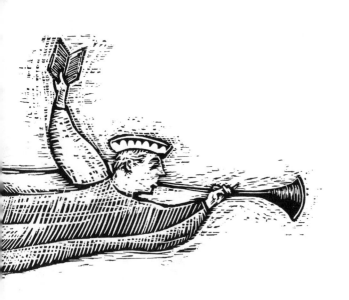

Moroni: *a brief theological introduction*

This publication was made possible by generous support from the Laura F. Willes Center for Book of Mormon Studies, part of the Neal A. Maxwell Institute for Religious Scholarship at Brigham Young University.

Published by the Neal A. Maxwell Institute for Religious Scholarship, Brigham Young University, Provo, Utah. The copyright for the 2013 text of The Book of Mormon is held by The Church of Jesus Christ of Latter-day Saints, Salt Lake City, Utah; that text is quoted throughout and used by permission.

Printed in the United States of America

ISBN: 978-0-8425-0013-5

LIBRARY OF CONGRESS CONTROL NUMBER: 2020902730

# Moroni

*a brief theological introduction*

BRIGHAM YOUNG UNIVERSITY

NEAL A. MAXWELL INSTITUTE

PROVO, UTAH

David F. Holland

*The Book of Mormon: brief theological introductions* series seeks Christ in scripture by combining intellectual rigor and the disciple's yearning for holiness. It answers Elder Neal A. Maxwell's call to explore the book's "divine architecture": "There is so much more in the Book of Mormon than we have yet discovered. The book's divine architecture and rich furnishings will increasingly unfold to our view, further qualifying it as '*a marvelous work and a wonder.*' (Isaiah 29:14) . . . All the rooms in this mansion need to be explored, whether by valued traditional scholars or by those at the cutting edge. Each plays a role, and one LDS scholar cannot say to the other, '*I have no need of thee.*'" [1] (1 Corinthians 12:21)

For some time, faithful scholars have explored the book's textual history, reception, historicity, literary quality, and more. This series focuses particularly on theology—the scholarly practice of exploring a scriptural text's implications and its lens on God's work in the world. Series volumes invite Latter-day Saints to discover additional dimensions of this treasured text but leave to prophets and apostles their unique role of declaring its definitive official doctrines. In this case, theology, as opposed to authoritative doctrine, relates to the original sense of the term as, literally, reasoned "God talk." The word also designates a well-developed academic field, but it is the more general sense of the term that most often applies here. By engaging each scriptural book's theology on its own terms, this series explores the spiritual and intellectual force of the ideas appearing in the Latter-day Saints' "keystone" scripture.

Series authors and editors possess specialized professional training that informs their work but, significantly, each takes Christ as theology's proper end because he is the proper end of all scripture and all reflection on it. We, too, "talk of Christ, we rejoice in Christ, we preach of Christ...that our children may know to what source they may look for a remission of their sins" (2 Nephi 25:26). Moreover, while experts in the modern disciplines of philosophy, theology, literature, and history, series authors and editors also work explicitly within the context of personal and institutional commitments both to Christian discipleship and to The Church of Jesus Christ of Latter-day Saints. These volumes are not official Church publications but can be best understood in light of these deep commitments. And because we acknowledge that scripture demands far more than intellectual experimentation, we call readers' attention to the processes of conversion and sanctification at play on virtually every scriptural page.

Individual series authors offer unique approaches but, taken together, they model a joint invitation to readers to engage scripture in their own way. No single approach to theology or scriptural interpretation commands preeminence in these volumes. No volume pretends to be the final word on theological reflection for its part of the Book of Mormon. Varied perspectives and methodologies are evident throughout. This is intentional. In addition, though we recognize love for the Book of Mormon is a "given" for most Latter-day Saint readers, we also share the conviction that, like the gospel of Jesus Christ itself, the Book of Mormon is inexhaustible.[2] These volumes invite readers to slow down and read scripture more thoughtfully and transformatively. Elder Maxwell cautioned against reading the Book of Mormon as "hurried tourists" who scarcely venture beyond "the entry hall."[3] To that end, we dedicate this series to his apostolic conviction that there is always more to learn from the Book of Mormon and much to be gained from our faithful search for Christ in its pages.
—The Editors

# Contents

# Introduction

*a theologian of the gifts*

Moroni comes to us as a proclaimer of gifts. We first encounter him in the record of the restoration as the herald of a buried scriptural treasure. We then hear his voice on the title page of the Book of Mormon, where he introduces us to a sacred text that he describes as coming forth "by the gift and power of God" and as having been translated "by the gift of God." He eventually reappears in the later portions of the book, bearing the records of his father and of Ether, offerings that he has completed and conveyed for his readers' benefit. In Richard Rust's judgment, Moroni's gifting of other writer's words unmistakably proceeds "out of his own generosity of spirit."[1] Generous giving lies at the heart of Moroni's message and his sense of mission.

Moroni's theology—embodied in his ministry and expressed in his writing—unmistakably points us toward the generosity of God. A giver leads us toward the Giver. Moroni draws our attention to godly grace and its charisms—those endowments of the Spirit that grant fallen humans a measure of divine ability. His record contains an account of the proper conferral of the gift of the Holy Ghost; it presents his father's theologically profound sermon on the gifts of faith, hope, and charity; and it concludes (and thus completes the Book of Mormon as a whole) on a discussion of spiritual gifts.[2]

The term *gift* appears more frequently in the writings of Moroni than in any other portion of the Book of Mormon. In a characteristic editorial gloss on the record of Ether, Moroni summarizes Jesus Christ's redemptive work by declaring that the Savior "prepared a way that thereby others might be partakers of the heavenly gift" and, thus, "ye may also have hope, and be partakers of the gift" (Ether 12:8, 9). Moroni's closest rival in the frequency of references to *gifts* is his father. Mormon's book offers an especially striking sequence: He opens with the declaration that because of Nephite wickedness "there were no gifts from the Lord" bestowed upon that people; Moroni concludes that same book with an earnest plea for all to believe unceasingly that the "gifts" of God can and will continue (Morm. 1:14; 9:7). Where Mormon laments the temporary absence of the gifts, Moroni declares their eternal promise. The book that bears Moroni's name repeatedly affirms that message.

His book, this witness to a giving God, is specifically addressed to his "brethren, the Lamanites [of] some future day" (Moro. 1:4). He thus opens with the conviction that God will preserve the Lamanite people, that the Book of Mormon is an offering intended primarily for them, and that Moroni can deliver to them an expression of faith, hope, and love across hundreds of years of history and despite centuries of violent antagonisms. His whole book thus rests on a belief in divine gifts that can transcend time and outlast human conflict. The implicit message is that some gifts take a very, very long time to have their intended effect.

One of the motifs running through Moroni's book is that God's gifts often come in complementary or even contrasting pairings. Most notably, Moroni repeatedly alternates references to the blessings of stabilizing ecclesiastical structures and the promise of personal spirituality. The disciple's life, as he frames it, is both embedded in a well-ordered community and endowed with the ability to connect directly with the divine.

These complementary gifts of Church formality and spiritual freedom balance, check, and enrich each other. To lay hold "upon every good gift" is to cling to both of them, even when they seem to pull us in differing directions (Moro. 10:30). Moroni's theology repeatedly calls on us to live gratefully at the convergence of competing truths, recognizing the shared divinity of God's diverse gifts. His book attests to a divine plan that elevates us on the tension of contrast and complement.

As the book opens, we find Moroni roaming through a forbidding environment. As it closes, we envision him ascending toward heaven. His personal transformation over the course of his book, from plodding wanderer to soaring angel, illustrates the redemptive impact of God's greatest gift, Jesus Christ. Both human and divine, both embodied and spirit, both just and merciful, both crucified and alive, Jesus himself represents the elevating contrasts that often lie at the heart of God's giving.

The theology woven through Moroni's writings raises a series of essential questions: What is the relative agency of the giver and the receiver in the exchange of a gift? Do true gifts come with obligations or are they given freely? How does a diverse distribution of divine gifts affect the way our communities function and our relationships develop? To study the book of Moroni is both to encounter these questions and to find resources for answering them. It is to shed light on some of the most central pillars of our faith.

Most importantly, through Moroni's work we come closer to understanding the character of a God whose nature is to give.

# A Note about Order

*the soteriological sequence*

The thematic progression of this book almost always mirrors the thematic progression of the book of Moroni. That is, this book begins where Moroni begins and ends where he ends, marching through his themes in roughly the same order he has established. It does so because I suspect that the book of Moroni—like various other sections of the Book of Mormon—is consciously arranged for a specific theological purpose. The order matters.

Note that Moroni has composed his book from a mix of materials: brief histories of earlier events, the centuries-old wording of the sacrament prayers, a sermon by his late father, a pair of letters from the same, and a concluding declaration of his own testimony. No other section of the Book of Mormon does so little to narrate contemporary events, and no other section rests so heavily on such a montage of sources from former periods. Severely isolated, with only the records of previous generations as his companions, Moroni knows more about the past than about what is happening in his present moment. The book of Moroni, in contrast to the books that precede it, cannot be an account of the titular figure's own times. It is more an assemblage of artifacts than the chronicle of an era.

Largely freed from the role of chronicler, Moroni enjoys a particular liberty to assemble his historically disparate materials according to his own purposes. The question, then, is whether he has ordered them with some larger point in mind. It looks to me very much like he has.

To invoke a term that theologians often use for doctrines related to salvation, there is a *soteriological* sequence conveyed in the ordering of the book of Moroni. Consider the essential elements of the book's structure.

① It opens with a resolute witness of Jesus Christ and a reference to the uncertainty Moroni feels about his temporal circumstances and his ability to do the work asked of him.

② It then immediately bounces back four hundred years to discuss the ordinances that Christ outlined and modeled during his visit to the Americas.

③ It goes on to describe the church that coalesced around those ordinances, depicting a community of mutual care and mercy.

④ It subsequently jumps ahead four centuries to reproduce a sermon Mormon gave to the remnant of that church, a sermon that culminates in the highest of Christian virtues: pure love.

⑤ That sermon concludes with a promise that the Saints who receive the essential gifts of grace will come to resemble the soul of the Savior, a soul in which love is the defining quality.

⑥ The sermon is followed by two letters from Mormon that—at first glance—seem somewhat arbitrarily placed but ultimately appear to be included as guards against a misreading of the material that precedes them.

⑦ Finally, the book concludes with a declaration of God's gifts to humanity and an expression of profound confidence that, through Jesus Christ, Moroni will be redeemed.

Looking at these elements with a sense of Moroni's purpose in mind, the steps of his soteriological sequence begin to emerge. The book opens and closes with an expression of faith in Jesus: first as an anchor in a time of earthly insecurity and finally as the source of eternal assurance. Between this beginning and end, within the interior chapters of his book, Moroni's path to salvation runs as follows: The Savior gives the rituals that form the church. The church then helps inform the soul. The soul then conforms to Christ. And every step on that path acknowledges the generosity of a giving God, whose gifts flow through the greatest Gift of all—his only begotten Son.

Moroni's materials are positioned to suggest a particular relationship among these saving elements. For this reason, I have—with one early exception—followed his topics in the order he has arranged them.

# 1

## Resolute and Unsure

*"I had supposed not to have written more, but I have not as yet perished."* —*Moroni 1:1*

*"And I, Moroni, will not deny the Christ."* —*Moroni 1:3*

The book of Moroni opens on a complex note of uncertainty and conviction. As the war-weary prophet begins the record, his suppositions have proved faulty. He is surprised still to be alive. Having outlived his self-predicted passing, his next steps are unsure. The one thing he knows is that he must preserve his testimony of Jesus Christ.

Moroni is strikingly transparent about his lack of clarity. He will not pretend to know more than he does. It is almost as if, in his state of unsettled expectations, he is determined to challenge his reader's easy assumptions: We expect the prophetic voice to be confident, but his is hesitant. We expect a prophesied future to be clear, but his is cloudy. We do not expect prophets to flee from a fight with the forces of evil, but Moroni is on the run.

Or, more precisely, he *wanders* (Moro. 1:3). The meaning conjured by such a verb suggests indeterminacy, motion without a set destination. The wanderer does not know where the journey leads, only that he must keep moving.

He is certain about the Christ. So much else seems unsure.

*"I write a few more things, contrary to that which I had supposed . . . that perhaps they may be of worth unto my brethren, the Lamanites, in some future day."*
—*Moroni 1:4*

His book is for the Lamanites. He believes that it will be received by them at some point, but he does not know exactly when or how. Given the great atrocities Nephites had committed against Lamanites, Moroni's offer to them rests on an audacious hope, a dream that they will eventually accept the sincere gift of an erstwhile adversary. Surely the apparent odds against such a future add to his sense of uncertainty.

An eminent scholar of American culture, Richard Brodhead, in a lecture on prophetic figures in the history of the United States, listed "inmitigable certainty" as the first of any self-proclaimed prophet's characteristics.[1] That description only partially fits the opening chapter of Moroni, where the prophetic author's certainty is deeply compromised by the language of contingency. Note the recurring tone of the words in Moroni 1:4: *a few, perhaps, may, some . . . day.* It would be difficult to pack more equivocation into one sentence.

One of the things about which Moroni is consistently uncertain is the quality of the text he is composing. He fears that it may contain errors. In fact, in earlier books he seems rather convinced that he and his father have made mistakes, but he is not sure where and what those flaws might be. The inability to pinpoint the source of one's unease can turn potentially motivating dissatisfaction into a kind of paralyzing anxiety. Moroni is clearly haunted by the thought that errors are lurking somewhere in this offering that he had hoped to perfect (Morm. 8:17).

Rather than succumb to such paralysis, however, Moroni resolves to press on, and he asks the readers to do likewise, holding out hope that God's work will be done despite human imperfection. Indeed, at some points he seems to take courage from the idea that God's work will be done *through* human imperfection.

In an editorial interjection at the end of his father Mormon's book, Moroni offers a representative bit of handwringing that invites readers to find personal benefit in the authors' errors "that ye may learn to be more wise than we have been" (Morm. 9:31). In a similar editorial moment in the book of Ether, he raises the issue again, reminding readers that imperfection is a call to meekness and to the divine grace that can make "weak things strong" (Ether 12:27). On the unattributed title page of the Book of Mormon, of which he is the most likely author, Moroni addresses the matter yet again, pleading with readers not to condemn the things of God because of the inevitable flaws in the humans tasked with conveying them. Everywhere Moroni appears, this issue comes up.

When Moroni seems to be at his most anxious about the errors in his record, he repeatedly comes to see his heightened awareness of his own imperfection as a source of potential power, a resource that can be mined for future capacity through the Lord's gifts of grace. The promise that God would turn weakness to strength—a process in which faith in Jesus Christ is paramount—is immediately fulfilled in Moroni's declaration of that principle. That is, he does not just preach it; in the preaching of it, he demonstrates it. His own anxiety has been the means to profound theological insight, his awareness of his own weakness a pathway to some of the record's most poignant moments.

In the sermon that forms Moroni chapter 7, Mormon puts a word on this quality—this deep recognition of one's own deficiency coupled with a profound belief in God's empowering grace—which combination of humility and trust he posits as the activating agent of all divine gifts. Mormon calls it *meekness*. Moroni exemplifies it over and over again.[2]

Throughout his writings, then, Moroni conveys self-doubting questions about himself, his future, and his work. These questions are recurrently transformed into a source of light at that point where they intersect with enduring faith in Jesus Christ. The book of Moroni opens at just such an intersection.

The first two theological declarations of the book of Moroni intertwine in its opening verses: Jesus is the Christ, and uncertainty is an unavoidable part of our existence in this mortal world. The uncertainty affects even the most devoted disciples at even their most urgent moments of need. The sustaining gifts of faith in Christ are the necessary complement to that uncertainty, and those gifts come not only despite our inadequacies but also sometimes through them. A prophet on the lam—troubled by the specter of his mistakes, inclined to worry and self-doubt in a world falling apart around him, and determined to hold on to his faith—shows these things to be true as he composes the final chapters of an epic book.

14

# 2

# The Gifts of Sacred Community in a Time of Chaos

*"And on as many as they laid their hands,*
*fell the Holy Ghost."* —*Moroni 2:3*

Against the backdrop of the high drama in which Moroni finds himself—a flight for survival against mounting odds—the next chapters of the book of Moroni head in a decidedly undramatic direction. Instruction on the proper way to confer the gift of the Holy Ghost, the steps for ordaining priests and teachers, and the specific wording for consecrating the sacrament of the Lord's Supper follow in rapid succession. These things come from a man well aware that he will not live to see a church community capable of implementing these practices. They are offered to a people, the Lamanites, who at that point showed very little interest in the message and had very little reason to trust the messenger.

The prosaic, procedural elements of these passages stand in such stark contrast to the existential saga that is playing out all around Moroni that they force us to confront some challenging questions: Why would a fugitive prophet, running for his life, suddenly begin etching specific ritual procedures onto the plates? If these things were so important for a future church, why have they been left for this unexpected appendix to the record? If these instructions are not that critical for the projected readers—after all, greater detail on all these ordinances would be directly revealed to future prophets —why devote these precious final words to them at all?

A possible explanation lurks in Moroni's unsettled context. And in that explanation lies another essential theological truth: We need each other. Indeed, this truth fuels the next steps in the *soteriological* sequence that follows.

*the sociality of creature and creator*
*"We ask thee..."*   *—Moroni 4:3; 5:2*

Aristotle famously argued that human beings are—by nature and by necessity—social creatures. We need community. He wrote that any being incapable of living a communal life, or so self-reliant as to have no need for such an association, must not be human. Such a figure would have to be either a beast or a god.[1]

Aristotle's assertion about a humanity built for community resonates powerfully in Latter-day Saint theology, which promises both temporal gathering and eternal sociality (D&C 33:6; 130:1–2). However, his claim about the self-sufficiency and isolation of divinity runs directly counter to our understanding of a God whose glory and joy—and, indeed, whose very essence—are profoundly relational (Ex. 25:8; Luke 15:11–32; Moses 7). Both the humanity we have *and* the godliness we seek are essentially social.

The absence of such interpersonal connection can be devastating. Note that for the first great post-fall sin, Cain killing his brother, Cain's punishment was to wander this earth without a community (Gen. 4:12–14). Interestingly, the Book of Mormon scholar Matthew Bowen has given us reason to believe Cain was on Moroni's mind in these final years of his ministry.[2]

Grant Hardy has noted that Moroni's tendency to speak in terms of "we" and "us"—grouping himself with all the other Book of Mormon writers—"is unexpected from someone who has spent more than a decade utterly alone."[3] Moroni's circumstances and his rhetoric may actually be closely related. Perhaps Moroni had conjured a fictive community of his fellow writers to make up for the isolation of his physical surroundings. He created a "we" with whom he could travel his difficult road. The human hunger for connection seems irresistible here, underscoring a central theological assertion of the restored gospel. No wonder Cain responded to his exile as "greater than I can bear" (Gen. 4:13). Moroni must have wondered how long he could bear his.

Unlike Cain, however, Moroni did have a choice. There were societies he could join—secret combinations and warring tribes—if he were willing to betray both his better nature and his testimony of the Christ. As agonizing as prolonged solitude is to souls wired for connection, Moroni concluded that there is in fact something worse: a community in which inclusion comes at the price of core convictions. And so he walks on, alone with his faith in Jesus, maintaining his mentally projected sense of place among a community of righteous writers and reflecting on what a well-ordered, Christ-centered people once looked like.

For him, that reflection begins with the ordinances.

*of ordinances, order, and a gospel of grace*
*"I am filled with charity, which is everlasting love;*
*wherefore, all children are alike unto me; wherefore,*
*I love little children with a perfect love; and they are*
*all alike and partakers of salvation."* —Moroni 8:17

*"It is mockery before God, denying the mercies of Christ, and the power of his Holy Spirit, and putting trust in dead works."*   —Moroni 8:23

*"They are seeking to put down all power and authority which cometh from God."*   —Moroni 8:28

*"They have lost their love, one towards another."*
—Moroni 9:5

The next five chapters of Moroni's book focus on ritual procedures relating to the gift of the Holy Ghost, the ordaining of church officers, the blessing of the sacrament, and the prerequisites of baptism. Jonathan Stapley has gone so far as to assert that "it was Moroni...who created the foundation of Mormon worship, ending his work with general instructions on church structure and liturgy."[4] Moroni seems to know that this early emphasis on ordinances could be easily misconstrued, and at the end of his record he offers a pair of correctives to make sure we do not misread him. The cautions come in the form of letters from his father. While Moroni places those warnings near his conclusion, I think there might be some value for our purposes in also noting them closer to the beginning. In this book's one major departure from the plan to mirror Moroni's ordering, I suggest that we temporarily jump ahead to the letters from Mormon, even though they do not appear in the book of Moroni until chapters 8 and 9.

I see these two letters functioning as complementary guardrails, or counterpoints, preventing the readers of Moroni's book from veering off to either side of the soteriological path that he is laying out. For instance, without the caveat provided in Mormon's letter in chapter 8, which warns against the doctrinal errors of infant baptism, Moroni's early preoccupation with the ordinances could be taken as a kind of formalism.

In Christian theological discourse, *formalism* refers pejoratively to an emphasis on ritual and outward observances to the neglect of the spiritual content and higher meaning of religious experience. Christian reformers stretching back to Jesus Christ himself have long critiqued the notion that religion is about going through ceremonial motions. Alma's account of the Rameumptom offers the Book of Mormon's most vivid depiction of a formalistic absurdity. Moroni's opening focus on ordinances could make him any easy target for this time-tested theological critique. He accordingly makes sure that we cannot misconstrue his meaning.

Throughout the modern era, the contrast between "cold formalism" and true "heart religion" has driven the theology of some of Western Christianity's most influential figures, such as Methodism's founder, John Wesley, who wrote that we must "guard those who are just setting their faces toward heaven . . . from formality, from mere outside religion, which has almost driven heart-religion out of the world."[5] Wesley retained more of the traditional rituals of Christian worship—including infant baptism—than did some of his more radically reforming contemporaries, but he was adamant that these things should not be allowed to supplant the soul's true piety. Like many other theologians, he sought the right relationship between the stability of outward forms and the elevation of sublime inward feeling. A balancing act between the dangers of formalism on one hand and structural instability on the other has long been the quest of Christian thinkers. Moroni's book shows him to be working on something of the same challenge.

When Moroni sorted through the artifacts at his disposal and decided to include his father's letter on infant baptism, which we now have in chapter 8, the intent may well have been to address that very specific doctrinal controversy of whether to baptize children. However, it may also have been to prevent his readers more generally from taking Moroni's own early focus on the ordinances too far. The letter contains Mormon's admonition that a belief in infant baptism risks promoting "dead works" to the point that they obscure the love of God and the atoning grace of the Savior (Moro. 8:23). The ordinances, stripped of the spirit of heartfelt devotion and divine love, are worse than empty shells, Mormon's letter cautions. They become obstacles to redemption.

Immediately after issuing a warning against dead works, Mormon and Moroni also prove mindful of the danger that lurks on the other side of the Christian's theological spectrum, an impulse that pushes so aggressively away from formalism that it ends up undermining all structure and outward coherence. Mormon actually begins to warn against this opposite error at the end of his letter on infant baptism: He laments a people antagonistic toward "all power and authority which cometh from God" (Moro. 8:28). The two terms here, *power* and *authority*, are not synonyms; rather, they suggest the importance of both content and form, substance and structure. The need for authoritative outward practices—the necessary complements to inward spiritual power—becomes even clearer in Mormon's second letter.

Writing in that letter of the rapid descent of his people into the most depraved kinds of inhumanity, Mormon explains to his son that "they have lost their love, one towards another" and "they are without order and without mercy" (Moro. 9:5, 18). In that latter

21

pairing, Mormon suggests a link between order and human decency, a sense in which the external structural bonds of community play an important role in developing the genuine sentiments of empathy housed within our hearts. Mormon's second letter—which contains the scriptural record's most nauseatingly graphic references to rape, murder and cannibalism—shows the steep fall of a nation living in *disorder*. Mormon defines them as a people devoid of "civilization," a word that here connotes both collective membership in orderly civil society and the individual's cultivation of the higher human virtues (Moro. 9:11). To lack "order," in this sense, is to risk losing our capacity to love.

Moroni's choice to include this particular pair of letters from Mormon establishes two poles through which his path of salvation proceeds. One letter warns against dead works. The other warns against disorder. Moroni appears to offer them at the end of his book to correct any misreadings that might have crept in along the way. I think it is just as well to preempt those misreadings from the start. As we move through his book, we should do so with those letters in mind, guarding against the threat of leaning too far toward the extremes of empty formalism on one hand or of anarchic antistructuralism on the other. The gifting of his father's two letters to us exemplifies Moroni's tendency to give us pairs of complementary principles meant to both balance and challenge the disciple's life.

Moroni portrays the ordinances as divine gifts. In the theology of gifting embedded in the book of Moroni, the human recipients must be prepared to receive both the gift *and* the high purpose for which it is intended. Separated from its ennobling end, a blessing can be a curse.

*"The manner..."* —Moroni 3:1
*"The manner..."* —Moroni 4:1
*"The manner..."* —Moroni 5:1

When considering that, as his book commences, Moroni is watching his world disintegrate into an anarchy of roving death squads, it hardly seems surprising that his opening chapters would gravitate toward the collective rituals of a unified society. He reflects on the stable procedures of the ordinances, "the manner" of a ceremonially careful church. He begins thinking about his people's most important experience, that moment of the past when Jesus Christ was in their midst and unity had obtained and the correct form of church procedures was clear. In the entire narrative of the Book of Mormon there is no starker contrast than that between the event Moroni reflects on and the reality he is living. Just as starving people dream of feasts, Moroni reacts to his anarchy-enforced isolation by dwelling on the promise of a well-ordered people.

That promise begins with Jesus Christ. With virtually no effort at a transition, Moroni jumps immediately from a brief description of his own lamentable state into an unannotated account of Jesus Christ conferring the ability to "give the Holy Ghost" on the twelve disciples (Moro. 2:2). Moroni reconstructs a system of conferrals that, like the ordering clarity of a line of authority, starts with the Savior and then runs through these apostolic figures, to local priests and teachers, and then to the sacramental bread and wine consumed by every saint. Where Moroni's testimony of Jesus serves as the centering point of his daily survival, his faith in the originating authority of the Christ forms an essential part of the foundation on which his vision of the orderly community rests.

*"And after ye have done this ye shall have power."*
*—Moroni 2:2*

And yet, even as these opening passages on ordination and authorization point to the official structures of a Christian community, Moroni's history of Christ's visit simultaneously reminds us that the authority of office is not the same thing as divine power. Indeed, these chapters seem to insist on driving home a distinction between the two. The act of ordaining may convey a role of particular responsibility within the church, but the power of God is something other than that. It is bigger in its capacity and more universal in its distribution than a narrow fixation on ordination could possibly accommodate.

Note that, in chapter 2, even though Christ gave his twelve disciples the assignment and the authority to confer the gift of the Holy Ghost, the apostles would not have the "power" to accomplish this thing until "after" they had sought the Lord in "mighty prayer" (Moro. 2:2). In other words, the power came not through ordination but through prayer; it was then to be used in a specific way to meet the ordained responsibilities of a particular office.

Consider also the similar implications of chapter 3, which contains Moroni's account of ordaining priests and teachers: "And after this manner did they ordain priests and teachers, according to the gifts and callings of God unto men; and they ordained them by the power of the Holy Ghost, which was in them" (Moro. 3:4). The manner and authorization to confer these offices was a function of the apostles' *calling*, but the *power* to accomplish this thing came from the Holy Ghost.

Moroni's chapters on the ordinances make clear that the power by which the work of God is accomplished proceeds according to gifts available to all followers of the Savior: the exercise of mighty prayer and the presence of the Spirit. Some of Christ's followers are distinctly tasked—called—to use that universal power in a particular way, but that does not privilege them with any different source of divine capacity than that which flows to all members throughout the body of Christ. To put this concept in the language of current Church usage, priesthood office carries the authority of specific community roles, but priesthood power is within the reach of every Saint.

*how to give and how to receive among the saints*
*"The disciples" and "the multitude"* —Moroni 2:3

The two-part processes that Moroni describes in chapters 2 and 3 involve both formal ritual authority and personal spiritual power, suggesting the inextricable intertwining of form and substance. During his visit Jesus seemed to insist that his disciples live and minister at that point where procedural clarity and spiritual profundity converge. To use Paul's metaphor, both the spiritual treasure and the structural vessel must be attended to (2 Cor. 4:7).

The book of Moroni thus sends a challenging message to those who would be the instruments through which divine things flow to others: When we seek to serve as the bearers of God's gifts to those around us, we take upon ourselves a weighty responsibility to be the best vessels of sacred cargo that we can be. Moroni's recounting of the history of Christ's visit reminds us that we can have official authority to convey a divine offering and still not carry the full power that God may be willing to grant us.

At one level, this union of form and substance seems obvious. How could it be otherwise? In his late nineteenth-century work "The Seventy's Course in Theology," B. H. Roberts cited Moroni 3 to establish the point that "priesthood and church organization [are] ineffective without the Holy Ghost."[6] But in this curriculum, Roberts—like so many other latter-day commentators—shifts the focus of this passage to the potency of a charismatic ministry rather than sticking with Moroni's original implications about a particular ordinance's power. This distinction between ministerial potency and ritual efficacy is quite significant.

It is one thing to say that I cannot be a very effective ministering sister or brother without the Holy Ghost (what Roberts seemed to be saying); it is quite another to say that the conferral of the Holy Ghost on a new convert depends on the quality of the officiator's personal spirituality (what Moroni seems to suggest). The latter statement is an element of these verses that modern readers sometimes want to ignore. The small interjection of "mighty prayer" between Jesus's conferral of authority on the disciples and their access to spiritual power, along with the next chapter's clear suggestion that the power to ordain is largely a function of the sanctified spirit that lies within the administrator rather than an inevitable accompaniment to formal ecclesiastical position, raises a series of provocative questions.

Would Moroni's description not imply that I have to feel some assurance that the person performing my ordinance was duly prepared in heart and mind before I could rest confidently in the efficacy of the ritual I received? Does a Latter-day Saint need to know that the woman conducting the initiatory ordinances at the temple is spiritually in tune before accepting that her washing and anointing have been ratified by heaven? Does the congregation need to know that the priest at the sacrament table is worthy and focused before they can believe that those crusts of bread and cups of water will work a gracious effect in their life? Today's Church certainly does not invite such questions and is clearly not keen on fomenting the sorts of suspicion and uncertainty—even *disorder*—that this kind of doctrine seems to entail. Rather, the Church assures recipients that their ordinances are valid simply by virtue of the formal authority and the proper procedure of the person officiating. In contemporary Latter-day Saint culture, in contrast to a potential implication of Moroni's account, there is no encouragement for members to inquire into the state of an officiator's soul.

But this is certainly *not* to say the modern Church has completely muted the place of a person's spiritual condition in the performance of a sacred role. Consider these lines from a modern church manual on the administration of ordinances: "Our ability to bless the lives of others through priesthood ordinances is determined by our faithfulness and obedience....Before we perform priesthood ordinances we should seek the Lord in prayer. Even fasting may sometimes be necessary in special circumstances."[7] Certainly today's Church leadership recognizes something of the same distinction the book of Moroni makes between power and office. In a general conference address, President Boyd K. Packer warned, "We have done very well at distributing the *authority* of the priesthood....But distributing the *authority* of the priesthood has raced, I think, ahead of distributing the *power* of the priesthood."[8] Like the Jesus of Moroni 2 and 3, President Packer called on his hearers to live at the junction of procedural legitimacy and personal spiritual depth.

So, are the ordinances dependent on the officiator's spirituality or not? One of the clues to that answer lies in the fact that, in today's Church, these teachings that emphasize the spiritual prerequisites of ritual power are directed to a specific audience: the administrators of the ordinances. They appear, for instance, in the training given to the women and men who serve as ordinance workers in the temple but not in instructions to the patrons. That is, these teachings are aimed at those who are called to give these sacred gifts, not those who are called to receive them. The clear implication of this distinction of audience is that, in the divine workings of God's grace, the recipient will not be penalized for a lack of spiritual preparation in the performer of the rite, but the officiator will be held accountable for the state of her or his soul as a representative of godly power.

It would be easy to see this as a distinction of mere convenience, developed by the modern Church to avoid the disruption that would undoubtedly be caused if the recipients of ordinances must constantly pass judgment on the spirituality of the people providing those rites. But I think there is much more to it. It is worth pointing out that Jesus Christ did the same thing when he instructed the Lamanites and Nephites about these ordinances. Here we might profitably take a closer look at the wording of Moroni 2:3: "Now Christ spake these words [about the ritual of conferring the Holy Ghost] unto them at the time of his first appearing; and the multitude heard it not, but the disciples heard it; and on as many as they laid their hands, fell the Holy Ghost."

The parallels between Jesus Christ's ancient discourse and the practical approaches of the modern Church are quite remarkable. When talking about the ordinances, Jesus likewise distinguished between the audiences. His detailed instructions were heard by the administrators of ritual, not the recipients (see also 3 Ne. 12:1; 18:37; 19:20–21). In Moroni's condensed version of these events, the concluding assurance that *everyone* who received the ordinance had the same effectual experience amplifies the central principle: those with calls to officiate should take their spiritual preparedness with heightened seriousness while the recipients can receive the gifts of the kingdom with confidence.

I hasten here to add that this point must not be confused with the claim that those who occupy position in the church should be above due scrutiny. The point about receiving the gifts with confidence is manifestly not the same as accepting the giver as personally infallible. Quite the opposite, actually. The latter is a recipe for spiritual imposition; the former is an echo of Paul's invitation to distinguish the treasure from its vessel. Flaws in one do not necessarily diminish the value of the other. If I have determined the doctrine of the temple to be divine, for instance, I can peacefully receive its ordinances even if the person offering them to me has fallen far short of its high ideals.

The significance of this easily overlooked fact—that Christ directed some messages to the bearers of gifts and others to the recipients—strikes me as rather profound for all of us. (And I do mean for *all* of us, as I will explain.) The lessons are these: First, if I believe I have a divine gift to offer to those around me, I also have a heavy and sacred obligation to work to be worthy to carry it. At the same time, if I believe the offering of a fellow saint to be good (a true principle taught, a helpful act of service rendered, a saving ordinance performed—what Moroni 3:4 calls "the gifts and callings of God"), I should not lose confidence in it because it was brought to me by a fellow fallen creature. In other words, when I am the giver, I should strive to meet the highest standards of spiritual power; when I am the receiver, I should not devalue the offering by the imperfect vehicle that bears it.

His theology of gifting involves both high personal spiritual standards and a community of generous acceptance. As his book opens, Moroni teaches us all something about how to give and about how to receive in the kingdom of our God.

### dispensational threshing

In our act of reading Moroni 2, we participate in a contradiction. And in that contradiction lies an implication for the Book of Mormon as a whole and, indeed, for the entire restoration.

Christ said something to the "disciples" that was not meant to be heard by "the multitude." And, yet, now every person who picks up the Book of Mormon reads that passage, which was originally intended for a select few. Why has Moroni done this? Why tell everyone what Jesus apparently reserved for a limited audience? Whatever his level of prophetic consciousness about our day, Moroni's decision to share openly what was originally addressed to apostolic leaders seems especially well suited to a dispensation in which we are progressively less inclined to distinguish between *disciples* and the *multitude* and more inclined to see the Church as a multitude of disciples. (To this point, I might note that a *Handbook of Instructions* that was once divided into public and privileged volumes is now published in its entirety online.)

The inclusion of Moroni 2 in a text read by every Church member gestures toward one of the defining features of the restoration, namely a complex confluence of dispensational cultures. The latter days are to be a time when the truths of every dispensation flow into one complete whole. The depth of our theology results from the overlapping interplay—and sometimes the outright collision—of ancient and modern revelations. Consider the meaningful relationship between Moroni's teachings and the contemporary practices of today's Church with regard to ecclesiastical office.

The callings described by Moroni are limited to a very small handful of offices. In today's Church, however, a person can't walk down the corridor of a meetinghouse without passing numerous "presidents" and "counselors" and "leaders," female and male, youthful and aged. Girls and boys as young as eleven lead their peers. The person at the pulpit in a sacrament meeting may be an unendowed adolescent speaking to a room of adults ordained to be priestesses and priests, wearing the priestly emblems of their ordination. Who, then, should take personally the book of Moroni's suggestion that spiritual leaders have distinctive obligations? Who are the givers and who are the receivers in this community of gifting? The special designations of position described in Moroni's account, combined with the current Church's culture of widely distributed priestly symbols and proliferating leadership roles, results in a striking mix of high office (with its ancient overtones of exclusive hierarchy) and increasingly broad dissemination (with its millennial promise of full inclusion). Givers and receivers have distinctive roles and obligations, but we all occupy both positions.

In recent years, a growing recognition of the kingdom's shared leadership has accompanied a shifting discourse on priesthood power, a greater readiness to highlight the part of the priesthood doctrine that transcends gendered distinctions (which, setting aside the specific assignments of particular Church offices, turns out to be all of it). This is playing out alongside the Church's continued struggle to move beyond the racialized thinking that distorted its discourses of priesthood with the poison of white supremacy. The questions of what the priesthood is and who enjoys both its power and its authority has evolved over the course of the restoration.

The modern Church's singular and paradoxical effort both to maintain a very high notion of priestly power and to impart it relatively widely has unleashed radical and conservative instincts, generating its share of ecstasy and agony. The effort to make the special common without reducing its specialness has been among the restoration's great audacities, its most exhilarating possibilities, and its most daunting aspirations, a task made all the more challenging when the process has been devastatingly entangled in surrounding cultures of racism and misogyny.

Given the gendered pain and the racialized harm that has circled around it, the whole idea of a priestly hierarchy has drawn sharp criticism. As with most tense relationships, the one between a community of well-ordered offices and a levelling diffusion of spiritual power can produce frictions and inconsistencies. The tension is also, however, an invitation to careful, prayerful reflection while we strive as a people to understand the competing demands of these complementary doctrines.

It might be simpler to sever the taut cord that connects them—to dismiss ancient authorities of office as archaic or to denounce the equalitarianism as mere concession to modern feeling—but the very point of the restoration is a creative dynamism between the recovery of old truths and the discovery of new light. It is a convergence of dispensations in which each can hold the others accountable. Certainly, the Book of Mormon's absence of women's voices can be held to account by modern prophetic calls for more inclusive councils; likewise, a Church culture affected by modern American white supremacy has been held to account by such ancient declarations as 2 Nephi 26:33 that function from outside the cultural frame of the United States' racial prejudices. When different dispensations converge in the fullness of times, the shearing tensions can winnow the gospel seed from its cultural chaff. Neither modern nor ancient husks should survive the threshing. And no eternal truth should be lost.

As breaking light reflects on ancient truths, the restoration unfolds. No one dispensation can be made perfect without the check and balance of the others. Moroni appears to believe this as his book begins by jumping back four hundred years and ends with an affirmation of continuing revelation. He writes in his present, to future readers, about a distant past. He knows that different eras have something sacred to say to each other. When in his opening chapters he places the exclusive knowledge of ancient apostles in plain sight for every latter-day reader, the theological effect is a call for us *all* to rise to the task of bearing well our sacred gifts to our fellow Saints.

# 3

# A Sacrament of Multiple Gifts

*"We know the manner to be true." —Moroni 4:1*

As Moroni's instructions on the ordinances turn toward the administration of the "flesh and blood of Christ unto the church," he offers the Book of Mormon's only statements on ritualized prayer (Moro. 4:1). He provides the precise wording of the blessings on the sacrament—wording that he indicates came from Jesus Christ four hundred years earlier, wording that would be essentially affirmed in a subsequent revelation to Joseph Smith fourteen hundred years later. These words clearly matter. They would thus seem to warrant our close attention.

The first thing to notice in the remarkable persistence of the wording is that it remarkably persists, and therein lies one of the gifts of this rite: it offers a moment of shared reliving, a chance to collapse the temporal distance between sacred times of the past and the regular occurrences of the present. When we show up on a Sunday and together listen to words that have been uttered (and partake of emblems that have been blessed) in just this way by people who lived many centuries before us, we momentarily transcend the barriers of time that separate generations of God's children.

Today, the presiding officer in every sacrament meeting is tasked with a solemn responsibility to preserve the ordinance's linguistic stability, policing each word with a kind of fastidiousness that is foreign to other aspects of our Sunday services. This meticulous preservation of the prayers is a kind of defiance of historical change. When we hear the sacramental words from Moroni 4 and 5, we share an auditory experience with ancient Lamanites and Nephites. (Similarly, with a morsel of bread we emblematically re-create the evening of the Last Supper, reaching through epochs to eat with the original apostles.) Where the march of history creates temporal divisions among humans, the careful maintenance of ceremonial practice affirms a sense of connection. This gift may reach its ultimate expression in the temple, where vicarious ordinances become offerings of love and service that explicitly burst free of our temporal limitations and flow fully to all generations, but elements of it are present in every ritual that links us to sacred moments of other eras.

As every Latter-day Saint knows, however, the sacrament prayer has changed in one significant respect between Moroni's day and today. The word *wine* has been changed to *water*. That alteration is a reminder that even the most stable of sacred rituals exists in a tension between the now and the then, an illustration of the fact that the timeless and the temporary elements of human life are constantly interacting in our religious practices. Complementary realities of persistence and change shape the sacrament experience, granting us the chance to be connected to both the past and the present in our day.

These are not the only gifts provided by the sacrament prayers. Attention to their form and content reveals an ordinance that offers multiple benefits to those who would receive them. In the seemingly simple ritual of the sacrament lies a host of blessings.

*"...and witness unto thee...and always remember him..."* —*Moroni 4:3*

Let us return for a moment to the internal order in which Moroni places his materials: instructions on ordinances, a description of a church community, a discourse on pure love leading to personal transformation. The sequencing of topics here—a process that starts with rituals and ends with the formation of a new being—bears resemblance to an argument made by the modern scholar of religion Saba Mahmood. Interviewing Muslim women in Egypt and observing these women in their devotion to the Islamic practice of daily prayer rituals, Mahmood noticed that their experience did not exactly correspond to some of the prevailing academic theories about ritualism. She concluded that the repetitive performance of religious rituals functions in people's lives in ways that modern scholars have too often overlooked.

Mahmood notes that the rituals are usually seen by their practitioners as a substantive way to connect with the divine while they are usually seen by academic observers as symbolic expressions of identity and an affirmation of group cohesion. In close observation of her subjects, however, Mahmood noticed a third implication of their ritual lives. She recognized that the women approached their prayer rituals as repeatable acts of spiritual training, disciplines whose repetition over time would facilitate a gradual internal transformation. They did them less as professions of faith and more as avenues toward faith. They did not observe their prayer practices *because* they self-identified as part of a righteous people; they observed them in the *hope of developing* into righteous people. Their rituals were about the diligent, repetitive work of forming a new self. They were not static symbols so much as active exercises. Mahmood's women did these things in order to *become*.[1]

Though focused on a cultural setting and a religious practice quite different from my own, Mahmood's research has helped me understand something powerful about the possibilities of our sacrament services. I do not take the sacrament because I always remember Jesus Christ, because I always keep his commandments, or because I always bear his name well. To eat those emblems under such pretenses would transform the Lord's Supper into the sin the Lord most frequently condemned: hypocrisy. No one perfectly lives the promises entailed in those prayers. Rather, I go to church and partake of the sacrament because I want to be more mindful, more righteous, and more courageous. I hope to remember, obey, and represent better. The sacrament is, in this sense, much less about who I am and much more about who I yearn to be.

In it, we bear "witness *unto him*." Again, audience matters here. If the sacrament prayers stated that I partake of this bread and water as a "witness unto the congregation" or a "witness unto the world" that I always remember him, that I keep his commandments and bear his name well, then—for the sake of truth and integrity—there would have to be a direct correlation between who I already am and what the sacrament declares. But the sacrament prayer makes no reference to any such messaging to fellow mortals.

Rather, I do these things as a witness unto God, the one Being who already knows absolutely everything about me. I am at no risk of deceiving him. He is fully familiar with the yawning gap between who I am and who he wants me to be. Thus, to declare to *him* that I am these things becomes a prayer of hope rather than an act of hypocrisy. It is a form of repentance rather than a profession of status. In addition to the sacrament's essential role as a *communal* act of connection, it is also an *individual* aspiration from a supplicant to a God who knows the petitioners are not yet everything promised through this ordinance but who is determined to help them become equal to that expression.

The ordinances are therefore not the culmination of my righteousness; rather, they are a foundational exercise that allows me to develop righteousness. That reading of the ritual is underscored by Moroni's sequencing. The ordinances described in chapters 2 through 6 are a staging ground for the personal transformation to which his book builds.

In rough calculation, a Latter-day Saint born into the Church and living to eighty will partake of the sacrament some four thousand times. This reliable punctation to our weekly calendar—a conscious effort to step repetitively into a state of remembrance toward Christ and into a covenantal conversation with our God—has the potential to create a kind of spiritual muscle memory. It constitutes what Mahmood, drawing from Aristotle, calls a "habitus." Its cumulative effect can rewire a soul. Like a pianist running through scales over and over again, this repetitive ordinance sharpens my reflexes of remembrance and covenanting. Scales do not an artist make, and neither are the ordinances sufficient for the full development of discipleship, but the conditioning exercises of the sacrament help shape a disciple's character. Week by week, crust by crust, sip by sip, I change.

Or, at least, I should.

When describing the sacramental practice of the ancient American church, Moroni reported that they did "meet together oft to partake of bread and wine, in remembrance of the Lord Jesus" (Moro. 6:6). Those Saints clearly saw the Lord's Supper as a matter of frequent replication. The modern Church does likewise, typically citing Moroni's words.

The current Latter-day Saint practice of receiving the bread and water every week sets the Church's sacramental rhythm apart from the communion cultures of many other Christians, especially among Protestants. (Frequent communion is standard, of course, for Catholics and their closest High Church relatives, such as Episcopalians, who place much heavier emphasis on the redemptive power of the sacraments than their Low Church Protestant counterparts.[2]) Though the restored Church's weekly calendar of communion often differs from many current Protestant practices, it actually corresponds to the original vision of various founding figures of Protestant denominations.

The two great theological forces running through the environment of the early restoration—the Reformed (e.g., Presbyterians, Congregationalists, and many Baptists) and the Wesleyan (e.g., Methodists)—had founders in John Calvin and John Wesley who believed in the importance of weekly communion. Calvin, for instance, adamantly insisted that it should be provided "at least once a week" to "feed us spiritually."[3] And yet, in the denominational practices of the early United States, groups such as the Presbyterians and Methodists were celebrating the Lord's Supper much less frequently—in some denominations as little as twice a year. In the case of the Calvinists, this was the product of centuries' worth of theological debate that moved them away from Calvin's original vision; for the Methodists, this reflected the practicalities of early American preaching circuits that circulated pastors through pulpits at infrequent intervals.[4] As part of a culture dominated by such denominations, early Latter-day Saints themselves played around with different cadences to the ordinance, but—often with the Book of Mormon in mind—they settled into a weekly repetition relatively quickly. Moroni's "oft" has prevailed.[5]

Latter-day Saints may have set themselves apart from other groups of Christians by their adherence to Moroni's description of a frequently administered sacrament, but their Protestant contemporaries have sometimes complained about another element of the Latter-day Saint practice. They have objected to the fact that the elements of the Lord's Supper were administered quite broadly, to almost all members, including even small children. This, the critics have felt, undermined the solemnity that should attend such a sacred ritual. It rendered the holy mundane.[6] Familiarity could bring irreverence. But, in combination with its weekly availability in Latter-day Saint worship, this extensive participation in the ordinance of the sacrament suggests its role as an exercise whose *lifelong* and *frequent* observance can help train a Saint's soul from her earliest years. Less a special observance and more a regular discipline, the sacrament and its culture lead us to consider the ordinance's steady and repetitive role in the gradual development of our being.

As Christian critics of such sacramental practices have rightly noted, however, that repetitiveness comes with certain spiritual dangers. Christians are hardly alone in fearing the threat of empty formalism. Saba Mahmood's Muslim women saw the same risks. They not only embraced the transformative implication of reiteration in our ritual lives; they also repeatedly expressed a warning. They constantly reminded themselves "that an act of [ritual] performed for its own sake, without regard for how it contributes to the realization of piety, is 'lost power.'"[7] To go through the motions of the sacrament, without consciously tuning its repetitive actions toward the formation of a new self, is to miss its purpose. Put simply, sacramental habit can be powerfully transformative, but only if it does not descend into thoughtlessness. I have to be intentional about my quest for holiness when I place that bread on my tongue and bring the water to my lips over and over again. Otherwise, I squander the gift. I have "lost power."

This, then, is one of the sacrament's central challenges: the relentless repetitiveness that lends it a particularly transformative capacity may also contribute to a certain mindlessness in the performance of it. Moroni's "oft" conveys both an opportunity and a risk, calling on us to embrace the former and guard against the latter. Only then is the gift of repetition truly realized.

*sacramental gift: transformation by divine sanctity*
*"...to bless and sanctify..."*   —Moroni 4:3

It would be terribly misleading to give the impression that the doctrine of the sacrament as recorded in Moroni is only about the transformation of the self through the vast, habituating accumulation of ritual repetitions. It is that, and it is also much more. I may see my regular participation in the ordinance as a reiterative process of internal formation but I can also—indeed, I *must* also—understand the bread and water to be carrying supernatural power, a grace well beyond the reach of my personal striving. The sacrament exceeds mere habit. A Latter-day Saint should recognize these gifts (the gift of repetitive discipline and the gift of supernatural grace) as coexisting and complementing each other rather than competing for prominence in our sacramental practices.

The sacrament prayers themselves—as laid out by Moroni—highlight the presence of an external agency. This element is made clear in the opening petition: "O God, the Eternal Father, we ask thee in the name of thy Son, Jesus Christ, to bless and sanctify this bread . . ." (Moro. 4:3). The prayer underscores that a power beyond mere symbols has been invoked, that these substances are being rendered into something other than what they were when the ordinance began. Before, they were unblessed and unsanctified; by the time they enter my mouth, they have been touched by the sanctifying power of the living God. This is not just a reverence that humans give them; this is a quality God imparts. The prayers are a reminder of the point made repeatedly in scripture—from the spit and dirt with which Jesus heals blindness in John 9, to the stones that become instruments of light in Ether 3, to the imperfect disciples who are made special witnesses throughout the standard works—that God can take the most mundane of materials and turn them into miraculous instruments of redemption. He is the Sanctifier of previously unhallowed elements. He changes things.

The rhetorical choices that Moroni and his translator make in chapters 4 and 5 create a conception of the sacrament that we might situate in a tense middle space between two theological positions. It reaches across a Christian continuum that runs from the Catholic conviction that the consecrating prayer of a priest transubstantiates the Eucharistic materials into the literal body and blood of Christ, on one end, to a low-church evangelical version of communion in which the bread and wine remain purely symbolic memorials without any intrinsic holiness to them. If those positions define the two ends of Christianity's sacramental spectrum, with different denominations taking up a vast variety of places along that line, Moroni's words stake out a place near the center. The prayers that he records partake of both theological impulses.

On one side, the sacrament prayers that Moroni quotes are much shorter than those a Catholic priest recites to consecrate the Eucharist, and they contain none of the explicitly transubstantiating language of the Mass or even the consubstantiating language of the Lutheran tradition; to that degree they sound more like a rather Reformed emphasis on symbolic meaning over sacerdotal power. The brevity and the simplicity of the prayers downplay the role of the priest and minimize the sense of anything ontologically miraculous occurring at the table. Certain elements of Moroni's sacrament, then, seem to push it toward the symbolic end of the spectrum. But some of its features simultaneously prevent it from traveling too far down that line.

As readers, for instance, we may too quickly pass over the words with which Moroni chooses to introduce the ordinance. He does not refer to it as "the sacrament" in the way of today's Latter-day Saints (even though he does use that term at Morm. 9:29), nor does he refer to it as "communion" or as the "Lord's Supper" as was typical of the Protestants of Joseph Smith's day. Strikingly, when presenting these two prayers he refers to the ordinance as "administering the flesh and blood of Christ" (Moro. 4:1). The phrase clearly has scriptural resonance, hearkening back to the language Jesus used in John 6 to describe his atoning sacrifice and the gifts it offers. It appears again in 3 Nephi, where the resurrected Lord uses it to describe this ordinance. Notwithstanding its origins in Christ's discourses, however, the phrase has reflected the presence of some historical controversy among Christians. For centuries, the phrase has been regularly invoked in debates between Protestants and Catholics—and among Protestants—concerning the meaning of the sacrament, typically attached to more substantive conceptions of the ritual's transformative nature. Moroni's—or his translator's—conspicuous invocation of the phrase draws our attention to the ordinance as something more than mere memorial.[8] It is for remembrance, to be sure, but there is also a presence beyond memory involved.

The phrasing of "administering the flesh and blood of Christ" unmistakably elevates the identity of the sacramental materials. This point need not go so far as to mean that the emblems were transubstantiated into Jesus's actual flesh and blood in order to convey the principle that we truly invite the investiture of Christ's being into the ritual elements. It certainly carries the connotation that the bread becomes more than mere flour and yeast, that the water is more than mere hydrogen and oxygen. The rhetorical mix of Moroni's description keeps us in this tense middle space—forces pushing us away from transubstantiation, forces pulling us away from mere symbolism—and we are left with bread and water empowered to carry the presence of our Redeemer into our lives. If this ordinance is not transubstantiation, but it is something more than simple symbolism, what then might it be? Moroni does relatively little to solve that riddle, but we might see the beginnings of an answer in the phrase "to . . . sanctify this" that appears in both prayers (Moro. 4:3, 5:2). This possibility was brought to my attention—as so many good things are—in a conversation with a student. In this case, Joseph Sorenson observed that maybe what is going on here is that through a shared process of sanctification Christ's body and the elements of the sacrament have become mutual partakers of the same sacred power. To put this bluntly, perhaps the principle is not that we are literally consuming the flesh and blood of the Savior in a transubstantiated sense but that the materials we consume in the sacrament have become infused with the very same sanctity that filled his physical frame. He is present through the process of sanctification. We are eating his flesh and blood in the sense that we are ingesting into our embodied existence the quality that made his flesh and blood *his*.

To this point, consider these lines in the Savior's intercessory prayer from the Gospel of John, another place where the concept of shared sanctification crops up: "And for their sakes I sanctify myself, that they also might be sanctified through the truth. . . . That they all may be one; as thou, Father, art in me, and I in thee, that they also may be one in us" (John 17:19, 21). The idea of mutual participation in sanctity prefaces Christ's discourse on our union with the divine; sanctification seems to be the quality that transforms us into joint partakers of godly nature. If we become one with him through sanctification, then the bread and water likewise become one with him through the same process. So, when the young priest at the sacrament table pleads with the Lord on behalf of the gathered Saints to "sanctify this bread," he is calling for the bread to take on the same defining quality that characterizes our Redeemer's redeeming nature (Moro. 4:3). To ingest this bread, then, is to partake of that nature.

Different from, but coexistent with, the act of memorializing, the consumption of *sanctified* materials transcends the cumulative processes of self-formation. There is in this ordinance something much more than just the repetitive habituations of discipleship. There is an intrinsic power in the very sacramental material I eat and drink, a sanctifying presence that can transform me every bit as much the first time I partake as the four-thousandth time I partake. This is the gift of the sacrament that corresponds to the Savior's parable of the laborers: whether to a lifelong member or a convert of one day, the gift is the same.

Moroni has brought us yet again to the convergence of the gospel's complementary truths. Time spent in the kingdom has value; the more often I get to partake of the sacrament the more episodes of spiritual habituation I get to experience. This is the side of the coin that pushes us to gather God's children into the Church with some urgency, to give people as many opportunities as life can afford to live the formative processes of membership. In this sense, the accumulation counts. On the other side, there is a transcendent power of godliness carried by these consecrated materials that comes from outside of myself and functions independently of me. The presence of this power is immediate; its influence goes well beyond the effects of repetitive motion, and its impact has nothing to do with its frequency. It can cleanse and heal in an instant.

Just as the discourse on ordination in the previous chapters invited us to live at the place where procedural authority and personal power intersect, so these chapters on the sacrament remind us that our redemptive experiences are most fully realized at that place where steady habits of devotion and the miraculous infusion of God's autonomous power overlap. We remember and he sanctifies. Such an overlap is possible at every sacrament meeting.

In the relatively brief observance of a Sunday morning sacrament, then, multiple realities converge: ① time and distance collapse as I connect with both the Saints of other eras and a community of my contemporaries; ② a repetitive devotional exercise continues a gradual process of discipling; and ③ the immediate sanctifying power of God's holiness and the Savior's atoning presence are truly ingested. In the act of consuming the flesh and blood of Christ, I simultaneously connect, condition, and receive. Not bad for a crust of bread broken by adolescent hands, or a drop of water in a little plastic cup. In the very ordinariness of our sacrament meetings a multitude of gifts unfolds.

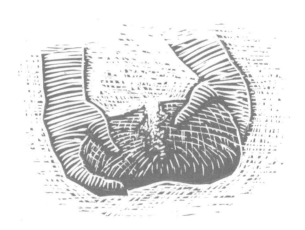

# 4

## To Gather Among and to Rely Alone

*"...they were numbered among the people..."*
—*Moroni 6:4*

*"...relying alone upon the merits of Christ..."*
—*Moroni 6:4*

As chapter 5 gives way to chapter 6, Moroni continues his discussion of ritual ordinances, moving from the sacrament prayers to baptism. The opening of chapter 6 maintains Moroni's recurring emphasis on the vertical links that these embodied ceremonies forge between a soul and its Maker, but the chapter also marks an increase in his attention toward the lateral bonds of human love as he begins to build from these sacred rituals toward the community of caring that coalesces around them. Beginning with baptism, chapter 6 is both explicitly descriptive of the church that came into being after Christ's visit and tacitly prescriptive of the sort of communal relationships that Moroni thinks we should emulate.

The chapter strikes, with considerable force, chords that Moroni has already touched on, such as our profound need of each other and the special accountability of those who would serve the faith community. It ends with a reminder that the Spirit should guide our shared worship.

*"And now I speak concerning baptism. Behold elders, priests, and teachers were baptized; and they were not baptized save they brought forth fruit meet that they were worthy of it."—Moroni 6:1*

Moroni is, throughout his book, mindful of distinctive demands on those who would administer gifts to the Saints. His opening emphasis on the baptism of leaders conveys a message about the responsibilities of sacred office and the risks of hypocrisy. The elders, priests, and teachers were baptized first, it seems, so that they could then baptize with a moral authority to match their authorization, an order of events that precludes the possibility of leaders presiding over a covenantal commitment that they themselves had not yet made. Community guides must have traveled the path along which they strive to lead others.

As previously noted, that message is now extended to all of us, for in the fullness of times we are all beckoned to be leaders. We thus are all subject to this high call for the moral authority of personal example. Moroni goes on to indicate that the first prerequisite of that personal example is "a broken heart and a contrite spirit" (Moro. 6:2).

*of broken hearts and contrite spirits*

*"Neither did they receive any unto baptism save they came forth with a broken heart and a contrite spirit."*
*—Moroni 6:2*

Discussing specific phrasing in the Book of Mormon is an inherently fraught endeavor. For instance, some version of the phrase "a broken heart and a contrite spirit" recurs in our English translations of expressions from Lehi, Nephi, and Mormon, as well as Moroni, both in Ether 4 and here in Moroni 6, but we have no way of knowing if those passages reflect the same original ancient words in each case. ☞ We are similarly unable to know how closely the original Book of Mormon words relate to the Hebrew phrases that get so translated in the King James Version of the Old Testament. With that difficulty acknowledged, the following discussion rests on an assumption of underlying connection—at least conceptual if not linguistic—among these various instances of the phrase in our English version.

That connection has some substantive justification. Note, for instance, that we find references to broken hearts and contrite spirits in Nephi's famous soliloquy in 2 Nephi 4—the passage in which Nephi most closely mimics the style of David's Psalms. This similarity is significant because it is in the Psalms that iterations of the phrase first appear in the King James Version of the Bible. That is, when Nephi's writing assumes a kind of Davidic form we also find Davidic phrasing, suggesting that the words have an intertextual relationship.[1]

The phrase "a broken heart and a contrite spirit" appears in the Psalms when David writes of the divine presence and of God's relationship with individual souls. Psalm 34 tells us that "the Lord is nigh unto them that are of a broken heart; and saveth such as be of a contrite spirit" (verse 18). Psalm 51 teaches that God "wilt not despise" those of "a broken spirit: a broken and contrite heart" (verse 17). David's psalmic pleading, of course, does not just teach about broken-heartedness and contrition; it also offers the biblical text's most exquisite example of a sinner self-aware in his own failings, bringing his broken heart before the

☞ In this book, all references to Lehi are to Lehi₁ (from Jerusalem) and all references to Nephi are to Nephi₁ (son of Lehi), not to any of their decendants mentioned in the Book of Mormon with the same name. Other series volumes use subscripts to distinguish people with the same name: Nephi, Mosiah, Alma, etc.

Lord. To lovers of that literature—as surely the Book of Mormon prophets were—the idea of a broken heart and a contrite spirit must have conjured up the image of a fallen king's agonizing search for redemption, the very epitome of abandoned pride and utter dependence.

David stood in the ruins of adulterated relationships—both earthly and heavenly—deeply regretting his betrayal of his Beloved and aching for reconciliation. He also knew, though, that in our God's ordering, hurt is never without hope. As David notes, in our relationship with divinity, broken-heartedness is both the experience of separation from a loved one and also the pathway of reconnection: "The Lord is nigh unto them that are of a broken heart" (Psalm 34:18).

Consider also the words of Isaiah, the biblical prophet who most conspicuously picks up David's concept of contrition. "For thus saith the high and lofty One that inhabiteth eternity, whose name is Holy; I dwell in the high and holy place, with him also that is of a contrite and humble spirit, to revive the spirit of the humble, and to revive the heart of the contrite ones" (Isaiah 57:15). To rise to divine heights, we must descend into the depths of humility. Isaiah, like David before him, connects these qualities to the presence of the Lord. The contrite and the broken hearted are the people with whom God "dwells."

Given Nephi's obvious affinity for Isaiah and David, the appearance of broken hearts and contrite spirits in his writing underscores their prophetic influence on him. Given the context of Moroni's writings, however, the appearance of the phrase "a broken heart and a contrite spirit" should probably point us to an even more proximate source. In light of the fact that Moroni, throughout this first portion of his book, is reflecting back on the impact of the Savior's visit to Bountiful and is using specific phrases from that visit (see, for example, "flesh and blood"), the most immediate reference for his use of the phrase is likely not David or Isaiah or Lehi or Nephi. The likeliest source is Jesus Christ. Note that the phrase appears three times in the account of Christ's discourses at the temple site as recorded in 3 Nephi:

> And ye shall offer for a sacrifice unto me a broken heart and a contrite spirit. And whoso cometh unto me with a broken heart and a contrite spirit, him will I baptize with fire and with the Holy Ghost, even as the Lamanites, because of their faith in me at the time of their conversion, were baptized with fire and with the Holy Ghost, and they knew it not. (3 Ne. 9:20)

> And behold, I have given you the law and the commandments of my Father, that ye shall believe in me, and that ye shall repent of your sins, and come unto me with a broken heart and a contrite spirit. Behold, ye have the commandments before you, and the law is fulfilled. (3 Ne. 12:19)

Jesus's use of the phrase, like David's and Isaiah's, suggests a link between broken hearts, contrite spirits, and the presence of the divine. As in Moroni's invocation, Christ's words connect the phrase to a concept of baptism. In the case of the Savior, however, that connection comes in the first-person singular. In each invocation, he links the phrase "a broken heart and a contrite spirit" with an invitation—"come unto me"—reinforcing the sense that these contrite spirits and broken hearts are the passports to our connection with our Lord. They enable us to dwell with him. When the phrase appears in the writings of Moroni's father, Mormon, it carries the same connotation that Jesus gave it. Writing—unlike Lehi and Nephi—*after* the Savior's visit, Mormon laments that the Nephites "did not come unto Jesus with broken hearts and contrite spirits" (Morm. 2:14). Mormon was clearly affected by the Savior's phrasing.

Here in chapter 6, Moroni also uses the Christic verb "to come," noting that the early church did not "receive any unto baptism save they came forth with a broken heart and a contrite spirit." When Moroni invokes these qualities in reference to baptism, he sheds a particular light on the nature of that ordinance. Such an invocation of the phrase not only indicates the importance of recognizing one's own dependence and cultivating true meekness in order for this saving rite to have its full effect; it also vividly reinforces the doctrine that baptism is a gateway to the companionship of the divine. If a broken heart and a contrite spirit are the prerequisites both for the baptismal covenant and for the presence of God, then to enter into one is to come unto the other. By establishing this quality as essential to the ordinance, Moroni associates it with an actual shift in our spiritual location, a moment of rapprochement in which we are drawn further into closeness with our Father and his Son.

The brokenhearted will not be barred from the presence of God—in heaven or on earth. Indeed, it seems, the brokenhearted are the only invitees.

*the imperfect tense of repentance*
*"They truly repented."* —Moroni 6:2

Among the meaningful word choices in the book of Moroni is the decision *not* to include a word. In his list of baptism's requirements, Moroni writes that those who were received as baptismal candidates "witnessed unto the church that they truly repented of all their sins. And none were received unto baptism save they took upon them the name of Christ, having a determination to serve him to the end" (Moro. 6:2–3). It would have been a small rhetorical or translation choice, but one with major theological implications, to insert a word into this phrase that a reader might reasonably expect in such a statement: "had." That is, one could easily imagine a version of this verse that read as follows: They "witnessed unto the church that they *had* truly repented of all their sins and that they *had taken upon* them the name of Christ." To add the "had" would have rendered the sentence in what grammarians call past-perfect tense. Such a formulation would convey that repentance is something that can be completed as a finite act or that one could take on themselves the name of Christ once and for all.

The absence of the past-perfect tense recurs in both clauses of that sentence and seems quite intentional. Because Moroni's description of the church is—understandably, given his circumstances—written entirely in the past tense, the imperfect formulation can be obscured. It comes through more clearly, however, in relation to other sentences in which the past-perfect does occur, such as in the observation that they "*had* been received unto baptism" (Moro. 6:4). This grammatical contrast drives home the difference between the singular deed of baptism and the ongoing process of repentance. This word choice opens up the possibility for conceiving of repentance and Christian commitment as continual efforts rather than isolated actions. It seems significant that Moroni writes of these things in an imperfect tense.

The wording of Moroni's teachings here reminds me very much of a sacrament meeting talk my brother, Matt, gave when he was in his mid-twenties and I was in my late teens. It left an indelible impression on me; I still regularly draw from it some three decades since. One of the lines from the talk that I recall most distinctly is that "discipleship is not a matter of commitment. It is a matter of recommitment." Matt's declaration and Moroni's formulation—which characterizes the Saints not as people who *have* repented and *have* taken upon them the name of Christ, but as people who *do* repent and who *do* take upon them the name of Christ—reinforces the idea that the life of a disciple is a matter of continual rededication. Repentance as an act of imperfection reminds us that on the journey of Christian discipleship, it is the choice to continue that makes all the difference.

*a community of endless love*
*"Their names were blotted out."* —*Moroni 6:7*

*"But as oft as they repented . . . they were forgiven."*
—*Moroni 6:8*

The messaging embedded in the grammar gets reinforced in the substance of Moroni's account a few verses later, when he describes the disciplinary policies of the church. Here Moroni details a procedure by which unrepented sins would result in the transgressors having their names "blotted out" (Moro. 6:7). The spiritual integrity of the flock seems to require an honest and firm boundary around what constitutes acceptable behavior within the flock. The imagery of "blotting" suggests not only that the names were written indelibly and could not merely be erased—that is, they were not easily removed and the possessors of those names were presumed to be permanently within the fold—but also that willful rebellion against the commandments would result in a dark obscuring of one's place among the people of God.

The image of the blot is unsettling; its connotation of a spreading stain threatens those whose names have thus been concealed, and its suggestion of bleeding ink depicts the loss of even a single sister or brother as a kind of seeping wound on the body of Christ.

The stark language of blotting and counting out transgressors reads quite heavily, indeed. Yet the following sentence immediately casts a steady light of hope on the matter: "But as oft as they repented and sought forgiveness, with real intent, they were forgiven" (Moro. 6:8). Even more so than the "oft" Moroni uses in the recurring invitations to the sacramental altar, the promise of return seems limitless here. Moroni quite specifically does not reference the wrestle that our guilty souls must have with our God as part of our repentance, but he does say that the believers, as a body, have an obligation to pardon all. God will forgive whom he will forgive, but the Saints should forgive everyone (D&C 64:10).

Note, too, that Moroni does not speak in the procedural language of *readmission* but in the emotionally substantive language of *forgiving*. This is a matter of hearts as well as process. The church is about real relationships and real relationships regularly require forgiveness. In Moroni's depiction of the church, repentance is ever on offer and its repeated enactment will not exhaust the patience or love of God's people. In a phrase like "as oft," repentance again looks less like a discrete event and more like a process that bears endless repetition. Its promise is perpetual.

The promise of repentance does not, however, mean that transgression comes without a price. Moroni's depiction of the church as a community where souls really are nourished with mutual care suggests that even a temporary severing from this collective—caused by a violation or rejection of its defining commitments—is a profound loss. As with the New Testament prodigal, separation from the body of Christ carries its own costs, not only for those who leave but also for those who are left. Rather than suggesting that sin is without consequence, Moroni's description of limitless repentance teaches that—precisely because that price of departure is so high, for both the member and the body—any sincere effort to return should be met with open arms.

*"among" and "alone"*

*"They were numbered among the people of the church of Christ; and their names were taken, that they might be remembered and nourished by the good word of God, to keep them in the right way, to keep them continually watchful unto prayer, relying alone upon the merits of Christ, who was the author and finisher of their faith."*
*—Moroni 6:4*

Moroni describes a faith community with both high standards of righteousness and a tireless capacity for forgiveness. He also depicts a church life that includes a robust culture of mutual human assistance and the promise of direct divine connection: The Saints were "numbered among the people of the church" and they relied "alone upon the merits of Christ." In this description of the Saints as existing "among" each other and depending "alone" on Christ we again catch a glimpse of Moroni's conception of a church sitting at the convergence of complementing truths. We are part of a community of mutual care; Christ is sufficient for our spiritual welfare. Such paradoxical phrasing suggests a community that keeps us attentive, nourished, and prayerful, while its church structures and relationships appear as means to an end, a collective scaffolding in support of a personal experience with divinity. The phrasing of the verse suggests paths of discipleship that are necessarily marked by elements of both solidarity and independence.

For Moroni, the communitarian and the liberating parts of the disciple's life are not at war with each other; indeed, they are not even really in tension. He notes their combination without much commentary. In his unremarked merging of these two principles—a rhetorical simplicity that seems utterly unconcerned with the fact that he has just uttered a paradox—he suggests his comfort with a gospel of counterpoints. We should ensure that his ease does not blind us to the dangerous temptations that lurk on either side of this binary.

On one hand, to insist that our spiritual life is a purely individual affair—that all we need is to rely on Christ—is potentially to atomize and isolate ourselves to our own great harm. A growing body of evidence illustrates the high price people pay for lives of self-oriented detachment—the sort of life to which modern culture has so often told us we should aspire. Loneliness is one of the great public health crises of our time, a crisis that manifests in deeply troubling consequences for our physical and mental health. We really do need each other—not only in some soft, sentimental way but even in the hard material realities of our existence, right down to our physiology.[2] Moroni understands that the impact of isolation is just as damaging on our spiritual health. He is, it is worth recalling, writing this as he wanders all alone. He knows whereof he writes.

It is also worth recalling, however, that Moroni had his chances to join with others around him. If only he would deny the Christ, he could have stepped out of his isolation and into a band of comrades. He really is relying *alone* on the grace of his Savior. In both his dangerous current circumstances and in his theological reflections, he recognizes the risks of oppressive community demands, of social bonds that impede rather than pull toward the intimate relationship between the individual soul and the God who loves each wandering lamb.

The French sociologist Emile Durkheim—and legions of scholars of religious studies and human society who followed him—insisted that the community *is* God, that the entire point of religion is to define and strengthen the collective.[3] They touch on a powerful truth; as previously noted, for Latter-day Saints divinity is inherently relational. But as so often happens in academic theorizing, these scholars' position can overreach in reducing complex religious forces to simple material explanations. Moroni's invitation to rely "alone" upon the merits of Christ is a powerful reminder that the religious impulse has not only been toward the gathering but also often away from it: to the mystic's grotto, to Nephi's mountain top, to Jesus's Judean wilderness, to Moroni's lonesome journey. Sometimes, for its own growth and well-being, the individual soul has to suspend those societal ties and remember that Christ alone can save. Yet, in turn, monastic isolation is never sufficient as a disciple's life: Christ comes out of the wilderness and back into Jerusalem, Nephi comes down the mountain with his insights to share, Moroni returns across the temporal expanse of fourteen hundred years to connect repeatedly with a bewildered young prophet. The disciple's devotion must function both "among" and "alone."

As noted previously, life in such tension can be taxing. In many ways it would be easier to lose all spiritual autonomy in complete deference to community authority, letting the voice of the collective exercise a sovereign influence. Conversely, it would also be easier to abandon tight community connection in an absolute quest for freedom, something in keeping with Thomas Paine's famed line, "My own mind is my own church."[4] The tougher task, it seems to me, is to figure out how to live simultaneously "numbered among" and "relying alone." Moroni's verse suggests that it is in just such a paradox that God's redemptive gifts lie.

Here we might reflect on the historical lessons of Alcoholics Anonymous (AA). The disease of alcoholism had been an American public health scourge for generations by the time AA began offering its distinctive path to sobriety. Many other programs and systems had been tried, including legal prohibitions that sought to eradicate the problem by the flex of coercive and criminalizing state power. None of these programs battled addiction quite like AA did. The piece of the Alcoholics Anonymous approach that most distinguished it from those that came before it was the role of the "sponsor," the person who had walked the difficult path of recovery and now returned to the trail to walk it with another. The secret to success revealed in the AA model is that this element of the process—the fact that a person does not graduate from the program but stays closely involved in a sponsoring role—is just as important for the sponsor as for the person sponsored. It turns out that recovery requires a chance to help others achieve what you have achieved. The AA description of sobriety draws on a language of gifting that Moroni would appreciate: "You keep it only by giving it away."[5]

This description may be true of our redemptive relationship with Jesus, as well. If the journey of my discipleship gives me a community of fellow travelers with whose help I achieve the ability to rely confidently on my immediate connection with Christ—if my "among" facilitates my "alone"—that process is never fully finished. It is written in an imperfect tense. There is always someone else to walk that trail with, someone who needs the among, and in the process of providing to others what was given to me, my personal union with my Savior continually deepens.

Like Jesus, we may always alternate between lonely wilderness retreats and the bustling congregation of the faithful, each enriching the other. To be part of a faith community certainly has its burdens: problematic histories to carry, challenging personalities to navigate, uncomfortable collective decisions to swallow. To pursue a life of spiritual isolation likewise comes at a cost: self-centeredness, echo chambers formed by one's own opinions, loneliness. In the parlance of our moment, to be religious but not spiritual or spiritual but not religious may look like a welcome reprieve from the shearing demands of community commitments and personal devotions, and we may in fact need to focus on one or the other at any particular moment on our journey of redemption. But to reject one of these in favor of the other may be to shut down one of the pistons that drives the engine of faith; without the dynamic tension between the two, discipleship may coast for a time but it cannot really progress. The among and the alone, it turns out, are mutually constitutive and inextricably linked. Perhaps that is why Moroni shows absolutely no hesitancy to throw them into the same sentence.

### whether to supplicate or to sing

*"Their meetings were conducted... after the manner of the workings of the Spirit."*   —*Moroni 6:9*

One of the striking features of Moroni's theology of contrast and complement is that he presents it with

very little concern for the potential contradictions. The counterpoints of the gospel don't have to be explained, he seems to say; they simply need to be lived. True to form, as he comes to the conclusion of his section on the practices of the church, he unapologetically offers us yet another striking juxtaposition of two competing principles. After repeated references to the proper manner of performing ordinances, right down to the precise and unchanging wording of the sacrament prayers, he ends on a contrasting note of charismatic worship. Church meetings were based on the unscripted movements of the Spirit, with the Saints following the direction of the Holy Ghost wherever it led. When they were prompted to preach, they preached. And when they were inspired to pray, they prayed. When they felt to sing, they sang. They do not seem to have been bound to a preprinted bulletin.

This combination of clear ecclesiastical forms and free-flowing spirituality is characteristic of Moroni's penchant for contrapuntal theology. Just when he seems to be leaning into a kind of ritualistic formalism, up crops a vibrant culture of spiritual spontaneity, preventing us from pushing our reading too far in the direction of formulaic worship. Once again, he wants us to enjoy both the blessing of good order and the ongoing gifts of the Spirit. These are not at odds for Moroni. Rather, the disciples he describes live resolutely at their junction.

# 5

## The Sermon: Part I

*"And now I, Moroni, write a few of the words of my father."*
—Moroni 7:1

*"All things which are good cometh of Christ."*
—Moroni 7:24

Moroni is known for delivering the words of others. He finishes and presents Mormon's account. He interjects Ether's record into the final portion of the unsealed plates. Even in the book that bears Moroni's own name, major portions of the text consist of him conveying words that others had previously expressed: what Christ said to his disciples, what elders said to priests, what priests said over the sacrament, what his father said to the church, and finally what his father directly wrote to him. (This personality trait seemed to continue into immortality, as his first angelic visit to Joseph Smith was marked by his recitation of numerous writings from various ancient prophets.)[1]

It may be that his offering of Mormon's address on faith, hope, and charity—what we now call chapter 7—constitutes Moroni's finest gift to his readers. In his characteristically modest willingness to cede space to Mormon, Moroni brings forth one of the record's most important moments of theological reflection.

The chapter's opening verse reminds the readers, however, that Moroni is something other than a purely passive conduit through which Mormon's words pass to us. It explains that Moroni writes "a few" of the things that Mormon taught, indicating that Moroni took an active editorial role in assessing his father's teachings and choosing what he considered most important from Mormon's discourses. The sermon that follows, then, comes with two witnesses to the power and importance of the doctrine it contains—that of author-father and that of curator-son.

*of deeds and character*
*"A bitter fountain cannot bring forth good water."*
*—Moroni 7:11*

*"All things which are good cometh of God."*
*—Moroni 7:12*

Mormon shared his son's interest in the concept of the divine gift. Indeed, he likely bequeathed that interest to Moroni. In the speech that Moroni has selected, Mormon opens with the language of gifting in an expression of gratitude for the blessing of being allowed a place in the work of the Lord. "It is by the gift of his calling unto me," Mormon tells his audience, "that I am permitted to speak unto you at this time" (Moro. 7: 2). His opening indicates that one's specific place in time and space is a chance to make a particular contribution to the divine work of redemption. This is the "gift of his calling." As Mormon frames his ministry in these terms he reminds us why in the Church we refer to a calling as something "given" and "received."

Mormon's introductory acknowledgment of divine sovereignty—the notion that our work is a gift of God, that we act only by his allowance—is more than an opening cliché. It helps set the stage for the remarkable theology that follows. From the sermon's very beginning it orients us away from our own initiating capacity and toward God's overruling providence. It is an acknowledgement of our dependence on divine grace. Mormon did not begin this way by accident.

And yet, his next statement initially appears to cut in an opposing theological direction. The shift occurs as he turns from himself to his audience. Looking over his listeners, he declares them to be the "peaceable followers of Christ," people who "have obtained a sufficient hope" and "rest" in the Lord and who maintain "a peaceable walk with the children of men." That is, he sees a certain level of spiritual preparedness in his listeners, a kind of maturation—emphatically marked by their peacemaking—that seems both to enable and to encourage Mormon to speak to them of hopeful things. He emphasizes their Christlike way of living to the point that some readers might begin to think of these people as having been redeemed by their own good deeds. He cites a scriptural sentiment that by one reading certainly could reinforce that interpretation: "By their works ye shall know them; for if their works be good, then they are good also" (Moro. 7:3–5).

If left to stand on their own, such statements might point toward a theology of "works righteousness"—the doctrine that we become holy, and thus qualify for heaven, on the basis of good works. Mormon, however, does not let these statements stand on their own. He immediately follows them with a set of rapid-fire correctives, assertions to assure us that the righteousness of which he speaks is something more than the simple pieties of outward behavior. He takes pains to establish that external actions may in fact be misleading measures of the heart. His implication is that *truly* good lives are the *result* of redemption, not the *source* of redemption.

In chapter 7 verse 6 Mormon states, "For behold, God hath said a man being evil cannot do that which is good; for if he offereth a gift, or prayeth unto God, except he shall do it with real intent it profiteth him nothing." The hypothetical "man" in Moroni's declaration seems able to do an ostensibly good deed, to extend a gift and to utter a prayer, but he *cannot* do it with the right kind of heart, and it is the heart that matters. The grudging offer of a gift not only fails to register a credit on the giver's ledger of righteousness, it also is counted by God as a compounding of sin. In this rendering, behavioral projections of righteousness may only be a mask for inward depravity. The colorful early Church authority J. Golden Kimball drew this meaning from Mormon's message: "I find that a man can act good and talk good and look good and not do any good."[2] Mormon warns, "God receiveth none such" (Moro. 7:9).

To drive home his point, Mormon then places a vivid metaphor on this doctrine: "A bitter fountain cannot bring forth good water," he declares, "neither can a good fountain bring forth bitter water" (Moro. 7:11). The water flowing from a clean spring and the water flowing from a corrupted spring may *look* exactly the same, but in their unseen nature they unavoidably carry the characteristics of their source, whether life-giving or poisonous. And the God who looketh not on the outward appearance but on the heart will never be fooled by the inauthentic sanctimonies of an impure soul.

I might accept a church calling out of pride. I might seek peace out of fear of conflict. I might attend the temple in the belief that I am building a bigger mansion in heaven. To a mortal observer these things could look like sainthood, but to the God who cares about our inward character, those acts come from the exact same source that could turn down a church calling out of fear, or spark conflict out of pride, or not make it to the temple because I was building a bigger mansion on earth. Those two versions of me have different calculations of interest but they do not evidence a fundamentally different kind of soul. They are simply alternative strategies of the same heart. This is far from the mighty redemptive change upon which so many previous prophets insisted.

*Mormon's foundational determinism*
*"Except he shall do it with real intent it profiteth him nothing."*   —Moroni 7:6

Mormon's fountain analogy, and the logic that surrounds it, insist that the good or evil quality of our deeds necessarily results from the good or evil of our character, not the other way around. An act stemming from fear is an act of cowardice, whether it ends up looking like peacemaking or bullying. An act generated by pure love is an act of charity, whether it appears humble or harsh. The nature of the source defines the essence of the output regardless of appearances. This is a challenging notion, but Mormon's language seems unrelenting on the matter.

Rather than affirming a theology of works righteousness, then, Mormon's phrases push radically away from such a doctrine, coming remarkably close to undermining notions that Latter-day Saints have long identified as central features of their faith: free moral agency and the intrinsic, elective power to self-improve. If a bitter fountain can never bring forth good water, how can that fountain ever change its ways? If an act by a corrupt heart counts for nothing—including even the act of prayer—what can that heart ever do to alter its own character? If an entity cannot produce anything other than what it already is, it is eternally stuck. What, then, can a sinner do to pursue salvation?

Nothing at all. Or, at least that is what multitudes of thoughtful Christians, beginning with Mormon's same premises, have reasonably concluded.

As Latter-day Saints, we have traditionally rejected that answer. On the question of human capacity to choose salvation, we are more inclined to quote James than Paul. Given that Latter-day Saints have for much of their history been locked in a kind of antagonistic theological struggle with Protestant Christians, a contest in which the restoration's emphasis on human capacity frequently conflicts with the Reformation's commitments to human depravity, we are often better versed in the arguments for free agency than we are in the notion of unmerited gifts from above. If we are all waiting on the arbitrary election of God, we frequently say to our grace-focused interlocutors, then we have emptied our lives of all responsibility and, thus, of all meaning. Why preach, why teach, why try? As a famous bit of anti-Calvinist doggerel had it during Joseph Smith's day, such theology says, "You can and you can't / You will and you won't / You'll be damned if you do / And you'll be damned if you don't."[3] We're pretty good at finding absurdity in caricatured versions of doctrines of human inability.

We are typically less aware of the actual logic of the arguments arrayed against the notion that humans can simply choose to be something better than what they are, but those arguments are extensive and profound. Indeed, they have been profound enough to sustain a powerful stream of Christian thinking for two thousand years: from the patristic figures of the early Christian church to the Puritan settlers of British North America to the neo-orthodox theologians of the present century.

One of the most compelling arguments on this question, one that closely relates to Mormon's metaphor, was developed with particular incisiveness by the eighteenth-century American theologian Jonathan Edwards.[4] Its logic runs like this: If you are presented with a choice, you will always choose the thing for which you have the more powerful internal inclination. I act in a certain way because my internal motivations have determined that direction. If I had acted differently, it could only be because my inclinations had a different orientation. In this sense I have free will—I can do what I really want to do—but I am bound by that supreme desire, a force over which I cannot have any control because I possess no inclination stronger than it.

This does not mean I always act in accordance with my *interest* or my *pleasure*. I may "choose" to avoid the job I really wanted because I was afraid of failure, or I may "choose" to run into a burning building to save others at the risk of my life, but this is not saying that I chose something other than my strongest inclination. Rather, it is simply indicating that my inclination to fear was stronger than my interest in the job and that my interest in the safety of others was stronger than my inclination to fear. If my actions are logically bound to reflect my strongest internal motivation—which, by definition, they are—I cannot *choose* in any morally meaningful sense unless I can somehow opt to alter my own internal mix of motivations. And this, I am afraid, is a logical impossibility. On this point, I find Edwards (and Mormon) utterly unanswerable. I see no compelling exit from this logical dead-end. A corrupt heart cannot cleanse itself.

The questions provoked by this point are quite predictable. Are we not capable of choosing selflessness over greed, or self-denial over appetite, or courage over fear? In answer to such questions, consider the logical impasse at the heart of a concept like "self-discipline." Does this mean that *I* discipline *me*? Does not this suggest there are at least two of me? Who is the governing "I" that can discipline the governed "me" for the better? I may choose to listen to my spirit over my flesh, but what is the part of me making *that* choice (something other than either spirit or flesh that can thus choose between them), and where did its character come from? Even if we could identify these multiple kinds of "me," how could the one calling the shots ever act otherwise than in accordance with its own existing inclinations? The "I" who sincerely wants "me" to be more righteous and thus bends the subordinate "me" to its will must itself already be more righteous, ergo there is no real change or choice. My choices thus simply display what "I" already was. The logical impossibility of improving one's character goes on and on. Thus, a bitter fountain cannot bring forth good water.

What difference does it make to see this? Why does Mormon begin here? Well, for one thing, it is difficult to appreciate a gift or its giver until you realize just how desperately you need them.

When we recognize both ① the need to change and ② the logical impossibility of changing ourselves, perhaps we should be willing to acknowledge that our Christian sparring partners are not so thoroughly illogical when they insist that the only viable conception of redemption is one in which a sovereign Lord graciously reaches into our hearts and changes us. We can be a bit more willing to see the reasons behind their argument that, of ourselves, we literally can do nothing to warrant such amazing grace. We can recognize why they reject our notion that a heaven based on our self-determined choices makes any more sense than a heaven based on predestined election. We can be a little slower to assume that a doctrine of free grace is merely a mask for moral laziness. We can more readily see sincerity in the tears they weep at the thought that a freely giving Savior has chosen to rescue them from themselves. We do not have to accept their ultimate conclusions—indeed, I do not—but I believe we absolutely must recognize the magnitude of the conceptual problem that they are willing to meet head-on and that we often sidestep. Mormon, after all, at the outset of his sermon is calling on us to pay close attention to these very things. He wants us to understand the need for a gift from which all others will flow.

*the importance of these things*
*"It is given unto you..."* —*Moroni 7:15*

Historically, one of the primary counterarguments to Jonathan Edwards's sort of determinism has rested heavily on what philosophers called "facts of consciousness," those self-evident truths that we simply experience as true. On the question of agency, an argument from facts of consciousness runs something like this: We are *conscious* of an act of choosing to change; we *experience* the sensation of having our willpower overcome strong desires and habits within us; we *feel* the capacity to enact self-discipline; and, thus, we *know* ourselves to be free to become something better than we have been. When famed American psychologist and philosopher William James struggled to make a case for human agency, he felt he broke through—at least temporarily—with the following: "My first act of free will shall be to believe in free will."[5] The simple experience of choosing becomes our strongest argument for the self-contained ability to change.

Every day of my life, from the morning when I choose scriptures over TikTok, to the late evening when I opt for a bowl of ice cream over twenty push-ups, I enact agency. This experience of freedom has made many of us supremely confident in the truth of our position that we can choose to change ourselves. Even if the conceptual argument against moral freedom is insurmountable, our own internal awareness of our own endless acts of volition renders all that philosophizing moot. Why worry about ideas, however logically sound, that seem disproven by the simple truths of our own experience, the endless witness of our own consciousness?

And yet, when we simply tune out the philosophical problem of human freedom (a problem which has now actually been *strengthened* by neuroscientific research) we may woefully underappreciate the wonder of the Savior's atonement. If we do not fully confront the necessarily unbreakable bars of the prison cell that is our own character, we cannot fully recognize the abundant gift of the Brother whose blood has set us free. Mormon wants us to understand that gift and the freedom it facilitates.

He was not the first, even in the Book of Mormon, to want us to understand the agentive implications of the atonement. The book's founding prophet, Father Lehi, made a similar point when he pleaded with his children to understand that it was only "because [we] are redeemed from the fall" that we "have become free forever, to know good from evil; to act for [ourselves] and not to be acted upon" (2 Ne. 2:26). Recall the declaration of King Benjamin: "And under this head ye are made free, and there is no other head whereby ye can be made free" (Mosiah 5:8). We are not free until we are "made free." Otherwise I am locked in a nature that cannot possibly progress. I think Mormon's phrasing is actually the most poignant of all: a man, being evil, cannot give a good gift. This is an impasse in which existence would seem utterly pointless.

Christ, then, really is our Alpha and Omega, our beginning and our end. Even before he saved me from my sins he made the very notion of "me" meaningful.

I owe him *everything*.

*the spirit of Christ, human freedom,*
*and angelic ministrations*
"How is it possible that ye can lay hold upon every good thing?"   —Moroni 7:20

Like a combination of Edwards and James, Mormon unmistakably establishes the logical impossibility of choosing to change ourselves and then unapologetically insists that we try to do exactly that. In preaching these contrasting truths, he repeatedly returns to the gifts of God. For instance, the capacity to distinguish light from darkness is a faculty that must be given before it can be exercised. "It is given unto you to judge," "the Spirit of Christ is given to every man," everything that pulls us toward the good comes from "the power and gift of Christ...wherefore ye may know..." (Moro. 7:15–16). Only after God has given us a set of choices, *and* the ability to see their qualities, and the power to follow one over the other, can we begin to speak meaningfully of our freedom. Mormon leaves us in no doubt about where this all comes from. Jesus is the gift through which *all* other gifts are made possible. Mormon insists on the principle he states with special clarity in verse 22: "[I]n Christ there should come every good thing."

He also insists on the precept expressed in verse 24: "All things which are good cometh of Christ; otherwise men were fallen, and there could no good thing come unto them." On a superficial reading, the doctrinal points in verses 22 and 24 sound essentially the same, repetitions for the sake of emphasis. But the verses actually contain phrases that form two different statements. Where verse 22 says that Christ makes possible the embrace of *every* good thing, the end of verse 24 indicates that Christ is necessary in order to obtain any good thing. He is both the modest start (any good thing) and the glorious finish (every good thing). To put this another way, Jesus gives us both the power to choose and the ability to choose well, the capacity to see at all and the light by which to see it all. The former seems to have been universally given through Christ, but the latter seems to rest on faith in Christ (Moro. 7:25). And that faith in him begins with revelations about him, which have been abundantly extended through the miraculous ministrations of angels and prophets (Moro. 7:22–23).

*the affirming miracle of our experience*
*"Have miracles ceased?"   —Moroni 7:29*

As Mormon weaves back and forth through complicated and interrelated themes of inability, agency, and illumination, he begins in chapter 7 verse 26 to articulate a recurring affirmation of the reality of miracles. He hammers his message home repetitively. He's serious about this. Without a commitment to the miraculous, the whole thing falls apart.

For instance: "And now, my beloved brethren, if this be the case that these things are true which I have spoken unto you, and God will show unto you, with power and great glory at the last day, that they are true, and if they are true has the day of miracles ceased?... If these things have ceased, then has faith ceased also; and awful is the state of man, for they are as though there had been no redemption made" (Moro. 7:35, 38). Redemption and a faith in miracles go hand-in-hand.

Why this turn to the miraculous? There may be multiple reasons for it. In Mormon's telling, wonders will happen as long as people have enough faith in Christ. Miracles therefore serve as something like the canary in the mineshaft; when they cease, we're all in trouble. But that point does not seem a sufficient explanation for his dramatic turn to this topic mid-sermon. Why would a sermon that begins with the immovable problem of impure hearts and ends with the irresistible promise of pure love be preoccupied in the middle with miracles? Perhaps because a miracle is exactly what it takes to get us from the problem to the promise.

In Mormon's theology, it turns out that both the Calvinistic proponents of determinism and the modern defenders of human will were correct. Jonathan Edwards was right that there is no logical defense of moral agency. William James was right that we in practice enact such agency every day. What should we call something that we know we have experienced but that logically cannot be? *Miracle* seems to be the right word for such a thing.

The divine act that has enabled us to choose and change is actually a more inexplicable wonder than the moving of mountains or the parting of seas. When we appreciate the existential miracle involved in the former we will see both the necessity and the possibility of believing in miracles like the latter. When we understand that we carry within us a witness of Christ's power to overcome the fetters of logical constraint, we may come to understand more thoroughly that God is ready and willing to work any other necessary marvel in our lives. And to lose faith in one is to undermine the other.

Mormon's sermon here brushes up against Paul's epistle to the Romans, even using the same formulation of "all things." Paul reasoned, "He that spared not his own Son, but delivered him up for us all, how shall he not with him also freely give us all things?"[6] (Rom. 8:32). If Christ can, through the atonement, punch through the prison walls of my character to offer me real freedom, everything else we ask of him should be easy. "Christ hath said," Mormon reports, that "if ye will have faith in me ye shall have power to do whatsoever thing is expedient in me" (Moro. 7:33). *Whatsoever* is a comprehensive word. Christ's is a comprehensive power.

Maybe it is the ultimate act of human ingratitude that across time and around the globe we all experience this undeniable reality of moral freedom—the sensation that we can be better than we are, a chance to choose a better way, a possibility we taste and feel and live but for which our best philosophizing and even our neuroscience can make no convincing account—and speak about it as if it were anything other than a miraculous gift. Every change and choice I make, each of a thousand big and little decisions that I enact in a typical day and that make my existence meaningful and the prospect of improvement possible, scream out to me and to all other human beings that we have a Savior.

This is something we can hear only if we start where Mormon starts.

There are also things we can see only if we end where Mormon ends: in the pure love of Christ.

# 6

# The Sermon: Part II

*"Charity is the pure love of Christ."*    —*Moroni 7:47*

Among the most important implications of this theology is a reminder of why we must leave judgment to the Lord. Note that if agency is gifted rather innately and universally present, its limits are set by the Giver and its extent may be individually specific. I will thus encounter others who quite literally *cannot* do what I might otherwise expect them to do. Capacity is constrained by inherited mental health, physiological structure, the paralyzing impact of trauma, and a million other obstructions to action. When we say that the ability to act and choose is given by God, we necessarily also acknowledge that its limitations often lie beyond our understanding and within the veil of his superior wisdom. Were I to tell a severely depressed soul to rise up and be of good cheer, and condemn her for her failure to do so, I might rest that judgment on the belief that the ability to act on that command is a capacity all humans have by nature. In the process, I might also fail to comprehend that her ability to choose forgiveness and patience exceeds my own. Conversely, in seeing agency as a gift, I can better recognize its divine diversity of forms; I will be both more appreciative of what other human beings can do and more patient with what they cannot do. (Maybe that is why Mormon said that the telltale characteristic of those who understand the doctrine of Christ is their peaceable walk with the rest of humanity.) Through this theological lens, each soul's endowment of agency—its lengths and its limits—begins to look very personalized, just as one would expect from the gifts of a thoughtful Giver.

This is precisely why grace and works must coexist in their ever-dynamic relationship, so resistant to precise definition. With every person, at any given moment, the interaction of the two will take a distinctive form. Each soul needs its own mix; each event of our life will require us to strive and to be still in differing proportions. Only with an eye single to the Giver can we understand the nature of what he is giving us at any particular point in our lives. The recurring theme of the book of Moroni—God's repeated offering of contrasting gifts that complement and counterbalance each other—reaches something of a climax in Mormon's sermon, where the gospel appears as fully infused with both utter dependence on God's unmerited generosity and unmistakable calls to the high exercise of human agency. Apparently uninterested in providing any kind of clear formula for the relationship of grace and the ability to work, what Mormon wants us to understand most is the giftedness of both. He invites us to understand them as givens.

When the children of Israel began their redemptive journey home—a metaphor for our own path to exaltation —they needed both to be released from bondage by the blood of the Lamb and the chance to walk the trail with manna and light. They needed, in short, an endless series of gifts—an initial offering of agency and the chance to use it well—if they were ever to make it back to the place they had been promised. And what the Lord most asked of them was to appreciate the giftedness of it all even as he called on them to keep pressing on. So it is with us. Paradoxical as it may be, when we humbly accept as givens both the offer of grace and the opportunity to work, the practical result of such a combination is the promise of peaceful exertion. We get the chance to try, the blessing of a morally meaningful existence, even as we know that the attributes of godliness will ultimately be conferred according to God's own giving and forgiving. The result of such a theology can be nonjudgmental, resolute, life-affirming effort. The yoke becomes easier, the burden becomes lighter, and we may find rest to our souls. Mormon unapologetically declares both that we cannot change ourselves and that we must change: rather than locking us into a maddening conundrum, Christ transforms that paradox into a grateful life of patient progress.

Having established both our natural inability to move beyond our character and the miraculously conferred gift of an ability to seek and find something better, Mormon begins to lead us toward the three culminating graces: faith, hope, and charity. His thematic progression affirms that, because of the Savior, God can draw us out of our natural inclinations, over the limits of the human condition, and toward a triumvirate of divine attributes—the highest of which is pure love. We can choose to change, he holds, but only because the process of becoming like Christ is a path marked by repeated acts of divine giving. We can claim no credit for the progress even as we are called on to embrace the opportunities God grants. Mormon insists that a life lived in full acknowledgement of our dependence on God's giving, a life lived focused on the divine generosity of it all—to borrow his word, a life lived in *meekness*—is the essential feature of a disciple's pilgrimage toward redemption.

86

*"because of your meekness"*
*"I judge that ye have faith in Christ because of your meekness."* —Moroni. 7:39

*"I say unto you that he cannot have faith and hope, save he shall be meek, and lowly of heart."* —Moroni 7:43

*"If a man be meek and lowly of heart... he must needs have charity."* —Moroni 7:44

We think of Mormon 7 as the sermon on faith, hope, and charity. Rightly so. But in fact a fourth attribute also makes repeated appearances, intertwining with the other three. In the last portion of Mormon's sermon, the quality of "meekness" recurrently emerges as both the conclusive sign and the fundamental prerequisite of the more famous trio of Christian graces.

Mormon is hardly alone in emphasizing meekness. Gospel commentators have highlighted it frequently over the past two millennia, noting Christ's striking call and promise: "Come unto me, all ye that labor and are heavy laden, and I will give you rest. Take my yoke upon you, and learn of me; for I am meek and lowly in heart: and ye shall find rest unto your souls" (Matt. 11:28–29). When Jesus most explicitly described both who he is and who we should be, he featured the quality of meekness. When he offered the paradoxical chance to take up a yoke that brings rest, he highlighted meekness. Christians have taken note.

Yet, despite its obvious importance, an exact sense of what it means to be meek has proved rather elusive in Christian theology. At times, modern scriptural commentators have seemed more interested in telling us what meekness is *not*. An internet search of the phrase "meekness is not weakness" returns over eighteen thousand hits. One *Christianity Today* article, which takes that phrase as its title, opens with the declaration that "blessed are the meek for they shall inherit the earth" is the "most misunderstood, mistrusted, and neglected" of all the beatitudes.[1] It is quite striking how eagerly, almost anxiously, Christian writers assure us that meekness can be compatible with power and strength. Don't mistake the meek for the merely passive, we are regularly warned. After all, Jesus Christ, the meek One, flipped tables in the temple.

Fair enough. There is clearly truth in this caution. But do we risk an overcorrection on such a vital principle? Some of the towering premodern theological figures of the Christian tradition were far less concerned than we seem to be with protecting meekness from the libel of feebleness. Rather, they placed their full emphasis on the principle of humble submission to the will of God. To teach about meekness, St. Augustine used the example of the adolescent donkey on which Jesus chose to ride into Jerusalem: a relatively weak and lowly beast carrying the King of Kings, chosen over the greater strength and status of a fully grown stallion for no other reason than its greater submissiveness to the will of its rider. "Our Lord would have meek beasts to ride upon," Augustine wrote. "You must be the Lord's mount, that is, you must be meek.... He governs you: do not be afraid of stumbling and falling."[2] If we submit to God's authority, Augustine argues, he will both keep us on the right path and secure our steps along the way. The blessing of meekness lies not in pursuing some stealthy strength but in humbly bearing the Lord who knows precisely where to lead us.

Part of our struggle with the meaning of meekness is that various terms get translated as meek in our English Bibles. In the Greek New Testament the original word is often *praus*, which connotes a mild and gentle demeanor. Emphasizing this meaning, St. Thomas

Aquinas wrote extensively about a Christian obligation to restrain one's anger and to show magnanimity in the face of frustration. This call to meekness-as-mildness certainly has scriptural warrant and its own theological beauty. It presents meekness as a matter of forbearance, a question of self-control.[3]

But Mormon, writing in Reformed Egyptian, may not have referenced the New Testament's Greek. *Praus* was likely not his source for his calls to meekness. Again, it is difficult to know the original of any word in our English translation of the Book of Mormon, but the Hebrew term that seems the most likely candidate for Mormon's use is *anav*—which appears in Psalm 37:11, a verse Jesus clearly drew from in his blessing of meekness in the Sermon on the Mount (Matt. 5:5). *Anav* connotes deep humility, a kind of self-aware impoverishment. This profound sense of personal lack and inadequacy serves as the natural companion to the phrase that both Jesus and Mormon paired it with: "lowliness of heart." Rabbis Dov Peretz Elkins and Abigail Treu have indicated that anav carries an "aware[ness] of one's limitations and of God's awesome power."[4] The venerable Hebraist Bruce Waltke equates the meek to "those who humbly acknowledge their dependence on God's power."[5] Also drawing on Hebrew meanings, the biblical scholar Charles Quarles has insisted that "the meek are those who...live in complete dependence on God."[6] Mormon, in the letter to his son that has become Moroni 8, reinforces this connection by linking meekness to God's gift of forgiveness: "The remission of sins bringeth meekness and lowliness of heart" (Moro. 8:26). We are made meek in the recognition of our need for God's intervention in our life, an unavoidable experience for those of us who have begged for and received atoning mercy.

Clearly some people are gifted in certain virtues, and the full cultivation of meekness seems to come much easier to one than another, but the foundational opportunity to be meek may be the most universally experienced element of our humanity. The awareness of having needs whose satisfaction must lie beyond ourselves is in part what it means to be human. It begins the moment we were born, the instant we cry for help. We need things we cannot, of ourselves, create. Revelation teaches it directly; life demonstrates it inevitably. Mere honesty about our lack is the beginning of meekness and may be the foundation of all religion. The famed German theologian Friedrich Schleiermacher surely overstated his case but still touched on a truth in arguing that the essence of true religion is a "consciousness of our absolute dependence." Schleiermacher insisted, "This feeling of absolute dependence, in which our self-consciousness in general represents the finitude of our being, is therefore not an accidental element, or a thing which varies from person to person, but is a universal element of life."[7]

Whether or not meekness universally lies within our natural reach, we have endless prophetic witness that God has graciously given us a chance to choose it. One of the most striking examples of this witness appears in Ezra Taft Benson's famous address on the Book of Mormon and pride. President Benson's climax to that speech reminds us that the Book of Mormon is not just a warning against pride; by definition, it is also a relentless call to humility. Note the emphasis President Benson places on our agentive capacity in relation to humility. His culminating passage begins with a single-sentence paragraph: "Let us choose to be humble." The passage then goes on to offer no less than *eight* repetitions of this phrase: "We can choose to humble ourselves." And then he concludes his reiterations with these striking lines: "Let us choose to be humble. We can do it. I know we can."[8] I know of no other moment of prophetic witnessing that so intertwines a Christlike attribute with a declaration of human capacity to choose.

Apparently meekness, in its Hebraic sense of deep humility, is something we can cultivate. It is also, Mormon indicates, the foundation of all other essential virtues. It turns out that the secret to escaping our inability is to acknowledge our inability. This humble recognition of desperate need, a lowliness of heart, a simple candor about the gaping chasm between who we are and who we hope to be, is the foundation of our faith, our hope, and our love.

In the mid-nineteenth century, American Transcendentalism's leading candidate for the title of theologian—Theodore Parker—insistently argued that the best way to know whether God has provided something in the universe is first to recognize our own need of it.[9] My observations of the faith journeys unfolding all around us has shed a revealing light on one part of Parker's point: I have noted that it is markedly easier to have faith that Jesus of Nazareth is our Savior once we realize how very much we need a savior. Note that King Benjamin, in his mighty sermon, brought his audience to a sense of their utter need—their "nothingness"—before he then called on them to have faith (Mosiah 4).The true gift of saving faith seems to be activated by a recognition of personal inadequacy. The same principle appears to apply equally well to the other graces. It is actually easier to rest securely in the hope of Christ's redemption when I realize that those hopes cannot rest wholly on me. It is easier to offer gifts of pure love when I realize how much I depend on them myself. If meekness is the activating force for the other virtues, then the conduit to these gifts is a recognition of their giftedness.

When we acknowledge that we can't, then God will. This may be why Mormon began his sermon with the problem of our necessity and our inescapable inability to change ourselves. This may be why Mormon spent so much time talking about Christ's willingness to do the miraculous for us, why he needs us to know that there is "no good thing" without our Redeemer. Mormon knows that meekness is the key to the theology of the gift.

*faith and hope*
*"If a man have faith he must needs have hope; for without faith there cannot be any hope."* —Moroni 7:42

In our common English idiom, hope can seem like a sort of watered-down version of faith (e.g., "I'm not sure I believe it's true, but I hope it's true"). That is clearly not the way Mormon is using it in Moroni 7:42 (or elsewhere; see Alma 25:16). Note that, in Mormon's formulation, faith is as much a prerequisite of hope as hope is of faith. Neither is a simple waystation to the other. Rather, faith and hope appear to be two distinct but interdependent forms of belief. They stabilize us by tethering our Christian conviction to different anchor points on the same rock of salvation.

Here, as his son would do in Ether 12, Mormon connects hope with the promise of personal salvation: "I say unto you that ye shall have hope through the atonement of Christ and the power of his resurrection, to be raised unto life eternal, and this because of your faith in him according to the promise" (Moro. 7:41). Mormon thus touches on a relationship that gets borne out elsewhere in the scriptures, a sort of division in which faith seems to refer to our belief in the being and nature and declarations of divinity, while hope has to do with the personal application and implication of those truths. For instance, if faith is the belief that God is good, hope is the belief that he will be good to *me*; if faith is the conviction that God keeps his promises, hope is the assurance that those promises apply to *us*. (For other verses linking hope to the prospect of personal redemption or blessing, see 1 Ne. 19:24; 2 Ne. 31:20; Jacob 2:19; Alma 5:10; 13:29; 22:16; 28:12; 34:41; Ether 12:24; Moroni 7:48; 9:25.)

Mormon's explanation in Moroni 7, then, helps explain the mutual dependence of faith and hope. If I don't believe God will be good to me, then I don't really believe he is good. And if I don't really believe he is good, then I cannot really believe he will be good to me. Faith is in this sense the substance of things hoped for: My recognition of the existence and character of God, and my conviction about the atonement of Jesus Christ, serve as the objective foundation on which my subjective hopes rest. "Without faith there cannot be any hope," Mormon states flatly. But "how can ye attain unto faith," he asks, "save ye shall have hope?" We must possess one to have the other (Moro. 7:42, 40). God's nature and his relationship with me are inextricably intertwined. In the former I have faith, through the latter I have hope, and neither half of the pairing can survive alone.

*charity*
*"For charity never faileth."*   —*Moroni 7:46*

Faith and hope, when actuated by meekness, are here characterized as profoundly powerful forces. But, Mormon explains, they are not the culminating virtues. Indeed, without the third and final gift, all others are for naught. He declares, "If a man be meek and lowly in heart, and confesses by the power of the Holy Ghost that Jesus is the Christ, he must needs have charity; for if he have not charity he is nothing;

wherefore he must needs have charity" (Moro. 7:44). Love is the final answer.

As in Paul's letter to the Corinthians, Moroni's sermon characterizes pure love as the counterforce to every destructive natural instinct that inheres in humanity. Our self-preservation instinct encourages self-interest, but charity seeketh not its own. Evolutionary biologists would tell us that we are hardwired to covet, but charity envieth not. In a human existence that is defined by limitations of energy and attention, charity beareth *all* things, believeth *all* things, hopeth *all* things, and endureth *all* things. Some loves are natural. This one is supernatural.

Such love sets a very high standard for humans to emulate. Indeed, it is an impossible standard. And yet, the absence of such love is—according to Mormon—a guarantee of nothingness. "If you have not charity," he insists, you are "nothing." Passages of scripture that call us to this kind of love can be demoralizing if we understand Mormon to be arguing that an inability to love like this, a life lived short of the Christian ideal, is a sign of existential failure.

To "have" such love can mean two things, however. It can be that we hold such love for others, or it can mean that we have received it from someone else. For example, I have love *for* my wife; I also have love *from* my wife. Same verb, different experiences. It may be this latter sense of "having love" that Mormon has in mind at some points in this discussion. Elder Jeffrey R. Holland has written, "The greater definition of 'the pure love of Christ'...is not what we as Christians try but largely fail to demonstrate toward others but rather what Christ totally succeeded in demonstrating toward us. *True* charity has been known only once."[10] Note in verse 44 that if we are to be meek and declare our faith in Jesus Christ, we "must needs have charity," for if we "have not charity" we are "nothing." I think this clearly means we could not even start on the redemptive process—we cannot even cultivate the foundational graces of meekness and faith—until Christ's love first empowers us to do anything. To borrow a phrase from the first epistle of John, we love God because he "loved us first" (1 Jn. 4:19). We can "have" charity only because we already "have" charity.

What does it mean that those who do not have this love "are nothing"? Surely, it does not mean that those who have not embraced Jesus Christ, or who do not yet live lives of perfected love, are "nothing" in God's eyes. If that were true, why do the scriptures record our Father as weeping over his unbelieving and inhumane children? Gods do not weep over nothing. Rather, the line about those without Christ's love being nothing should again turn our attention to the reality that without the liberating love of the atoning Savior our entire experience of self would be bound to static and passive meaninglessness. We would be nothing without him.

The phrase should also suggest to us that this love is universally distributed. He has released us all from nothingness; by making us *all* objects of a perfect love, he has made us *all* agentive subjects with meaningful choices and chances to change. If charity endureth all things, then it endures with all of us. If charity beareth all things, then it bears all of us. If charity hopeth all things, then there is hope for all of us. There is a law of transitive property at play here: if to be without his love is to be nobody, then by definition nobody is without his love.

Having described the limitless capacities of charity, Mormon then offers one of the sermon's most striking promises: "Whoso is found possessed of [pure love] at the last day, it shall be well with him" (Morm. 7:47). After all the many millennial preparations we undertake as a people—from stockpiling food to reading the signs of the times—it turns out that the essential prerequisite for being well in the last day boils down to one true thing: the love of Jesus Christ.

### *"that ye may become"*

If these verses emphasize that redemptive love is available to all who would receive it, making Christ the active saving agent and us the saved recipients, the ensuing passages remind us that an element of this gift is both the opportunity and the obligation to take active part in our own transformation. Again, Mormon interweaves dependence and ability. We may not be able to change ourselves, but the light of Christ has given us the chance to seek a soul like our Savior's. It has also given us the gift of prayer, a key to the progressive development of the graces within us.

Note that the verbs associated with the gift of charity change as Mormon's discourse unfolds. First we "have" it. Then we "cleave" unto it. Then we "possess" it. Then we must "be filled" with it. As the verbs change, so do the subjects: *Everyone* "has" it, but only the *true followers of Christ* are "filled" with it. The path of discipleship, defined as an increasingly comprehensive relationship with the Savior's love, facilitates conformation to the very character of Christ. Mormon concludes by inviting us to "pray unto the Father with all the energy of heart, that ye may be filled with this love, which he hath bestowed upon all who are true followers of . . . Jesus Christ; that ye may become the sons of God; that when he shall appear we shall be like him, for we shall see him as he is" (Morm. 7:48). This is the ultimate hope.

This relationship among the divine love that is given to all of us, the divine love that is prayerfully cultivated within is, and the divine love that is expressed through us is captured in a phrase that sometime sits awkwardly in Latter-day Saint culture: "that they may become the sons of God." Evangelical critics often use similar phrasing found in the Bible to challenge the Latter-day Saint tendency to characterize all people as the children of a Heavenly Father. Why, they wonder, would we say that every human being is the "child of God" when Paul wrote to the Romans that only "as many as are led by the Spirit of God, they are the sons of God" (Rom. 13:14)?

What such conversations miss is that in our common parlance there are two ways to be the child of a parent. When I look at my niece and say, "She is her mother's daughter," I am either making an inanely obvious statement about the biology of maternity or I am saying that she is conspicuously demonstrating the attributes of her parent. To say the latter is not to deny the generative relationship that her siblings also share with their mother, but it is to emphasize a particular fact of resemblance. Thus, the notion that we are all God's children and the idea that some are actively developing into his children are not mutually exclusive. These conceptions of childhood capture two equally true kinds of connections: one that is about being and one that is about becoming. The first is a universal reality of life; the second is a chosen way of living. God is always our father; I hope I am becoming his son.

So, too, with the pure love of Christ. I already "have" it in the sense that Christ has given it to me. I am also striving to cleave to it (living my life in connection to it) and praying to "possess" it (making the attribute mine) and to eventually "be filled" with it (letting it inform everything about me and my presence in the world). This progression of verbs ultimately points us to the second sense of charity—which involves the love we have for others—suggesting an additional expression to the formula articulated previously for the relationship of faith and hope: if faith is the knowledge that God is good, and hope is the assurance that he will be good to me, charity is the experience of him being good *through* me. When that occurs, we have evidence of its fullness in our life. When that occurs, we grow in the recognition that Christ's gift to us has empowered our offerings to others. As Nicholas J. Frederick has written, "We become 'sons of God' because we learn to love others with the same love that both the Father and the Son demonstrate toward each other and toward us."[11]

In those moments we convey God's love to others, we find ourselves approaching Mormon's culminating stage of our relationship with the Savior. When divine love flows through us, we begin to "see him as he is"; that is, having experienced for someone else a taste of the love God has for us, we have come to understand his character more fully. In that process, we have also begun "to become like him," increasingly definable by his defining quality. Both our faith in who he is and our hope for who we can be are fulfilled in pure love. Like a river running through a sandstone canyon, the divine love that passes through us toward others simultaneously reveals its full force and lastingly carves out our very character. In the use of the gift we come to resemble the Giver.

# 7

# The Letters

After reproducing his father's sermon, Moroni proceeds to insert into his record correspondence from Mormon. As noted previously, the two letters warn against the extremes of religious formalism on one side and anarchic disorder on the other. Moroni's choice to include this communication further extends his call for disciples to hold resolutely to the gospel's complementary demands, the counterweighted truths that both stretch and stabilize us.

Beyond their roles as guardrails against ecclesiastical extremism, the letters also harmonize as twinned warnings about contention. They each lament a kind of division, one concerned with theological disagreement within the church and the other with violence among communities. From the high point of pure love with which chapter 7 concludes, the descent into doctrinal controversy and war crimes is nauseatingly steep. No wonder "it grieveth" Mormon "that there should disputations rise" (Moro. 8:4). Within a few verses the book shifts from its most transcendent expressions of divine goodness to its most graphic depictions of human cruelty, the light and the darkness setting each other in especially sharp relief. Mormon's depiction of the ease with which human nature—and society—can slide into viciousness underscores the urgency of the gospel message.

With a profound parental concern, Mormon counsels his son—and by extension the rest of us—that the only way to survive such a fall is to keep Christ at the center of our story. Jesus is the author and the finisher of our narrative, and he must also be at its heart. He is the fulcrum on which the contrasting truths of the gospel must balance. The first letter opens with the hope that Christ can, "through his infinite goodness and grace...keep [us] through the endurance of faith on his name to the end" (Moro. 8:3). The second letter closes with the call to let "Christ lift [us] up" even when everything else in the world seeks to drag us down (Moro. 9:25). The Redeemer will "lift" and "keep" us in the most challenging of times. For that promise to have full effect, Mormon insists, we must have an accurate sense of God's parental character.

*little children and love; inequity and divine impartiality*
*"My beloved son" and "his Holy Child" Mormon 8:2–3*

*"I love little children with a perfect love; and they are all alike and partakers of salvation."* —*Mormon 8:17*

Chapter 8 opens on a note of parental love. Mormon begins his letter by signaling that he cares deeply for his own son, that he is "mindful" of Moroni and "praying" for him "always." He then immediately characterizes Jesus Christ as God's "Holy Child," the only use of this biblical phrase for Jesus in the entire record (Moro. 8:3; Acts 4:27–30). Mormon clearly has parenthood and progeny on his mind. He thus starts his epistle with a striking statement of affection for children, touching on both his own personal parental instinct and the familial dynamics of the Godhead. Where Moroni 7 ended with an abstract call to become the children of God, Moroni 8 commences with the rich emotional content that fills such a relationship.

Mormon insists that Jesus Christ's atonement makes a special provision for children. Three times in the course of the letter, Mormon explains that little ones are "alive in Christ" (Morm. 8:12, 19, 22). It is an arresting phrase, bringing us back to the doctrine embedded in Mormon's sermon from the previous chapter. If the atonement releases us from the prison house of our innate character, making existence something more than mere stagnation, it grants us life in a very real sense. It makes us "alive." This is one of the ways in which the Savior can be characterized as our "father," the generator of our being. Christ is a life-giver. And for those whose temporal circumstances prevent the full exercise of moral agency—such as small children—his atoning power takes a further step, filling their existence with life and meaning and the promise of redemption even in a period of incapacity and especially in the face of human inequality.

While wrestling with this topic, Mormon's letter makes clear that our understanding of the gospel cannot turn a blind eye to the lived realities of privilege and disadvantage. He specifically castigates those who were promoting a doctrine of infant baptism because he believes they had failed to consider fully the disparate circumstances into which God's children are born. To save some children because the situation in which they were raised was conducive to baptism, and to damn others because their situation was different, would make God a "partial God" (Moro. 8:12). And this kind of God could never do, neither for Mormon nor for the theology Moroni has been building through Mormon's writings. The love described in Moroni 7 would be incompatible with such an inequitable system and such an unfair Father. Mercy must account for circumstance.

Mormon uses this letter both to extol the goodness of God and to encourage the emulation of his divine character. Here, the godly attribute in question is fairness. When in verse 17 Mormon declares himself "filled with charity"—that is, when he puts himself forward as an example of the call to love issued in Moroni 7:48—his premier evidence of being filled with Christ's pure love is that "all children are alike unto" him. By such reasoning it would seem that the measure of our progress in the disciple's quest for a soul like the Savior's is the degree to which we have laid aside prejudice and partiality.

The implications of Mormon's doctrinal intervention here are actually larger than just the matter of childhood. He acknowledges as much in verse 22, where he extends this principle to all people who are "without the law." The big questions he raises in this letter—about inequality of circumstance and about the high theological importance of accounting for that inequality—resonate well beyond the particular practice of pedobaptism. Mormon's letter leaves us to contemplate how we can best answer those questions in relation to the other forms of injustice that may lurk in our own doctrinal errors.

It is worth noting that Mormon here made the goodness and parental devotion of God the firm standard against which one's theology must be tested. By implication, doctrines that fail that test should be discarded. In Mormon 8 the fairness of the Great Parent of us all becomes the great check on false gospels. The rhetorical intensity of his letter forces us to pause over this point.

*the tone of Mormon's preaching*
*and the character of his God*
*"It is mockery before God, denying the mercies of Christ, and the power of his Holy Spirit, and putting trust in dead works." —Moroni 8:23*

The tone of Mormon's attack on the doctrine of infant baptism is razor sharp. Infant baptism, Mormon tells

Moroni, is a "gross error," a "mockery before God." He goes on to insist that those who believe in this doctrine "have neither faith, hope nor charity." They are bitter, iniquitous, and on a slippery slope to damnation. He is not pulling punches (Morm. 8:6, 9).

Those who have known sincere and devoted Christians who believe in infant baptism—and surely we have all known such adherents to this practice—must pause at what seems to be Mormon's characterization of our friends and associates. At first blush, Mormon appears to insist that the mere fact of acceding to this doctrine disqualifies a person from faith, hope, and love and destines the heretic for perdition. This is challenging material. It is hard to picture Mother Theresa as a leading candidate for "death, hell and an endless torment" (Morm. 8:21).

But this implication needs to be amended by the fact that Mormon writes here about the *initiators* of this error, not its inheritors. Indeed, he is not even condemning all its initiators in the abstract, but he is specifically referring to particular people who have consciously corrupted the pure doctrine they had once received. Still, even with that qualification, we can certainly recognize that something about this doctrine has Mormon especially fired up. The exaggerated outrage of his epistle may not be very convincing as a description of broad swaths of Christian believers, but it is an unmistakable signpost to what he sees as the pressing importance of the underlying issues.

Mormon's view of the gospel hinges on the character of the God guiding its redemptive process. The sermon in Moroni 7 characterizes us as a species of beings who cannot change ourselves but whom the Lord generously empowers to seek salvation. If the Deity at the heart of that account of the gospel either cannot, or will not, make up for our inabilities, the whole thing falls apart. In

Mormon's mind, to say that children must—upon pain of damnation—make a choice for change before they have yet been fully enabled to do so is to say that God does not offer the requisite gifts to those who lack. Mormon's theological construct would collapse under the weight of such a God. After all, this category of the needy—the great congregation of the inadequate and the inequitably situated—ultimately includes us all.

If we don't believe God will right inequity for little ones and make up for their inheritance of inability, what chance would there be for the rest of us? The doctrine of infant baptism eats away at the heart of Mormon's gospel understanding and thus provokes his most energetic rebuttal. Without faith in the proper character of God there is no hope in the promise of pure love. But there *is* a good God, and pure love *is* on offer. A highly agitated Mormon refuses to let his son, or us, miss those essential truths.

*rapid descent*
*"They have lost their love, one towards another."*
—*Moroni 9:5*

While Mormon's first letter to his son indulges in an angry and amplified warning against a doctrinal risk to his theology, his next letter shows in disturbing detail what can happen in practice when humans lose sight of the divine love they have been granted. It also demonstrates what prejudice and partiality can look like in horrific actuality. In its description of the genocidal conflict between Lamanites and Nephites, Mormon's account depicts humanity at its lowest: sadistic torture, sexual violence, forced cannibalism, and a gory cycle of vengeance. The depths to which people could fall, and the frightening rapidity with which they might make that descent, serve as a stark reminder of what is at stake in the effort to retain a sense of faith, hope, and love. In the absence of these virtues, hatred can quickly win.

When that hatred is on the ascent, those who seek to promote charity frequently find their words falling on deaf ears. The throbbing pulse of bloodlust can drown out a call to love God and neighbor. Lamenting his inability to reach his people, Mormon puts the matter this way: "When I speak the word of God with sharpness they tremble and anger against me; and when I use no sharpness they harden their hearts against it" (Moro. 9:4). The fact that his listeners would respond to neither angle of appeal convinced Mormon that they were moving past feeling. The deadening of one's spiritual response marks a truly ominous state of affairs.

Given the graphic content of this letter, and Mormon's obvious frustration at his inability to lead his people out of their spiraling descent, it is worth reflecting on the reasons why Moroni chose to include such a troubling artifact. Why make this effort to provide material that is so hard to stomach and even harder to discuss with one's children? Why, in a text we often turn to for comfort and consolation, must we take this hard look at human depravity? Certainly, as previously noted, it serves as a warning against the breakdown of ecclesiastical order. But that surely could have been accomplished without passages on intentionally starved children being forced to eat the flesh of their fathers.

Some sense of Moroni's rationale may be found in an argument made by renowned literary critic—and Latter-day Saint—Wayne C. Booth. Booth argued that when encountering repulsive violence (or other forms of vice) in a literary text, we can decide whether this journey into darkness is gratuitous or essential, merely salacious or morally enriching, by considering whether our own capacity to distinguish goodness from evil has been expanded by the encounter. Has the author given us materials in the text that help us assess the squalor rather than merely be provoked by it? Are there enticements not only for reinforcing our own existing moral judgments but also for further developing our critical ethical faculties? If there are, the darkness can point us toward the light.

Appropriately, Booth uses the metaphor of the gift to discuss our assessment of the books we encounter, especially of those that contain disturbing material: "To tell a story, and especially to publish one, is to offer a gift," Booth writes. "Does this gift seem to me, I ask, now that I have lived with it intimately, like the gift of a friend?"[1] Moroni 9 reads to me as the gift of a friend.

This disturbing chapter can improve our moral reasoning in a variety of ways. Consider, for instance, Mormon's insistence on maintaining a critical distance in relation to the crimes of his own people—exemplifying the sort of ethical positioning that Booth believes an authorial friend should encourage. There is a strong invitation to better moral reasoning in the fact that Mormon's love for his people, and his resolve to press on in their service, do not blinker him to his people's viciousness. He clearly strives to emulate the attribute he ascribed to God in his previous letter: that he is no respecter of persons, that he will assess all people with equity. Chapters 8 and 9 both seem to show Mormon's basic agreement with David Hume, the eighteenth-century Scottish philosopher whose work on moral inquiry inspired Booth's modern theory of literary critique: "Prejudice is destructive of sound judgment, and perverts all operations of the intellectual faculties."[2] Had Mormon indulged in ethnic or national chauvinism here—excusing his own people's atrocities in light of Lamanite aggressions—a key lesson in moral reasoning would be lost. Instead, his prophetic integrity leaves him loyal to truth above tribe.

Mormon's unflinching gaze at the crimes of his own people, unobscured by the justifying instincts of nationalism, offers us a lesson in moral reasoning that elevates the low brutality of his description into a call to higher ground. Moroni's willingness to let this indictment stand in the historical record brings the benefits of Mormon's letter across time. That, too, is the work of a friend.

*a look at human depravity*
*"O the depravity of my people!"* —*Moroni 9:18*

Mormon and Moroni encourage us to resist naivete about the depth to which human nature can sink. At one level Moroni 9 is about Lamanites and Nephites, but in describing abominations on both sides of that divide, the chapter also becomes a commentary on the character of humanity as a whole. It confronts us with a nauseating portrait of our own capacity for evil.

Neither Mormon in writing the letter nor Moroni in including it has been reluctant to raise our awareness of human depravity. And neither will coddle a defensive reflex to attribute evil to others. They both know that evil's potential lurks within and among us. This prophetic realism places them at odds with philosophical and theological trends that were gaining strong religious momentum at the time the Book of Mormon was first published. It also places them in some tension with a tendency that can prevail within current Latter-day Saint culture.

The history of Western modernity has long been marked by a resilient belief in the essential goodness of humanity. This belief asserts that if the human spirit could just be free of its artificial fetters, if society would remove its distorting pressures, the individual conscience would intuitively point toward the light. This emphasis on the reliable moral compass of the liberated conscience marked one of the telltale features of American optimism, a view of humanity that seemed determined to leave its Calvinist opposite in the shadows of the past. It also gradually undermined a sense of need for scripture or any other external check on human instinct. Just listen to your heart, it said. The human soul, figures like Ralph Waldo Emerson were confidently declaring, should be "self-reliant."[3]

By the mid-twentieth century, however, that cheering view of humanity had taken a beating: the death and destruction wrought by two world wars and other genocidal conflicts gave the lie to the idea that human society was on a naturally upward curve of liberated decency. Instead, the world saw murderous nightmares of unprecedented scale. Some chastened theologians began to come back to the Puritans' rather dark views on humanity's unfathomable capacity for evil. One of these "neo-orthodox" theologians, H. Richard Niebuhr, famously pushed back on an overly optimistic mode of modern Christianity that he described as preaching a gospel in which "a God without wrath brought men without sin into a kingdom without judgment through the ministrations of a Christ without a cross."[4]

Even with such critiques, however, the siren song of humanity's self-sufficient goodness has proved persistent. Sometimes that persistence comes from a willful doctrinal rejection of the fallen depravity of the natural man about which Abinadi taught (Mosiah 16:5). Sometimes it comes simply from a culture oriented toward the escapism of sanitized stories and happy endings. The famed Latter-day Saint affinity for all things Disney suggests the degree to which we are prone to a whitewashed image of human existence and cartoonish depictions of evil.

Moroni 9 serves as a check on both tendencies. There is no neat wrap-up to the Nephite story. Mormon's letter, rather, stands starkly as a reminder that our capacity for cruelty is real. It will not let us escape from a full encounter with the effects of the fall. Note that in Mormon's narrating of his nation's depravity, the people's precipitous transformation into savagery did not come through the corrupting presence of external forces. It came in a moment when his people seemed most fully liberated from structural constraint. It came from within.

Mormon encourages his son—and us—to look that reality squarely in the face. The meekness of which he taught, after all, insists that we should exercise considerable skepticism with regard to the moral self-sufficiency of our own fallen natures.

Joseph Smith famously said that any person who wants to lead another toward the light would have to step out of a naively thoughtless optimism about our existence: "Thy mind, O Man, if thou wilt lead a soul into Salvation must stretch as high as the utmost Heavens, and search into and contemplate the darkest abyss."[5] Moroni 9 gives us a harrowing glimpse over that edge. When so many around us have lived in the murky recesses of the abyss—dragged into its darkness by abuse and injustice and, even after escaping, continuing to carry the traumatic consequences of humanity's inhumanity—we can be of little use to them until we have resolutely faced the actual evil of which our species is capable. We cannot be healers if we shield our eyes from the wounds.

This realism about human nature need not be a source of pessimism. Indeed, it must not be. Karl Barth, the most influential of the twentieth century's neo-orthodox theologians, put the matter this way: "We cannot forget how man is revealed to us in the light of God's Word—that he is a sinner, but that as such and in spite of himself he is also the object of divine grace, the partner in the covenant which God has made with him."[6] Barth insisted that we must resist fairytales about the irrepressible goodness of our souls, but we also need to preach the hope of a superior grace against which even the depravity of the natural man will yield. This is precisely what Mormon does.

*The Suffering Savior*
*"May his sufferings and death... rest in your mind forever."*
—*Moroni 9:25*

Mormon ends his disturbing letter on a hopeful note, and he calls on his son not to lose heart. "May Christ lift thee up," Mormon wrote to Moroni in the midst of the war's ugliest elements, "and may his sufferings and death, and the showing his body unto our fathers, and his mercy and long-suffering, and the hope of his glory and of eternal life, rest in your mind forever" (Moro. 9:25). It is interesting to me that Mormon's path to hope does not require him to draw a curtain on the agony around him but to pay closer attention to Christ's suffering and to his eternally wounded body. Mormon's concluding move—his emphasis on Christ's sufferings and the showing of his body—reminds me of a poignant observation made by the Latter-day Saint scholar Patrick Mason.

Mason has recently noted, "In my church we don't like to think very much about the crucified Jesus. We focus instead on the resurrected Christ. We like the glow, the glory, the happily ever after story. We don't much like the mangled, tortured, bloody body hanging limply on the cross. But Jesus doesn't want us to look away. When Jesus revealed himself after his resurrection, he showed the people the scars in his hands and feet and side. When you look at me, Jesus insists, don't forget my murdered body on the cross. And don't forget the violent system that did it.

"The resurrected, glorified Christ points us to the crucified Jesus. 'Behold the wounds which pierced my side, and also the prints of the nails in my hands and feet.' 'These wounds are the wounds with which I was wounded in the house of my friends.'"[7]

Jesus's broken body, like Moroni 9, is a lasting witness to humanity's bottomless capacity for depravity. We killed the Prince of Peace; we relish the destruction of others. Both Jesus's violent death and Moroni's gut-wrenching epistle, however, also testify to the power of divine love to pull us even out of those depths. They remind us that our skepticism about our nature should not become cynicism about our potential: pure love is possible, contingent on meekness. And for those who have been traumatized by their encounters with the dark nature of humanity, a faith attuned to Christ's history of descending below them all before ascending on high provides the hope that sustains a godly walk in a fallen world. The ugliness of Christ's death was bound to the beauty of his resurrection, and that arc of uplift is intended to carry all who will let it. With Jesus at the center, the moral of the story can be redeemed—even when surrounded by the sort of national nightmare through which Moroni had to live. His father pleaded with him to hold on to that as the world came down around him. Moroni clearly took that counsel to heart.

# Conclusion

*"Deny not the gifts of God, for they are many."*
—*Moroni 10:8*

Immediately after Mormon's stark letter on the destructive power of human hatred, with its concluding call to keep our hearts centered on the Savior's atoning sacrifice, Moroni draws his volume toward its close. He does so on the note of hope that his father had encouraged, wrapping up by reminding us of all God has done and is still willing to do for his fallen children.

Moroni is well aware that God's gifts may be temporarily rejected, but he is equally sure that they will be extended again. His conclusion helps us understand why his book bothered to describe how the gift of the Holy Ghost should be conferred, why it explained what the sacrament prayers should sound like, why it depicted a community united in covenants of caring. Moroni knows these gifts will come once more. The theme of hope weaves throughout his book because he understands God's bounty to be ever on offer.

For Moroni, this is not a naive hope. It has survived the worst that humanity could throw at it.

*remembering and anticipating gifts of mercy*
*"I write unto my brethren, the Lamanites."*
—*Moroni 10:1*

Moroni addresses his concluding testimony to future Lamanite readers. He has watched Nephite society disappear into political chaos and moral dissolution, but he knows that the Lamanites live on. He writes in the hope that these, his "brethren," will receive the message he has labored to compose. To begin his conclusion in these terms is itself a statement on the gifts that may come in time. After all the violence and the brutality—after all the hatred that Lamanites felt for the Nephites, who had committed unspeakable abominations against them—Moroni believes that the moment will come when Lamanites will receive a record from a Nephite as the offering of a friend. As he anticipates such a future of unwarranted reconciliation, he has gifts of mercy on his mind.

In verse 3 Moroni seeks to capture the overall meaning of his people's story. Their history looks like an abject disaster in so many ways, but to Moroni the message of the millennium-long history seems to come down to this: we should "remember how merciful the Lord hath been unto the children of men" (Moro. 10:3). This concluding assessment of the Book of Mormon's meaning squares remarkably well with Nephi's statement of some thousand years and five hundred pages earlier: "I will show unto you," Nephi wrote, "that the tender mercies of the Lord are over all those whom he has chosen" (1 Ne. 1:20). The book opened with a statement on the gifts of God's mercy, and now it ends on the very same point. God is good, the Book of Mormon has taught us from its first chapter to its last, and the ultimate evidence of that goodness is the mission of his beloved Son.

One aspect of this divine mercy is that God has granted us the ability to know his wisdom and his will. Mormon's sermon had emphasized such gifts of illumination, a promised ability to "know good from evil," and Moroni comes back to this point here in conclusion (Moro. 7:19). He affirms that this promise applies even to the book making such promises. Indeed, he assures us that "by the power of the Holy Ghost ye may know the truth of all things" (Moro. 10:5). The Father who has pledged to make up for what his children lack has gifted us a power to know things that lie beyond mere mortal cognition.

In this remarkable offering, we again run up against the recurring problem of human hearts. God's gift of enlightenment comes "if ye shall ask with a sincere heart, with real intent, having faith in Christ" (Moro. 10:4). That is a daunting standard for mortal seekers. Once more: How can we will ourselves to sincerity we don't feel? How does a person seeking faith ask in faith? This challenge reads differently here at the end of Moroni's book than it would have at the beginning. This is true in two ways, one exemplified by the structure of Moroni's promise and one embedded in the theology of his book.

The phrasing of Moroni's promise reveals a set of authorial assumptions. Most importantly, the invitation to pray is phrased in the negative. We are to ask "if these things are not true" (Moro. 10:4; emphasis added). That grammatical choice suggests Moroni's belief that after we have read and pondered the preceding pages—including his father's argument for the absolute need for a Savior—the meekness that activates faith, hope, and love will have already begun to work its effect prior to our prayer. Moroni imagines a reader who has already peered into the darkest abyss, who already sees humanity's absolute dependence on grace, who has encountered in the narrative so many examples of God's miraculous mercy that the gift of faith in a Savior has already begun to germinate sufficient to the posing of a meaningful prayer. The point of the prayer is thus only to theoretically disprove what, for Moroni, is already the obvious hypothesis.

The hope for those who are not quite as transformed by the book as Moroni presumes them to be may lie in the recurring theological weight his father placed on meekness. If meekness is the essential element and the chief generator of faith, then the initial prayer may need rest on only two admissions from the supplicant: that we need to know whether this is true and that we cannot determine that on our own. Not everyone is ready to make those admissions at a particular moment in their life. The thrust of the Book of Mormon's theology, however, is that, eventually, we will all confront such need.

When we do, it will be much easier to see why we must pray in the name of Jesus Christ. And this may be the ultimate answer to the conundrum. Why do we pray in Jesus's name? Because we recognize that the character of our hearts is in fact insufficient to carry our petitions through the veil. However, if we pray in *Jesus's name*, we get the imputed credit for praying with his kind of heart. Thus, the mere mechanical act of praying in his name begins to grant our petition the blessings of sincerity, of true intent, of saving faith. The Father and the Son have both mercifully offered a chance to convey our petitions in a spirit purer than we can generate on our own. And in recurrently borrowing his heart, by prayerfully invoking his name, we begin to be conformed to the soul of our Redeemer. As we ask, with his faith, for more faith, our own faith grows.

As we've seen before, in our use of the gifts we become more like the Giver.

*and we can search together*
*"...to one...and to another..."*   —*Moroni 10:9–10*

From this assurance to his readers that we can pray in Christ's name and that the Holy Ghost will affirm the truth of this record, Moroni then launches into a broader discussion of spiritual gifts. "I exhort you," Moroni pleads, "that ye deny not the gifts of God, for they are many; and they come from the same God" (Moro. 10:8). His list of gifts is extensive: to teach wisdom, to teach knowledge, to have exceedingly great faith, to heal, to work miracles, to prophesy, to see angels, to speak in tongues, and to interpret tongues. He emphasizes the diversity of these offerings, implying the image of God's family as an ensemble of diversely gifted individuals, each bringing their endowments to bear in our collective quest for divine truth. God appears to have designed this world in such a way that his children need each other in order to find his fullness.

Importantly, Moroni does not limit these gifts to a specific group. They seem to be on offer to all who would receive them, all who will not resist the "manifestations of the Spirit of God" (verse 8). In verse 25 Moroni indicates that *any* one doing *any* good in the world does it through the gifts of God—an echo of his father's sermon in Moroni 7. In like spirit, the First Presidency has declared that "the great religious leaders of the world such as Mohammed, Confucius, and the Reformers, as well as philosophers including Socrates, Plato, and others, received a portion of God's light. Moral truths were given to them by God to enlighten whole nations and to bring a higher level of understanding to individuals."[1] The distribution of spiritual gifts, broadly scattered among the children of our Heavenly Parents, is an invitation for us to learn from one another and to deepen our understanding by engaging with those whose gifts differ from ours in both their varied substance and their diverse "administr[ation]" (Moro. 10:8).

In other words, a person will have different gifts from God than I do, and those gifts may have come to her in a very different way than mine did; that difference

118

does not mean her gifts are any less essential or any less divine. After all, as Moroni emphasized, they come from "the same God." I dismiss such offerings to others at my own peril. To deny them is to deny something of the Savior. Moroni accordingly pleads with us to receive all the gifts. Both Mormon and Moroni repeatedly teach the principle that not only is everything from God good, but everything that is good is from God. Should not his children seek those gifts out from every sister and brother around them? As Mormon's sermon had declared, the mark of a true disciple of Christ is to "lay hold upon every good thing" (Moro. 7:20).

*the same God, different people*
*"He is the same..."*    —*Moroni 10:19*

Having emphasized that a diversity of gifts comes from the "*same* God," Moroni proceeds to use that identical adjective to describe God's relation to the passage of time: "He is the *same* yesterday, today, and forever...[and] all these gifts of which I have spoken...never will be done away, even as long as the world shall stand, only according to the unbelief of the children of men" (Moro. 10:19; emphasis added). Across all human difference, God's giving character persists.

In taking this theological stand on God's eternally unchanging inclination to give, and by assuming it so directly in relation to an opening statement on the variety of spiritual endowments, Moroni speaks to an issue that has proved deeply vexing to modern philosophers and has spilled over into theology. This daunting question asks whether human existence is best understood as a product of particularities (a view that emphasizes differences of time, location, and embodied existence in particularizing all lives) or whether our humanity is meaningfully informed by universals—principles of truth or common experience that unite us across difference.

The reason this question has been so challenging is that all answers to it—whether an emphasis on particularity or an emphasis on universality—can and have been put to evil purpose. On one hand, I might highlight the inescapable reality of difference, acknowledging that my culture, my race, my gender, my history, and my generation have so shaped my being—filtering all I encounter through these facts—that my perception of transcendent truth might merely be a reflection of my particular experience. This position can encourage meekness and tolerance, but it might also discourage the pursuit of common understanding and leave us splintered into mutually unintelligible and perpetually antagonistic tribes. On the other hand, I might insist that there are universal standards and shared principles that define the best of human existence, self-evident truths that we can all recognize. This position has been productive of global discourses of human rights and great cooperative endeavor, but it has also often been used by people (claiming to have the best understanding and to be the closest approximation of that universal truth) to suppress the cultures and deny the diversities—and police or punish the bodies—of those who have experienced the world differently. What, then, do we do with universals and particularities? Moroni offers an answer.

This is not the first place in the Book of Mormon where we encounter material relevant to this question. In 2 Nephi 29, there is a description of a world of different scriptures that will ultimately converge, under divine design, to provide the history of God's work in the world by the vast accumulation of various sacred stories from every nation on earth. That 2

Nephi solution—the universal as the collected whole of particular histories—bears a resemblance to the recent argument of Emilie Townes. Townes, an influential Womanist theologian, argues that when we really dive into the distinctive experience of a people—letting them narrate their own lives in their own terms—we will also see that no story can "be told in a vacuum. It is a story that can only be understood in relation to other stories—this is the universal or the first dawning of it."[2] One metaphor that might capture the Book of Mormon's implied answer to the dilemma of universals and particulars is the image of a global chorus in which every people that sings their note, and does so in a slightly different way, adds to the rich harmony of the whole. The descendants of Lehi have blessed us with one such note.

The chorus would be impoverished by the insistence on the dominance of any one part. It would be a lack of meekness to assume that any one group of mortals has the perfect melody in relation to which everyone else must position themselves. Conversely, the absence of a shared director or a common musical scale would result in cacophony. In answer, Moroni's theology repeatedly presents *God* as the stable and unchanging note with which we all seek to harmonize. Moroni recognizes that time changes but God is the same. He professes that the gifts are diverse but God is the same. His model depends on a profound appreciation of difference and on a shared search for the promised illumination of our Father. This is why humanity needs both resolute faith in him and a wide degree of respect for each other: "For they are many; and they come from the same God" (Moro. 10:8).

This emphasis, given in a concluding witness, seems especially relevant for a writer who has future Lamanite readers in his thoughts. This is his bond between the generations and the substance of his hope that he and his Lamanite kin might one day reconnect.

*his grace is sufficient*
*"...then are ye sanctified in Christ by the grace of God..."*   —*Moroni 10:33*

As Moroni's concluding chapter wends on, it swiftly weaves through a number of issues—such as the dangers of dying in our sins, prophecies on the coming forth of the Book of Mormon, and the interdependence of faith, hope, and charity—but it eventually, inexorably, returns to the concept of gifting: "Again I would exhort you that ye would come unto Christ, and lay hold upon every good gift" (Moro. 10:30).

This passage provides a telling formulation of the doctrine of the gift. These are offerings (offered independently of human ability), and we have the chance to choose them. Coming unto Christ, the act that requires broken hearts and contrite spirits, is the key. The gifts are available through the Gift. Moroni presents a Son of God who makes all of God's giving possible, the grace beyond our merit that includes the opportunity to choose and change: "Yea, come unto Christ, and be perfected in him, and deny yourselves of all ungodliness; and if ye shall deny yourselves of all ungodliness, and love God with all your might, mind and strength, then is his grace sufficient for you, that by his grace ye may be perfect in Christ" (Moro. 10:32). Note that in Moroni's formulation, Christ is both the beginning and the end. We start by coming unto him, and we end by being perfected in him. He empowers us to love, with our whole souls, the God who loved us first. He is he Author and the Finisher. He is the Giver and the Gift. And he is sufficient.

*"I bid unto all, farewell. I soon go to the rest in the paradise of God, until my spirit and body shall again reunite, and I am brought forth triumphant through the air."* —Moroni 10:34

When his book opens, Moroni is walking the earth—wandering, wondering, experiencing mortality in all its brokenness. In this final passage, we envisage him soaring through the air, liberated from the gravitational pull of the fallen planet he has been plodding. The Moroni of the last verse is transformed from the figure we met at the beginning. There may be less historical narrative in the book of Moroni than in almost any other portion of the Book of Mormon, but there is a plot arc: from low to high, from dark to light, from uncertainty to full assurance.

Between his introduction and his farewell, Moroni has laid out a soteriological sequence: ordinances, a covenant community, personal transformation through the love of Christ. All along the way he has emphasized the sustaining gifts of God that enable God's children to follow this path toward redemption. The irony of all this is that Moroni wrote his book in the absence of the very things of which he testified. The ordinances were not functioning. The covenant community had given way to anarchy. He had no living being to whom he could offer or from whom he could receive Christlike love. No one ministered to him with their spiritual gifts, and he had no living companions to minister to with his. And yet his sense of salvation was unshakable. He knew he would ascend.

The triumphant arc of Moroni's book, set against the vast landscape of spiritual emptiness through which Moroni travels, thus witnesses to the character of the God he and his father have been working to help us see: a God who makes up for what we lack, a God who fully compensates for the unfair and uneven circumstances in which his children are placed. Our faith in such a God, our hope in his promises to us, and the experience of encountering his love within us, will raise us up just as surely as Moroni has been raised.

His God is the provider of all good gifts. And, as Moroni has labored diligently to teach us, so is ours.

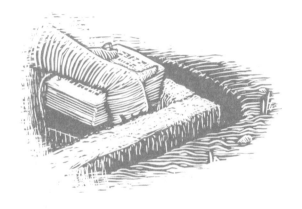

# Further Reading

Bell, Catherine. *Ritual: Perspectives and Dimensions.* New York: Oxford University Press, 1997. In her widely cited introduction to the academic study of religious rituals, Bell provides rigorous analytical frameworks for reflecting on the sorts of "oft"-repeated ordinances with which the book of Moroni opens.

Edwards, Jonathan. *A Careful and Strict Inquiry into the Modern Prevailing Notions of the Freedom of the Will which Is Supposed to Be Essential to Moral Agency, Virtue and Vice, Reward and Punishment, Praise and Blame.* 1754; London 1790. One of the most thorough and influential treatments of the theological problem of human agency to appear in English in the last three hundred years, Edwards's discourse on the will provides a useful starting point for any inquiry into the logical and scriptural issues that swirl around this topic.

Faulconer, James E. *The Book of Mormon Made Harder: Scripture Study Questions.* Provo: Maxwell Institute, 2014. A remarkably generative set of questions to inform our Book of Mormon study, Faulconer's text provides an especially helpful guide to the key issues at stake in the book of Moroni.

Hardy, Grant. *Understanding the Book of Mormon: A Reader's Guide.* New York: Oxford University Press, 2010. Though largely focused on Moroni's writings in the books of Ether and Mormon, rather than the book of Moroni itself, Hardy's study provides profound insight into Moroni as author and theologian.

Holland, Jeffrey R. *Christ and the New Covenant: The Messianic Message of the Book of Mormon.* Salt Lake City, UT: Deseret Book, 1997. A careful examination of Book of Mormon Christology, Elder Holland's treatment considers Mormon and Moroni as both theologians of the doctrine of Christ and as witnesses of the Savior himself.

Maxwell, Neal A. *Meek and Lowly.* Salt Lake City: Deseret Book, UT 1987. Meekness, a critical element of the theology of Mormon and Moroni, was also a theological preoccupation of Elder Maxwell. This book draws from the book of Moroni, as well as from a vast array of other texts, in its analysis of what it means to be meek.

Stapley, Jonathan. *The Power of Godliness: Mormon Liturgy and Cosmology.* New York: Oxford University Press, 2018. In his highly valuable assessment of the praxis of worship in the Latter-day Saint tradition, Stapley sees the book of Moroni as an important source for the development of the Church's liturgical culture.

# Endnotes

SERIES INTRODUCTION

1. Elder Neal A. Maxwell, "The Children of Christ," university devotional, Brigham Young University, Provo, UT, 4 February 1990, https://speeches.byu.edu/talks/neal-a-maxwell_children-christ/.

2. Elder Neal A. Maxwell, "The Inexhaustible Gospel," university devotional, Brigham Young University, Provo, UT, 18 August 1992, https://speeches.byu.edu/talks/neal-a-maxwell/inexhaustible-gospel/.

3. Elder Neal A. Maxwell, "The Book of Mormon: A Great Answer to 'The Great Question,'" address, Book of Mormon Symposium, Brigham Young University, Provo, UT, 10 October 1986, reprinted in *The Voice of My Servants: Apostolic Messages on Teaching, Learning, and Scripture,* ed. Scott C. Esplin and Richard Neitzel Holzapfel (Provo, UT: Religious Studies Center, Brigham Young University; Salt Lake City: Deseret Book, 2010), 221–38, https://rsc.byu.edu/archived/voice-my-servants/book-mormon-great-answer-great-question.

INTRODUCTION

1. Richard Dilworth Rust, *Feasting on the Word: The Literary Testimony of the Book of Mormon* (Salt Lake City, UT: Deseret Book, 1997), 140–41.

2. Christian theologians often use the words grace and charism to distinguish between a general category of divine giving, including those heavenly gifts that all Christians alike need (such as faith, hope, and charity), and the specific divine gifts with which individuals can be distinctively endowed (such as tongues, prophecy, and healing). This categorical distinction persists despite the fact that the etymology of the terms—and the content of the apostle Paul's teachings—warn us against drawing that division too starkly. Moroni himself troubles the border a bit by listing especially "great faith" among the individual gifts, suggesting both a continuity and a difference between the kind of faith universally needed for salvation and an "exceedingly" strong faith that may be the privilege of specially

gifted individuals (Moro. 10:11). For a helpful treatment of a theology of charism, see Francis A. Sullivan, *Charisms and Charismatic Renewal: A Biblical and Theological Study* (Ann Arbor, MI: Servant Books, 1982).

# 1

1. Richard Brodhead, "Prophets, Publics, and Publication: The Case of John Brown," *Proceedings of the American Antiquarian Society 3* (2001): 531.

2. For a poignant discourse on meekness, with repeated examples from Mormon and Moroni, see Neal A. Maxwell, "Meekness—A Dimension of True Discipleship" (delivered at Brigham Young University, September 5, 1982), https://www.churchofjesuschrist.org/study/ensign/1983/03/meekness-a-dimension-of-true-discipleship?lang=eng.

# 2

1. Aristotle, *Politics* (New York: Penguin Books, 1992), 1253a.

2. Matthew Bowen, "Getting Cain and Gain," *Interpreter: A Journal of Latter-day Saint Faith and Scholarship* 15 (2015): 115–41, https://journal.interpreterfoundation.org/getting-cain-and-gain/.

3. Grant Hardy, *Understanding the Book of Mormon: A Reader's Guide* (New York: Oxford University Press, 2010), 220.

4. Jonathan Stapley, *The Power of Godliness: Mormon Liturgy and Cosmology* (New York: Oxford University Press, 2018), 14.

5. Quoted in Isabel Rivers, "John Wesley and the Language of Scripture, Reason and Experience," *Prose Studies*, 4:3 (1981): 252.

6. B. H. Roberts, *The Seventy's Course in Theology: Years One through Five*, ed. David Hamer (Createspace Independent Publisher, 2013), 738; originally published as *The Seventy's Course in Theology: Fifth Year: Divinity Immanence of the Holy Ghost* (Salt Lake City, UT: Deseret News, 1912), 120.

7. *Duties and Blessings of the Priesthood: Basic Manual for Priesthood Holders, Part B* (Salt Lake City, UT: Church of Jesus Christ of Latter-day Saints, 2000), 41.

8. Boyd K. Packer, "The Power of the Priesthood," *Ensign* (May 2010): 7.

# 3

1. Saba Mahmood, *Politics of Piety: The Islamic Revival and the Feminist Subject* (Princeton: Princeton University Press, 2005), 128.

2. Randall Balmer and Lauren F. Winner, *Protestantism in America* (New York: Columbia University Press, 2002), 26.

3. Jean Calvin, *Institutes of the Christian Religion*, ed. John T. McNeill (Louisville, KY: Westminster John Knox Press, 2006), 1424.

4. D. G. Hart and John Muether, "The Lord's Supper: How Often?" *Ordained Servant* 6, no. 4 (October 1997): 96–98, https://opc.org/OS/pdf/OSV6N4.pdf; "Methodist History: Why Isn't Communion Every Sunday?" United Methodist Church, October 3, 2018, https://www.umc.org/en/content/methodist-history-why-isnt-communion-every-sunday.

5. Terryl Givens, *Feeding the Flock: The Foundations of Mormon Thought: Church and Praxis* (New York: Oxford University Press, 2017), 197–202.

6. Givens, *Feeding the Flock*, 203.

7. Mahmood, *Politics of Piety*, 128; Jonathan Z. Smith, "The Bare Facts of Ritual," *History of Religions* 20 (August–November 1980): 112–27.

8. From the era of the Book of Mormon's translation, see, for instance, "On the Mass," *Washington Theological Repertory*, December 1, 1820, 144; "Transubstantiation," *The Calvinistic Magazine*, February 1, 1829, 44; "Transubstantiation Versus Trinity," *Christian Register*, May 10, 1828; "The True Church," *The Jesuit or Catholic Sentinel*, February 20, 1830, 203, accessed through ProQuest digital database, "American Periodicals."

# 4

1. On intertextuality in the Book of Mormon, see Philip L. Barlow, *Mormons and the Bible* (New York: Oxford University Press, 1991), 26–33.

2. Kerstin Gerst-Emerson and Jayani Jayawardhana, "Loneliness as a Public Health Issue: The Impact of Loneliness on Health Care Utilization among Older Adults," *American Journal of Public Health* 105, no. 5 (May 2015): 1013–19.

3. Emile Durkheim, *The Elementary Forms of Religious Life,* trans. Carol Cosman (New York: Oxford University Press, 2008).

4. Thomas Paine, *Collected Writings* (New York: Library of America, 1995), 666.

5. Ernest Kurtz, *Not-God: A History of Alcoholics Anonymous* (Center City, MN: Hazelden Publishing, 1979), 89.

# 5

1. Larry E. Morris, *A Documentary History of the Book of Mormon* (New York: Oxford University Press, 2019), 55.

2. J. Golden Kimball, *J. Golden Kimball: His Sermons,* ed. Bonnie Taylor (n.p.: Latter-day Publishing, 2007), 281.

3. See Peter J. Thuesen, *Predestination: The American Career of a Contentious Doctrine* (New York: Oxford University Press, 2009), 116.

4. Jonathan Edwards, *The Freedom of the Will* (1754); see Allen Guelzo, *Edwards on the Will: A Century of American Theological Debate* (Middletown, CT: Wesleyan University Press, 1989).

5. Quoted in Gerald E. Meyers, *William James: His Life and Thought* (New Haven, CT: Yale University Press, 1986), 46.

6. Mormon actually uses the phrase "all things" eight times in this sermon. See Moroni 7:12, 22, 24, 45, 46.

# 6

1. Derek Rishmawy, "Meekness Is Not Weakness," *Christianity Today* 63, no. 5 (June 2019):28, https://www.christianitytoday.com/ct/2019/june/meekness-is-not-weakness.html.

2. Scholastica Hebgin and Felicitas Corrigan, trans., St. Augustine on the Psalms, *Ancient Christian Writers: The Works of the Fathers in Translation* (London: Longmans, Green and Co., 1961), 161–62.

3. See Thomas Aquinas, *Summa Theologica*, II-II, Q.157, article 4.

4. Dov Peretz Elkins and Abigail Treu, *The Bible's Top 50 Ideas: The Essential Concepts Everyone Should Know* (Eugene, OR: Wipf and Stock, 2013), 184.

5. Bruce K. Waltke, *An Old Testament Theology: An Exegetical, Canonical and Thematic Approach* (Grand Rapids, MI: Zondervan, 2007), 583.

6. Charles Quarles, *Sermon on the Mount: Restoring Christ's Message to the Modern Church* (Nashville, TN: B&H Publishing, 2011), 55.

7. Friedrich Schleiermacher, *The Christian Faith,* 2nd ed. (London: Bloomsbury, 2016), 133.

8. Ezra Taft Benson, "Beware of Pride," *Ensign*, May 1989, https://www.churchofjesuschrist.org/study/general-conference/1989/04/beware-of-pride?lang=eng.

9. Theodore Parker, *A Discourse of Matters Pertaining to Religion* (Boston, MA: Little and Brown, 1842), 187–88, 192.

10. Jeffrey R. Holland, *Christ and the New Covenant* (Salt Lake City, UT: Deseret Book, 1997), 336–37.

11. Nicholas J. Frederick, *The Bible, Mormon Scripture, and the Rhetoric of Allusivity* (Lanham, MD: Fairleigh Dickinson University Press, 2016), 69, 89n28.

# 7

1. Wayne C. Booth, "Of the Standard of Moral Taste," in *The Essential Wayne Booth* (Chicago: University of Chicago Press, 2006), 261.

2. David Hume, "Of the Standards of Taste," in *Selected Essays* (New York: Oxford University Press, 2008), 146.

3. Ralph Waldo Emerson, *Self-Reliance and Other Essays* (New York: Dover, 1993).

4. Martin E. Marty and H. Richard Niebuhr, *The Kingdom of God in America* (1937; repr., Middletown, CT: Wesleyan University Press, 1988), 193.

5. Joseph Smith, "History, 1838–1856, volume C-1 [2 November 1838–31 July 1842]," p. 904b. *The Joseph Smith Papers*, https://www.josephsmithpapers.org/paper-summary/history-1838-1856-volume-c-1-2-november-1838-31-july-1842/86.

6. Karl Barth, *Church Dogmatics: III.2 The Doctrine of Creation* (Edinburgh: T&T Clark, 1960), 32.

7. Patrick Mason, "George Floyd and Jesus: A Eulogy," *Medium*, June 5, 2020, https://medium.com/@pqmason/george-floyd-and-jesus-a-eulogy-b36c475d4694.

CONCLUSION

1. "Statement of the First Presidency Regarding God's Love for all Mankind," February 15, 1978.

2. Emilie M. Townes, *Womanist Ethics and the Cultural Production of Evil* (New York: Palgrave Macmillan, 2006), 23.

# Editions of the
# Book of Mormon

Most Latter-day Saints are familiar principally with the official edition of the Book of Mormon published in 2013 by The Church of Jesus Christ of Latter-day Saints. It contains the canonical text of the book, divided into chapters of relatively even length with numbered verses for ease of access. Its footnotes aim to assist readers in seeking doctrinal understanding.

Other Book of Mormon editions are available and often helpful. Among these are official editions from earlier in the scripture's publishing history, which are relatively accessible. There are also editions published recently by a variety of presses meant to make the text more readable. Both types of editions are referred to throughout *Book of Mormon: brief theological introductions*. Also of importance (and occasionally referred to) are the manuscript sources for the printed editions of the Book of Mormon.

### *manuscript sources*

Unfortunately, the original manuscript of the Book of Mormon was damaged during the nineteenth century, but substantial portions of it remain. All known extant portions have been published in typescript in Royal Skousen, ed., *The Original Manuscript of the Book of Mormon: Typographical Facsimile of the Extant Text* (Provo, UT: FARMS, 2001). A future volume of the Joseph Smith Papers will publish images of the extant manuscript, along with a typescript.

After completing the original manuscript's dictation, Joseph Smith assigned Oliver Cowdery to produce a second manuscript copy of the text. That manuscript has been called the printer's manuscript since it was designed for use by the first printer of the Book of Mormon. The printer's manuscript, which is more or less entirely intact, also contains corrections and other editorial markings inserted when the second (1837) edition of the Book of Mormon was being prepared. A typescript of the printer's manuscript can be found in Royal Skousen, ed., *The Printer's Manuscript of the Book of Mormon: Typographical Facsimile of the Entire Text in Two Parts,* 2 vols. (Provo, UT: FARMS, 2001). Full color images of the manuscript were subsequently published along with a transcript in the Joseph Smith Papers series: Royal Skousen and Robin Scott Jensen, eds., *Printer's Manuscript of the Book of Mormon*, 2 vols., vol. 3 of the *Revelations and Translations* series of The Joseph Smith Papers, ed. Dean C. Jessee, Ronald K. Esplin, and Richard Lyman Bushman (Salt Lake City: Church Historian's Press, 2015). The images and transcript of the printer's manuscript are also available at the Joseph Smith Papers website (www.josephsmithpapers.org/the-papers/revelations-and-translations/jsppr3).

*historical editions*

Multiple editions of the Book of Mormon were published during the lifetime of Joseph Smith. The first edition, published in Palmyra, New York, in 1830, appeared without versification and with fewer chapter divisions than the present canonical text. The text of the 1830 edition is available electronically at the Joseph Smith Papers website (www.josephsmithpapers.org/the-papers/revelations-and-translations/jsppr4) and in print through various publishers as a replica edition. The 1830 text is also available in Robert A. Rees and Eugene England, eds., *The Reader's Book of Mormon* (Salt Lake City: Signature Books, 2008), which is divided into seven pocket-sized volumes (each with an introduction by a scholar).

Joseph Smith introduced numerous minor changes into the text of the Book of Mormon when it was prepared for a second edition in 1837. Many of these changes are marked in the printer's manuscript. Most were aimed at correcting grammatical issues, but some, in a small handful of cases, were also aimed at clarifying the meaning of the text or its doctrinal implications. The 1837 edition is available electronically at the Joseph Smith Papers website (www.josephsmithpapers.org/the-papers/revelations-and-translations/jsppr4).

A third edition was prepared under Joseph Smith's direction in 1840, and evidence makes clear that the original manuscript was consulted carefully in preparing this edition. Some important errors in the earlier editions were corrected, further grammatical improvements were introduced, and a few other changes were made to the text for purposes of clarification. The 1840 edition can be read at the Joseph Smith Papers website (www.josephsmithpapers.org/the-papers/revelations-and-translations/jsppr4). It forms the basis for at least one printed edition as well: *The Book of Mormon*, trans. Joseph Smith Jr. (New York: Penguin Books, 2008), which contains

THE

# BOOK OF MORMON:

## AN ACCOUNT WRITTEN BY THE HAND OF MOR-
## MON, UPON PLATES TAKEN FROM
## THE PLATES OF NEPHI.

Wherefore it is an abridgment of the Record of the People of Nephi; and also of
the Lamanites; written to the Lamanites, which are a remnant of the House of
Israel; and also to Jew and Gentile; written by way of commandment, and also
by the spirit of Prophesy and of Revelation. Written, and sealed up, and hid
up unto the LORD, that they might not be destroyed; to come forth by the gift
and power of GOD unto the interpretation thereof; sealed by the hand of Moroni, and hid up unto the LORD, to come forth in due time by the way of Gentile;
the interpretation thereof by the gift of GOD; an abridgment taken from the
Book of Ether.

Also, which is a Record of the People of Jared, which were scattered at the time
the LORD confounded the language of the people when they were building a
tower to get to Heaven: which is to shew unto the remnant of the House of
Israel how great things the LORD hath done for their fathers; and that they may
know the covenants of the LORD, that they are not cast off forever; and also to
the convincing of the Jew and Gentile that JESUS is the CHRIST, the ETERNAL
GOD, manifesting Himself unto all nations. And now if there be fault, it be the
mistake of men; wherefore condemn not the things of GOD, that ye may be
found spotless at the judgment seat of CHRIST.

### BY JOSEPH SMITH, JUNIOR,
AUTHOR AND PROPRIETOR.

## PALMYRA:

PRINTED BY E. B. GRANDIN, FOR THE AUTHOR.

1830.

FIGURE 1 The title page of the original 1830 edition of
The Book of Mormon. © Intellectual Reserve, Inc.

a helpful introduction by Laurie Maffly-Kipp, a scholar of American religious history.

One other edition of the Book of Mormon appeared during the lifetime of Joseph Smith—an 1841 British edition, which was largely based on the 1837 edition and therefore lacked corrections and other improvements that appear in the 1840 edition. It, too, is available electronically at the Joseph Smith Papers website (www.josephsmithpapers.org/the-papers/revelations-and-translations/jsppr4).

In 1879, Latter-day Saint apostle Orson Pratt completed one of the more influential editions of the Book of Mormon published after Joseph Smith's death. Pratt lamented that too many Latter-day Saints left the scripture unread on the shelf. He sought to create an easier reading experience by dividing up the originally long chapters and adding verse numbers—revisions which have largely remained unchanged in the Church's official edition to the present. He also pioneered a system of cross-references and other explanatory footnotes. Most of Pratt's notes were removed or replaced in subsequent official editions—most thoroughly in the Church's 1981 edition when new descriptive chapter headings were introduced. These headings can still be found, with a few minor updates, in the 2013 edition.

A detailed and helpful devotional treatment of the publication history of the Book of Mormon can be found in Richard E. Turley, Jr. and William W. Slaughter, *How We Got the Book of Mormon* (Salt Lake City: Deseret Book, 2011). These authors trace developments in the format and study apparatuses used to present the text of the Book of Mormon to audiences from the 1850s to the present.

*study and reading editions*

The most important scholarly editions of the Book of Mormon are Grant Hardy, ed., *The Book of Mormon: A Reader's Edition* (Urbana and Chicago: University of Illinois Press, 2003); and Royal Skousen, ed., *The Book of Mormon: The Earliest Text* (New Haven, CT: Yale University Press, 2009).

Hardy's edition repackages the text of the 1921 public domain edition of the Book of Mormon. It contains a helpful introduction, a series of useful appendices, and a straightforward presentation of the text in a highly readable format. Footnotes are minimal—they are used only to clarify direct references or allusions within the text, to track dates, or to alert readers about original chapter divisions. This edition contains modern chapter and verse divisions, but they are unobtrusively typeset. The text is presented in straightforward paragraphs, with one-line headings marking text divisions. Poetry is set off in poetic lines, as in modern editions of the Bible.

Skousen's edition is the result of his quarter-century-long work with the manuscript and printed sources for the Book of Mormon text. The edition aims to reproduce as closely as can be reconstructed the words originally dictated by Joseph Smith to his scribes. Chapter and verse divisions familiar from recent editions are in the text (and symbols mark original chapter breaks), but the text is presented in what Skousen calls "sense lines"—each line containing (on Skousen's reconstruction) approximately what the prophet would have dictated at one time before pausing to allow his scribe to write. The edition contains helpful introductory material and a summary appendix noting significant differences between *The Earliest Text* and the current official edition. It is otherwise without any apparatus for the reader.

The most significant edition of the Book of Mormon deliberately constructed for a lay reading audience is Grant Hardy, ed., *The Book of Mormon: Another Testament of Jesus Christ, Maxwell Institute Study Edition* (Salt Lake City and Provo, UT: Neal A. Maxwell Institute, Deseret Book, and BYU Religious Studies Center, 2018). In this edition, Hardy uses the text of the 2013 official edition of the Book of Mormon but presents it in a readable way for everyday students of the volume. This edition reproduces the best of what appears in Hardy's *Reader's Edition* but adds further resources in the introductory and appendix materials. The footnotes are updated and expanded to include variant readings from the original and printer's manuscripts, and to provide notes about other textual details. The body of the text is presented, as in the *Reader's Edition*, in a straightforward fashion, readable and interrupted only by one-line headings. Modern chapter and verse divisions, as well as original chapter divisions, are easily visible.

# Index

# Colophon

The text of the book is typeset in Arnhem,
Fred Smeijer's 21st-century-take on late
18th-century Enlightenment-era letterforms
known for their sturdy legibility and clarity
of form. Captions and figures are typset in
Quaadraat Sans, also by Fred Smeijers.
The book title and chapter titles are typeset
in Thema by Nikola Djurek.

Printed on Domtar Lynx 74 gsm,
Forest Stewardship Council (FSC) Certified.

Printed by Brigham Young University Print & Mail Services

Woodcut illuminations **Brian Kershisnik**
Illumination consultation **Faith Heard**

Book design & typography **Douglas Thomas**
Production typesetting **Maria Camargo**

Moroni 1:4 Wherefore, I write a few more things, contrary to that which I had supposed; for I had supposed not to have written any more; but I write a few more things, that perhaps they may be of worth unto my brethren, the Lamanites, in some future day, according to the will of the Lord.

# CAESAR AND CLEOPATRA

## By GEORGE BERNARD SHAW

A Digireads.com Book
Digireads.com Publishing

Caesar and Cleopatra
By George Bernard Shaw
ISBN 10: 1-4209-4121-6
ISBN 13: 978-1-4209-4121-0

Please visit *www.digireads.com*

# CAESAR AND CLEOPATRA

## ACT I

*An October night on the Syrian border of Egypt towards the end of the XXXIII Dynasty, in the year 706 by Roman computation, afterwards reckoned by Christian computation as 48 B.C. A great radiance of silver fire, the dawn of a moonlit night, is rising in the east. The stars and the cloudless sky are our own contemporaries, nineteen and a half centuries younger than we know them; but you would not guess that from their appearance. Below them are two notable drawbacks of civilization: a palace, and soldiers. The palace, an old, low, Syrian building of whitened mud, is not so ugly as Buckingham Palace; and the officers in the courtyard are more highly civilized than modern English officers: for example, they do not dig up the corpses of their dead enemies and mutilate them, as we dug up Cromwell and the Mahdi. They are in two groups: one intent on the gambling of their captain Belzanor, a warrior of fifty, who, with his spear on the ground beside his knee, is stooping to throw dice with a sly-looking young Persian recruit; the other gathered about a guardsman who has just finished telling a naughty story [still current in English barracks] at which they are laughing uproariously. They are about a dozen in number, all highly aristocratic young Egyptian guardsmen, handsomely equipped with weapons and armor, very un-English in point of not being ashamed of and uncomfortable in their professional dress; on the contrary, rather ostentatiously and arrogantly warlike, as valuing themselves on their military caste.*

*Belzanor is a typical veteran, tough and wilful; prompt, capable and crafty where brute force will serve; helpless and boyish when it will not: an effective sergeant, an incompetent general, a deplorable dictator. Would, if influentially connected, be employed in the two last capacities by a modern European State on the strength of his success in the first. Is rather to be pitied just now in view of the fact that Julius Caesar is invading his country. Not knowing this, is intent on his game with the Persian, whom, as a foreigner, he considers quite capable of cheating him.*

*His subalterns are mostly handsome young fellows whose interest in the game and the story symbolizes with tolerable completeness the main interests in life of which they are conscious. Their spears are leaning against the walls, or lying on the ground ready to their hands. The corner of the courtyard forms a triangle of which one side is the*

*front of the palace, with a doorway, the other a wall with a gateway. The storytellers are on the palace side: the gamblers, on the gateway side. Close to the gateway, against the wall, is a stone block high enough to enable a Nubian sentinel, standing on it, to look over the wall. The yard is lighted by a torch stuck in the wall. As the laughter from the group round the storyteller dies away, the kneeling Persian, winning the throw, snatches up the stake from the ground.*

BELZANOR. By Apis, Persian, thy gods are good to thee.

THE PERSIAN. Try yet again, O captain. Double or quits!

BELZANOR. No more. I am not in the vein.

THE SENTINEL. [*poising his javelin as he peers over the wall.*] Stand. Who goes there?

[*They all start, listening. A strange voice replies from without.*]

VOICE. The bearer of evil tidings.

BELZANOR. [*calling to the sentry.*] Pass him.

THE SENTINEL. [*grounding his javelin.*] Draw near, O bearer of evil tidings.

BELZANOR. [*pocketing the dice and picking up his spear.*] Let us receive this man with honor. He bears evil tidings.

[*The guardsmen seize their spears and gather about the gate, leaving a way through for the new comer.*]

PERSIAN. [*rising from his knee.*] Are evil tidings, then, honorable?

BELZANOR. O barbarous Persian, hear my instruction. In Egypt the bearer of good tidings is sacrificed to the gods as a thank offering but no god will accept the blood of the messenger of evil. When we have good tidings, we are careful to send them in the mouth of the cheapest slave we can find. Evil tidings are borne by young noblemen who desire to bring themselves into notice. [*They join the rest at the gate.*]

THE SENTINEL. Pass, O young captain; and bow the head in the House of the Queen.

VOICE. Go anoint thy javelin with fat of swine, O Blackamoor; for before morning the Romans will make thee eat it to the very butt.

[*The owner of the voice, a fairhaired dandy, dressed in a different fashion to that affected by the guardsmen, but no less extravagantly, comes through the gateway laughing. He is*

*somewhat battle-stained; and his left forearm, bandaged, comes through a torn sleeve. In his right hand he carries a Roman sword in its sheath. He swaggers down the courtyard, the Persian on his right, Belzanor on his left, and the guardsmen crowding down behind him.*]

BELZANOR. Who art thou that laughest in the House of Cleopatra the Queen, and in the teeth of Belzanor, the captain of her guard?

THE NEW COMER. I am Bel Affris, descended from the gods.

BELZANOR. [*ceremoniously.*] Hail, cousin!

ALL. [*except the Persian.*] Hail, cousin!

PERSIAN. All the Queen's guards are descended from the gods, O stranger, save myself. I am Persian, and descended from many kings.

BEL AFFRIS. [*to the guardsmen.*] Hail, cousins! [*To the Persian, condescendingly*] Hail, mortal!

BELZANOR. You have been in battle, Bel Affris; and you are a soldier among soldiers. You will not let the Queen's women have the first of your tidings.

BEL AFFRIS. I have no tidings, except that we shall have our throats cut presently, women, soldiers, and all.

PERSIAN. [*to Belzanor.*] I told you so.

THE SENTINEL. [*who has been listening.*] Woe, alas!

BEL AFFRIS. [*calling to him.*] Peace, peace, poor Ethiop: destiny is with the gods who painted thee black. [*To Belzanor*] What has this mortal [*indicating the Persian*] told you?

BELZANOR. He says that the Roman Julius Caesar, who has landed on our shores with a handful of followers, will make himself master of Egypt. He is afraid of the Roman soldiers. [*The guardsmen laugh with boisterous scorn.*] Peasants, brought up to scare crows and follow the plough. Sons of smiths and millers and tanners! And we nobles, consecrated to arms, descended from the gods!

PERSIAN. Belzanor: the gods are not always good to their poor relations.

BELZANOR. [*hotly, to the Persian.*] Man to man, are we worse than the slaves of Caesar?

BEL AFFRIS. [*stepping between them.*] Listen, cousin. Man to man, we Egyptians are as gods above the Romans.

THE GUARDSMEN. [*exultingly.*] Aha!

BEL AFFRIS. But this Caesar does not pit man against man: he throws a legion at you where you are weakest as he throws a stone from a

catapult; and that legion is as a man with one head, a thousand arms, and no religion. I have fought against them; and I know.

BELZANOR. [*derisively.*] Were you frightened, cousin?

[*The guardsmen roar with laughter, their eyes sparkling at the wit of their captain.*]

BEL AFFRIS. No, cousin; but I was beaten. They were frightened [perhaps]; but they scattered us like chaff.

[*The guardsmen, much damped, utter a growl of contemptuous disgust.*]

BELZANOR. Could you not die?

BEL AFFRIS. No: that was too easy to be worthy of a descendant of the gods. Besides, there was no time: all was over in a moment. The attack came just where we least expected it.

BELZANOR. That shows that the Romans are cowards.

BEL AFFRIS. They care nothing about cowardice, these Romans: they fight to win. The pride and honor of war are nothing to them.

PERSIAN. Tell us the tale of the battle. What befell?

THE GUARDSMEN. [*gathering eagerly round Bel Affris.*] Ay: the tale of the battle.

BEL AFFRIS. Know then, that I am a novice in the guard of the temple of Ra in Memphis, serving neither Cleopatra nor her brother Ptolemy, but only the high gods. We went a journey to inquire of Ptolemy why he had driven Cleopatra into Syria, and how we of Egypt should deal with the Roman Pompey, newly come to our shores after his defeat by Caesar at Pharsalia. What, think ye, did we learn? Even that Caesar is coming also in hot pursuit of his foe, and that Ptolemy has slain Pompey, whose severed head he holds in readiness to present to the conqueror. [*Sensation among the guardsmen.*] Nay, more: we found that Caesar is already come; for we had not made half a day's journey on our way back when we came upon a city rabble flying from his legions, whose landing they had gone out to withstand.

BELZANOR. And ye, the temple guard! Did you not withstand these legions?

BEL AFFRIS. What man could, that we did. But there came the sound of a trumpet whose voice was as the cursing of a black mountain. Then saw we a moving wall of shields coming towards us. You

know how the heart burns when you charge a fortified wall; but how if the fortified wall were to charge you?

THE PERSIAN. [*exulting in having told them so.*] Did I not say it?

BEL AFFRIS. When the wall came nigh, it changed into a line of men—common fellows enough, with helmets, leather tunics, and breastplates. Every man of them flung his javelin: the one that came my way drove through my shield as through a papyrus—lo there! [*he points to the bandage on his left arm*] and would have gone through my neck had I not stooped. They were charging at the double then, and were upon us with short swords almost as soon as their javelins. When a man is close to you with such a sword, you can do nothing with our weapons: they are all too long.

THE PERSIAN. What did you do?

BEL AFFRIS. Doubled my fist and smote my Roman on the sharpness of his jaw. He was but mortal after all: he lay down in a stupor; and I took his sword and laid it on. [*Drawing the sword*] Lo! a Roman sword with Roman blood on it!

THE GUARDSMEN. [*approvingly.*] Good! [*They take the sword and hand it round, examining it curiously.*]

THE PERSIAN. And your men?

BEL AFFRIS. Fled. Scattered like sheep.

BELZANOR. [*furiously.*] The cowardly slaves! Leaving the descendants of the gods to be butchered!

BEL AFFRIS. [*with acid coolness.*] The descendants of the gods did not stay to be butchered, cousin. The battle was not to the strong; but the race was to the swift. The Romans, who have no chariots, sent a cloud of horsemen in pursuit, and slew multitudes. Then our high priest's captain rallied a dozen descendants of the gods and exhorted us to die fighting. I said to myself: surely it is safer to stand than to lose my breath and be stabbed in the back; so I joined our captain and stood. Then the Romans treated us with respect; for no man attacks a lion when the field is full of sheep, except for the pride and honor of war, of which these Romans know nothing. So we escaped with our lives; and I am come to warn you that you must open your gates to Caesar; for his advance guard is scarce an hour behind me; and not an Egyptian warrior is left standing between you and his legions.

THE SENTINEL. Woe, alas! [*He throws down his javelin and flies into the palace.*]

BELZANOR. Nail him to the door, quick! [*The guardsmen rush for him with their spears; but he is too quick for them.*] Now this news will run through the palace like fire through stubble.

BEL AFFRIS. What shall we do to save the women from the Romans?

BELZANOR. Why not kill them?

PERSIAN. Because we should have to pay blood money for some of them. Better let the Romans kill them: it is cheaper.

BELZANOR. [*awestruck at his brain power.*] O subtle one! O serpent!

BEL AFFRIS. But your Queen?

BELZANOR. True: we must carry off Cleopatra.

BEL AFFRIS. Will ye not await her command?

BELZANOR. Command! A girl of sixteen! Not we. At Memphis ye deem her a Queen: here we know better. I will take her on the crupper of my horse. When we soldiers have carried her out of Caesar's reach, then the priests and the nurses and the rest of them can pretend she is a queen again, and put their commands into her mouth.

PERSIAN. Listen to me, Belzanor.

BELZANOR. Speak, O subtle beyond thy years.

THE PERSIAN. Cleopatra's brother Ptolemy is at war with her. Let us sell her to him.

THE GUARDSMEN. O subtle one! O serpent!

BELZANOR. We dare not. We are descended from the gods; but Cleopatra is descended from the river Nile; and the lands of our fathers will grow no grain if the Nile rises not to water them. Without our father's gifts we should live the lives of dogs.

PERSIAN. It is true: the Queen's guard cannot live on its pay. But hear me further, O ye kinsmen of Osiris.

THE GUARDSMEN. Speak, O subtle one. Hear the serpent begotten!

PERSIAN. Have I heretofore spoken truly to you of Caesar, when you thought I mocked you?

GUARDSMEN. Truly, truly.

BELZANOR. [*reluctantly admitting it.*] So Bel Affris says.

PERSIAN. Hear more of him, then. This Caesar is a great lover of women: he makes them his friends and counselors.

BELZANOR. Faugh! This rule of women will be the ruin of Egypt.

THE PERSIAN. Let it rather be the ruin of Rome! Caesar grows old now: he is past fifty and full of labors and battles. He is too old for the young women; and the old women are too wise to worship him.

BEL AFFRIS. Take heed, Persian. Caesar is by this time almost within earshot.

PERSIAN. Cleopatra is not yet a woman: neither is she wise. But she already troubles men's wisdom.

BELZANOR. Ay: that is because she is descended from the river Nile and a black kitten of the sacred White Cat. What then?

PERSIAN. Why, sell her secretly to Ptolemy, and then offer ourselves to Caesar as volunteers to fight for the overthrow of her brother and the rescue of our Queen, the Great Granddaughter of the Nile.

THE GUARDSMEN. O serpent!

PERSIAN. He will listen to us if we come with her picture in our mouths. He will conquer and kill her brother, and reign in Egypt with Cleopatra for his Queen. And we shall be her guard.

GUARDSMEN. O subtlest of all the serpents! O admiration! O wisdom!

BEL AFFRIS. He will also have arrived before you have done talking, O word spinner.

BELZANOR. That is true. [*An affrighted uproar in the palace interrupts him.*] Quick: the flight has begun: guard the door. [*They rush to the door and form a cordon before it with their spears. A mob of women-servants and nurses surges out. Those in front recoil from the spears, screaming to those behind to keep back. Belzanor's voice dominates the disturbance as he shouts*] Back there. In again, unprofitable cattle.

THE GUARDSMEN. Back, unprofitable cattle.

BELZANOR. Send us out Ftatateeta, the Queen's chief nurse.

THE WOMEN. [*calling into the palace.*] Ftatateeta, Ftatateeta. Come, come. Speak to Belzanor.

A WOMAN. Oh, keep back. You are thrusting me on the spearheads.

[*A huge grim woman, her face covered with a network of tiny wrinkles, and her eyes old, large, and wise; sinewy handed, very tall, very strong; with the mouth of a bloodhound and the jaws of a bulldog, appears on the threshold. She is dressed like a person of consequence in the palace, and confronts the guardsmen insolently.*]

FTATATEETA. Make way for the Queen's chief nurse.

BELZANOR. [*with solemn arrogance.*] Ftatateeta: I am Belzanor, the captain of the Queen's guard, descended from the gods.

FTATATEETA. [*retorting his arrogance with interest.*] Belzanor: I am Ftatateeta, the Queen's chief nurse; and your divine ancestors were proud to be painted on the wall in the pyramids of the kings whom my fathers served.

[*The women laugh triumphantly.*]

BELZANOR. [*with grim humor*] Ftatateeta: daughter of a long-tongued, swivel-eyed chameleon, the Romans are at hand. [*A cry of terror from the women: they would fly but for the spears.*] Not even the descendants of the gods can resist them; for they have each man seven arms, each carrying seven spears. The blood in their veins is boiling quicksilver; and their wives become mothers in three hours, and are slain and eaten the next day.

[*A shudder of horror from the women. Ftatateeta, despising them and scorning the soldiers, pushes her way through the crowd and confronts the spear points undismayed.*]

FTATATEETA. Then fly and save yourselves, O cowardly sons of the cheap clay gods that are sold to fish porters; and leave us to shift for ourselves.

BELZANOR. Not until you have first done our bidding, O terror of manhood. Bring out Cleopatra the Queen to us and then go whither you will.

FTATATEETA. [*with a derisive laugh.*] Now I know why the gods have taken her out of our hands. [*The guardsmen start and look at one another.*] Know, thou foolish soldier, that the Queen has been missing since an hour past sun down.

BELZANOR. [*furiously.*] Hag: you have hidden her to sell to Caesar or her brother. [*He grasps her by the left wrist, and drags her, helped by a few of the guard, to the middle of the courtyard, where, as they fling her on her knees, he draws a murderous looking knife.*] Where is she? Where is she? or—[*He threatens to cut her throat.*]

FTATATEETA. [*savagely.*] Touch me, dog; and the Nile will not rise on your fields for seven times seven years of famine.

BELZANOR. [*frightened, but desperate.*] I will sacrifice: I will pay. Or stay. [*To the Persian*] You, O subtle one: your father's lands lie far from the Nile. Slay her.

PERSIAN. [*threatening her with his knife.*] Persia has but one god; yet he loves the blood of old women. Where is Cleopatra?

FTATATEETA. Persian: as Osiris lives, I do not know. I chide her for bringing evil days upon us by talking to the sacred cats of the priests, and carrying them in her arms. I told her she would be left alone here when the Romans came as a punishment for her disobedience. And now she is gone—run away—hidden. I speak the truth. I call Osiris to witness.

THE WOMEN. [*protesting officiously.*] She speaks the truth, Belzanor.

BELZANOR. You have frightened the child: she is hiding. Search—
quick—into the palace—search every corner.

[*The guards, led by Belzanor, shoulder their way into the palace
through the flying crowd of women, who escape through the
courtyard gate.*]

FTATATEETA. [*screaming.*] Sacrilege! Men in the Queen's chambers!
Sa— [*Her voice dies away as the Persian puts his knife to her
throat.*]

BEL AFFRIS. [*laying a hand on Ftatateeta's left shoulder.*] Forbear
her yet a moment, Persian. [*To Ftatateeta, very significantly*]
Mother: your gods are asleep or away hunting; and the sword is at
your throat. Bring us to where the Queen is hid, and you shall live.

FTATATEETA. [*contemptuously.*] Who shall stay the sword in the
hand of a fool, if the high gods put it there? Listen to me, ye young
men without understanding. Cleopatra fears me; but she fears the
Romans more. There is but one power greater in her eyes than the
wrath of the Queen's nurse and the cruelty of Caesar; and that is
the power of the Sphinx that sits in the desert watching the way to
the sea. What she would have it know, she tells into the ears of the
sacred cats; and on her birthday she sacrifices to it and decks it
with poppies. Go ye therefore into the desert and seek Cleopatra in
the shadow of the Sphinx; and on your heads see to it that no harm
comes to her.

BEL AFFRIS. [*to the Persian.*] May we believe this, O subtle one?

PERSIAN. Which way come the Romans?

BEL AFFRIS. Over the desert, from the sea, by this very Sphinx.

PERSIAN. [*to Ftatateeta.*] O mother of guile! O aspic's tongue! You
have made up this tale so that we two may go into the desert and
perish on the spears of the Romans. [*Lifting his knife*] Taste death.

FTATATEETA. Not from thee, baby. [*She snatches his ankle from
under him and flies stooping along the palace wall vanishing in the
darkness within its precinct. Bel Affris roars with laughter as the
Persian tumbles. The guardsmen rush out of the palace with
Belzanor and a mob of fugitives, mostly carrying bundles.*]

PERSIAN. Have you found Cleopatra?

BELZANOR. She is gone. We have searched every corner.

THE NUBIAN SENTINEL. [*appearing at the door of the palace.*]
Woe! Alas! Fly, fly!

BELZANOR. What is the matter now?

THE NUBIAN SENTINEL. The sacred white cat has been stolen. Woe! Woe!

[*General panic. They all fly with cries of consternation. The torch is thrown down and extinguished in the rush. Darkness. The noise of the fugitives dies away. Dead silence. Suspense. Then the blackness and stillness breaks softly into silver mist and strange airs as the windswept harp of Memnon plays at the dawning of the moon. It rises full over the desert; and a vast horizon comes into relief, broken by a huge shape which soon reveals itself in the spreading radiance as a Sphinx pedestalled on the sands. The light still clears, until the upraised eyes of the image are distinguished looking straight forward and upward in infinite fearless vigil, and a mass of color between its great paws defines itself as a heap of red poppies on which a girl lies motionless, her silken vest heaving gently and regularly with the breathing of a dreamless sleeper, and her braided hair glittering in a shaft of moonlight like a bird's wing.*]

[*Suddenly there comes from afar a vaguely fearful sound [it might be the bellow of a Minotaur softened by great distance] and Memnon's music stops. Silence: then a few faint high-ringing trumpet notes. Then silence again. Then a man comes from the south with stealing steps, ravished by the mystery of the night, all wonder, and halts, lost in contemplation, opposite the left flank of the Sphinx, whose bosom, with its burden, is hidden from him by its massive shoulder.*]

THE MAN. Hail, Sphinx: salutation from Julius Caesar! I have wandered in many lands, seeking the lost regions from which my birth into this world exiled me, and the company of creatures such as I myself. I have found flocks and pastures, men and cities, but no other Caesar, no air native to me, no man kindred to me, none who can do my day's deed, and think my night's thought. In the little world yonder, Sphinx, my place is as high as yours in this great desert; only I wander, and you sit still; I conquer, and you endure; I work and wonder, you watch and wait; I look up and am dazzled, look down and am darkened, look round and am puzzled, whilst your eyes never turn from looking out—out of the world— to the lost region—the home from which we have strayed. Sphinx, you and I, strangers to the race of men, are no strangers to one

another: have I not been conscious of you and of this place since I was born? Rome is a madman's dream: this is my Reality. These starry lamps of yours I have seen from afar in Gaul, in Britain, in Spain, in Thessaly, signalling great secrets to some eternal sentinel below, whose post I never could find. And here at last is their sentinel—an image of the constant and immortal part of my life, silent, full of thoughts, alone in the silver desert. Sphinx, Sphinx: I have climbed mountains at night to hear in the distance the stealthy footfall of the winds that chase your sands in forbidden play—our invisible children, O Sphinx, laughing in whispers. My way hither was the way of destiny; for I am he of whose genius you are the symbol: part brute, part woman, and part God—nothing of man in me at all. Have I read your riddle, Sphinx?

THE GIRL [*who has wakened, and peeped cautiously from her nest to see who is speaking.*] Old gentleman.

CAESAR. [*starting violently, and clutching his sword.*] Immortal gods!

THE GIRL. Old gentleman: don't run away.

CAESAR. [*stupefied.*] "Old gentleman: don't run away!!!" This! To Julius Caesar!

THE GIRL [*urgently.*] Old gentleman.

CAESAR. Sphinx: you presume on your centuries. I am younger than you, though your voice is but a girl's voice as yet.

THE GIRL. Climb up here, quickly; or the Romans will come and eat you.

CAESAR. [*running forward past the Sphinx's shoulder, and seeing her.*] A child at its breast! A divine child!

THE GIRL. Come up quickly. You must get up at its side and creep round.

CAESAR. [*amazed.*] Who are you?

THE GIRL. Cleopatra, Queen of Egypt.

CAESAR. Queen of the Gypsies, you mean.

CLEOPATRA. You must not be disrespectful to me, or the Sphinx will let the Romans eat you. Come up. It is quite cosy here.

CAESAR. [*to himself.*] What a dream! What a magnificent dream! Only let me not wake, and I will conquer ten continents to pay for dreaming it out to the end. [*He climbs to the Sphinx's flank, and presently reappears to her on the pedestal, stepping round its right shoulder.*]

CLEOPATRA. Take care. That's right. Now sit down: you may have its other paw. [*She seats herself comfortably on its left paw.*] It is very powerful and will protect us; but [*shivering, and with plaintive loneliness*] it would not take any notice of me or keep me

company. I am glad you have come: I was very lonely. Did you happen to see a white cat anywhere?

CAESAR. [*sitting slowly down on the right paw in extreme wonderment.*] Have you lost one?

CLEOPATRA. Yes: the sacred white cat: is it not dreadful? I brought him here to sacrifice him to the Sphinx; but when we got a little way from the city a black cat called him, and he jumped out of my arms and ran away to it. Do you think that the black cat can have been my great-great-great-grandmother?

CAESAR. [*staring at her.*] Your great-great-great-grandmother! Well, why not? Nothing would surprise me on this night of nights.

CLEOPATRA. I think it must have been. My great-grandmother's great-grandmother was a black kitten of the sacred white cat; and the river Nile made her his seventh wife. That is why my hair is so wavy. And I always want to be let do as I like, no matter whether it is the will of the gods or not: that is because my blood is made with Nile water.

CAESAR. What are you doing here at this time of night? Do you live here?

CLEOPATRA. Of course not: I am the Queen; and I shall live in the palace at Alexandria when I have killed my brother, who drove me out of it. When I am old enough I shall do just what I like. I shall be able to poison the slaves and see them wriggle, and pretend to Ftatateeta that she is going to be put into the fiery furnace.

CAESAR. Hm! Meanwhile why are you not at home and in bed?

CLEOPATRA. Because the Romans are coming to eat us all. You are not at home and in bed either.

CAESAR. [*with conviction.*] Yes I am. I live in a tent; and I am now in that tent, fast asleep and dreaming. Do you suppose that I believe you are real, you impossible little dream witch?

CLEOPATRA. [*giggling and leaning trustfully towards him.*] You are a funny old gentleman. I like you.

CAESAR. Ah, that spoils the dream. Why don't you dream that I am young?

CLEOPATRA. I wish you were; only I think I should be more afraid of you. I like men, especially young men with round strong arms; but I am afraid of them. You are old and rather thin and stringy; but you have a nice voice; and I like to have somebody to talk to, though I think you are a little mad. It is the moon that makes you talk to yourself in that silly way.

CAESAR. What! you heard that, did you? I was saying my prayers to the great Sphinx.

CLEOPATRA. But this isn't the great Sphinx.

CAESAR. [*much disappointed, looking up at the statue.*] What!

CLEOPATRA. This is only a dear little kitten of the Sphinx. Why, the great Sphinx is so big that it has a temple between its paws. This is my pet Sphinx. Tell me: do you think the Romans have any sorcerers who could take us away from the Sphinx by magic?

CAESAR. Why? Are you afraid of the Romans?

CLEOPATRA. [*very seriously.*] Oh, they would eat us if they caught us. They are barbarians. Their chief is called Julius Caesar. His father was a tiger and his mother a burning mountain; and his nose is like an elephant's trunk. [*Caesar involuntarily rubs his nose.*] They all have long noses, and ivory tusks, and little tails, and seven arms with a hundred arrows in each; and they live on human flesh.

CAESAR. Would you like me to show you a real Roman?

CLEOPATRA. [*terrified.*] No. You are frightening me.

CAESAR. No matter: this is only a dream—

CLEOPATRA. [*excitedly.*] It is not a dream: it is not a dream. See, see. [*She plucks a pin from her hair and jabs it repeatedly into his arm.*]

CAESAR. Ffff—Stop. [*Wrathfully*] How dare you?

CLEOPATRA. [*abashed.*] You said you were dreaming. [*Whimpering*] I only wanted to show you—

CAESAR. [*gently.*] Come, come: don't cry. A queen mustn't cry. [*He rubs his arm, wondering at the reality of the smart.*] Am I awake? [*He strikes his hand against the Sphinx to test its solidity. It feels so real that he begins to be alarmed, and says perplexedly*] Yes, I—[*quite panic-stricken*] no: impossible: madness, madness! [*Desperately*] Back to camp—to camp. [*He rises to spring down from the pedestal.*]

CLEOPATRA. [*flinging her arms in terror round him.*] No: you shan't leave me. No, no, no: don't go. I'm afraid—afraid of the Romans.

CAESAR. [*as the conviction that he is really awake forces itself on him.*] Cleopatra: can you see my face well?

CLEOPATRA. Yes. It is so white in the moonlight.

CAESAR. Are you sure it is the moonlight that makes me look whiter than an Egyptian? [*Grimly*] Do you notice that I have a rather long nose?

CLEOPATRA. [*recoiling, paralyzed by a terrible suspicion.*] Oh!

CAESAR. It is a Roman nose, Cleopatra.

CLEOPATRA. Ah! [*With a piercing scream she springs up; darts round the left shoulder of the Sphinx; scrambles down to the sand; and falls on her knees in frantic supplication, shrieking*] Bite him

in two, Sphinx: bite him in two. I meant to sacrifice the white cat—I did indeed—I [*Caesar, who has slipped down from the pedestal, touches her on the shoulder*] Ah! [*She buries her head in her arms.*]

CAESAR. Cleopatra: shall I teach you a way to prevent Caesar from eating you?

CLEOPATRA. [*clinging to him piteously.*] Oh do, do, do. I will steal Ftatateeta's jewels and give them to you. I will make the river Nile water your lands twice a year.

CAESAR. Peace, peace, my child. Your gods are afraid of the Romans: you see the Sphinx dare not bite me, nor prevent me carrying you off to Julius Caesar.

CLEOPATRA. [*in pleading murmurings.*] You won't, you won't. You said you wouldn't.

CAESAR. Caesar never eats women.

CLEOPATRA. [*springing up full of hope.*] What!

CAESAR. [*impressively.*] But he eats girls [*she relapses*] and cats. Now you are a silly little girl; and you are descended from the black kitten. You are both a girl and a cat.

CLEOPATRA. [*trembling.*] And will he eat me?

CAESAR. Yes; unless you make him believe that you are a woman.

CLEOPATRA. Oh, you must get a sorcerer to make a woman of me. Are you a sorcerer?

CAESAR. Perhaps. But it will take a long time; and this very night you must stand face to face with Caesar in the palace of your fathers.

CLEOPATRA. No, no. I daren't.

CAESAR. Whatever dread may be in your soul—however terrible Caesar may be to you—you must confront him as a brave woman and a great queen; and you must feel no fear. If your hand shakes: if your voice quavers; then—night and death! [*She moans.*] But if he thinks you worthy to rule, he will set you on the throne by his side and make you the real ruler of Egypt.

CLEOPATRA. [*despairingly.*] No: he will find me out: he will find me out.

CAESAR. [*rather mournfully.*] He is easily deceived by women. Their eyes dazzle him; and he sees them not as they are, but as he wishes them to appear to him.

CLEOPATRA. [*hopefully.*] Then we will cheat him. I will put on Ftatateeta's head-dress; and he will think me quite an old woman.

CAESAR. If you do that he will eat you at one mouthful.

CLEOPATRA. But I will give him a cake with my magic opal and seven hairs of the white cat baked in it; and—

CAESAR. [*abruptly.*] Pah! you are a little fool. He will eat your cake and you too. [*He turns contemptuously from her.*]

CLEOPATRA. [*running after him and clinging to him.*] Oh, please, PLEASE! I will do whatever you tell me. I will be good! I will be your slave. [*Again the terrible bellowing note sounds across the desert, now closer at hand. It is the bucina, the Roman war trumpet.*]

CAESAR. Hark!

CLEOPATRA. [*trembling.*] What was that?

CAESAR. Caesar's voice.

CLEOPATRA. [*pulling at his hand.*] Let us run away. Come. Oh, come.

CAESAR. You are safe with me until you stand on your throne to receive Caesar. Now lead me thither.

CLEOPATRA. [*only too glad to get away.*] I will, I will. [*Again the bucina.*] Oh, come, come, come: the gods are angry. Do you feel the earth shaking?

CAESAR. It is the tread of Caesar's legions.

CLEOPATRA. [*drawing him away.*] This way, quickly. And let us look for the white cat as we go. It is he that has turned you into a Roman.

CAESAR. Incorrigible, oh, incorrigible! Away! [*He follows her, the bucina sounding louder as they steal across the desert. The moonlight wanes: the horizon again shows black against the sky, broken only by the fantastic silhouette of the Sphinx. The sky itself vanishes in darkness, from which there is no relief until the gleam of a distant torch falls on great Egyptian pillars supporting the roof of a majestic corridor. At the further end of this corridor a Nubian slave appears carrying the torch. Caesar, still led by Cleopatra, follows him. They come down the corridor, Caesar peering keenly about at the strange architecture, and at the pillar shadows between which, as the passing torch makes them hurry noiselessly backwards, figures of men with wings and hawks' heads, and vast black marble cats, seem to flit in and out of ambush. Further along, the wall turns a corner and makes a spacious transept in which Caesar sees, on his right, a throne, and behind the throne a door. On each side of the throne is a slender pillar with a lamp on it.*]

CAESAR. What place is this?

CLEOPATRA. This is where I sit on the throne when I am allowed to wear my crown and robes. [*The slave holds his torch to show the throne.*]

CAESAR. Order the slave to light the lamps.

CLEOPATRA. [*shyly.*] Do you think I may?

CAESAR. Of course. You are the Queen. [*She hesitates.*] Go on.

CLEOPATRA. [*timidly, to the slave.*] Light all the lamps.

FTATATEETA. [*suddenly coming from behind the throne.*] Stop. [*The slave stops. She turns sternly to Cleopatra, who quails like a naughty child.*] Who is this you have with you; and how dare you order the lamps to be lighted without my permission? [*Cleopatra is dumb with apprehension.*]

CAESAR. Who is she?

CLEOPATRA. Ftatateeta.

FTATATEETA. [*arrogantly.*] Chief nurse to—

CAESAR. [*cutting her short.*] I speak to the Queen. Be silent. [*To Cleopatra*] Is this how your servants know their places? Send her away; and you [*to the slave*] do as the Queen has bidden. [*The slave lights the lamps. Meanwhile Cleopatra stands hesitating, afraid of Ftatateeta.*] You are the Queen: send her away.

CLEOPATRA. [*cajoling.*] Ftatateeta, dear: you must go away—just for a little.

CAESAR. You are not commanding her to go away: you are begging her. You are no Queen. You will be eaten. Farewell. [*He turns to go.*]

CLEOPATRA. [*clutching him.*] No, no, no. Don't leave me.

CAESAR. A Roman does not stay with queens who are afraid of their slaves.

CLEOPATRA. I am not afraid. Indeed I am not afraid.

FTATATEETA. We shall see who is afraid here. [*Menacingly*] Cleopatra—

CAESAR. On your knees, woman: am I also a child that you dare trifle with me? [*He points to the floor at Cleopatra's feet. Ftatateeta, half cowed, half savage, hesitates. Caesar calls to the Nubian*] Slave. [*The Nubian comes to him.*] Can you cut off a head? [*The Nubian nods and grins ecstatically, showing all his teeth. Caesar takes his sword by the scabbard, ready to offer the hilt to the Nubian, and turns again to Ftatateeta, repeating his gesture.*] Have you remembered yourself, mistress?

[*Ftatateeta, crushed, kneels before Cleopatra, who can hardly believe her eyes.*]

FTATATEETA. [*hoarsely.*] O Queen, forget not thy servant in the days of thy greatness.

CLEOPATRA. [*blazing with excitement.*] Go. Begone. Go away. [*Ftatateeta rises with stooped head, and moves backwards towards the door. Cleopatra watches her submission eagerly, almost clapping her hands, which are trembling. Suddenly she cries*] Give me something to beat her with. [*She snatches a snake-skin from the throne and dashes after Ftatateeta, whirling it like a scourge in the air. Caesar makes a bound and manages to catch her and hold her while Ftatateeta escapes.*]

CAESAR. You scratch, kitten, do you?

CLEOPATRA. [*breaking from him.*] I will beat somebody. I will beat him. [*She attacks the slave.*] There, there, there! [*The slave flies for his life up the corridor and vanishes. She throws the snake-skin away and jumps on the step of the throne with her arms waving, crying*] I am a real Queen at last—a real, real Queen! Cleopatra the Queen! [*Caesar shakes his head dubiously, the advantage of the change seeming open to question from the point of view of the general welfare of Egypt. She turns and looks at him exultantly. Then she jumps down from the step, runs to him, and flings her arms round him rapturously, crying*] Oh, I love you for making me a Queen.

CAESAR. But queens love only kings.

CLEOPATRA. I will make all the men I love kings. I will make you a king. I will have many young kings, with round, strong arms; and when I am tired of them I will whip them to death; but you shall always be my king: my nice, kind, wise, proud old king.

CAESAR. Oh, my wrinkles, my wrinkles! And my child's heart! You will be the most dangerous of all Caesar's conguests.

CLEOPATRA. [*appalled.*] Caesar! I forgot Caesar. [*Anxiously*] You will tell him that I am a Queen, will you not? a real Queen. Listen! [*stealthily coaxing him*] let us run away and hide until Caesar is gone.

CAESAR. If you fear Caesar, you are no true Queen; and though you were to hide beneath a pyramid, he would go straight to it and lift it with one hand. And then—! [*He chops his teeth together.*]

CLEOPATRA. [*trembling.*] Oh!

CAESAR. Be afraid if you dare. [*The note of the bucina resounds again in the distance. She moans with fear. Caesar exalts in it, exclaiming*] Aha! Caesar approaches the throne of Cleopatra. Come: take your place. [*He takes her hand and leads her to the throne. She is too downcast to speak.*] Ho, there, Teetatota. How do you call your slaves?

CLEOPATRA. [*spiritlessly, as she sinks on the throne and cowers there, shaking.*] Clap your hands.

[*He claps his hands. Ftatateeta returns.*]

CAESAR. Bring the Queen's robes, and her crown, and her women; and prepare her.

CLEOPATRA. [*eagerly—recovering herself a little.*] Yes, the Crown, Ftatateeta: I shall wear the crown.

FTATATEETA. For whom must the Queen put on her state?

CAESAR. For a citizen of Rome. A king of kings, Totateeta.

CLEOPATRA. [*stamping at her.*] How dare you ask questions? Go and do as you are told. [*Ftatateeta goes out with a grim smile. Cleopatra goes on eagerly, to Caesar*] Caesar will know that I am a Queen when he sees my crown and robes, will he not?

CAESAR. No. How shall he know that you are not a slave dressed up in the Queen's ornaments?

CLEOPATRA. You must tell him.

CAESAR. He will not ask me. He will know Cleopatra by her pride, her courage, her majesty, and her beauty. [*She looks very doubtful.*] Are you trembling?

CLEOPATRA. [*shivering with dread.*] No, I—I—[*in a very sickly voice*] No.

[*Ftatateeta and three women come in with the regalia.*]

FTATATEETA. Of all the Queen's women, these three alone are left. The rest are fled. [*They begin to deck Cleopatra, who submits, pale and motionless.*]

CAESAR. Good, good. Three are enough. Poor Caesar generally has to dress himself.

FTATATEETA. [*contemptuously.*] The Queen of Egypt is not a Roman barbarian. [*To Cleopatra*] Be brave, my nursling. Hold up your head before this stranger.

CAESAR. [*admiring Cleopatra, and placing the crown on her head.*] Is it sweet or bitter to be a Queen, Cleopatra?

CLEOPATRA. Bitter.

CAESAR. Cast out fear; and you will conquer Caesar. Tota: are the Romans at hand?

FTATATEETA. They are at hand; and the guard has fled.

THE WOMEN. [*wailing subduedly.*] Woe to us!

*[The Nubian comes running down the hall.]*

NUBIAN. The Romans are in the courtyard. [*He bolts through the door. With a shriek, the women fly after him. Ftatateeta's jaw expresses savage resolution: she does not budge. Cleopatra can hardly restrain herself from following them. Caesar grips her wrist, and looks steadfastly at her. She stands like a martyr.*]

CAESAR. The Queen must face Caesar alone. Answer "So be it."

CLEOPATRA. [*white.*] So be it.

CAESAR. [*releasing her.*] Good.

[*A tramp and tumult of armed men is heard. Cleopatra's terror increases. The bucina sounds close at hand, followed by a formidable clangor of trumpets. This is too much for Cleopatra: she utters a cry and darts towards the door. Ftatateeta stops her ruthlessly.*]

FTATATEETA. You are my nursling. You have said "So be it"; and if you die for it, you must make the Queen's word good. [*She hands Cleopatra to Caesar, who takes her back, almost beside herself with apprehension, to the throne.*]

CAESAR. Now, if you quail—! [*He seats himself on the throne.*]

[*She stands on the step, all but unconscious, waiting for death. The Roman soldiers troop in tumultuously through the corridor, headed by their ensign with his eagle, and their bucinator, a burly fellow with his instrument coiled round his body, its brazen bell shaped like the head of a howling wolf. When they reach the transept, they stare in amazement at the throne; dress into ordered rank opposite it; draw their swords and lift them in the air with a shout of HAIL CAESAR. Cleopatra turns and stares wildly at Caesar; grasps the situation; and, with a great sob of relief, falls into his arms.*]

## ACT II

*Alexandria. A hall on the first floor of the Palace, ending in a loggia approached by two steps. Through the arches of the loggia the Mediterranean can be seen, bright in the morning sun. The clean lofty walls, painted with a procession of the Egyptian theocracy, presented in profile as flat ornament, and the absence of mirrors, sham perspectives, stuffy upholstery and textiles, make the place handsome, wholesome, simple and cool, or, as a rich English manufacturer would express it, poor, bare, ridiculous and unhomely. For Tottenham Court Road civilization is to this Egyptian civilization as glass bead and tattoo civilization is to Tottenham Court Road.*

*The young king Ptolemy Dionysus [aged ten] is at the top of the steps, on his way in through the loggia, led by his guardian Pothinus, who has him by the hand. The court is assembled to receive him. It is made up of men and women [some of the women being officials] of various complexions and races, mostly Egyptian; some of them, comparatively fair, from lower Egypt; some, much darker, from upper Egypt; with a few Greeks and Jews. Prominent in a group on Ptolemy's right hand is Theodotus, Ptolemy's tutor. Another group, on Ptolemy's left, is headed by Achillas, the general of Ptolemy's troops. Theodotus is a little old man, whose features are as cramped and wizened as his limbs, except his tall straight forehead, which occupies more space than all the rest of his face. He maintains an air of magpie keenness and profundity, listening to what the others say with the sarcastic vigilance of a philosopher listening to the exercises of his disciples. Achillas is a tall handsome man of thirty-five, with a fine black beard curled like the coat of a poodle. Apparently not a clever man, but distinguished and dignified. Pothinus is a vigorous man of fifty, a eunuch, passionate, energetic and quick witted, but of common mind and character; impatient and unable to control his temper. He has fine tawny hair, like fur. Ptolemy, the King, looks much older than an English boy of ten; but he has the childish air, the habit of being in leading strings, the mixture of impotence and petulance, the appearance of being excessively washed, combed and dressed by other hands, which is exhibited by court-bred princes of all ages.*

*All receive the King with reverences. He comes down the steps to a chair of state which stands a little to his right, the only seat in the hall. Taking his place before it, he looks nervously for instructions to Pothinus, who places himself at his left hand.*

POTHINUS. The King of Egypt has a word to speak.

THEODOTUS. [*in a squeak which he makes impressive by sheer self-opinionativeness.*] Peace for the King's word!

PTOLEMY. [*without any vocal inflexions: he is evidently repeating a lesson.*] Take notice of this all of you. I am the firstborn son of Auletes the Flute Blower who was your King. My sister Berenice drove him from his throne and reigned in his stead but—but [*he hesitates*]—

POTHINUS. [*stealthily prompting.*]—but the gods would not suffer—

PTOLEMY. Yes—the gods would not suffer—not suffer [*he stops; then, crestfallen*] I forget what the gods would not suffer.

THEODOTUS. Let Pothinus, the King's guardian, speak for the King.

POTHINUS. [*suppressing his impatience with difficulty.*] The King wished to say that the gods would not suffer the impiety of his sister to go unpunished.

PTOLEMY. [*hastily.*] Yes: I remember the rest of it. [*He resumes his monotone.*] Therefore the gods sent a stranger, one Mark Antony, a Roman captain of horsemen, across the sands of the desert and he set my father again upon the throne. And my father took Berenice my sister and struck her head off. And now that my father is dead yet another of his daughters, my sister Cleopatra, would snatch the kingdom from me and reign in my place. But the gods would not suffer [*Pothinus coughs admonitorily*]—the gods—the gods would not suffer—

POTHINUS. [*prompting.*]—will not maintain—

PTOLEMY. Oh yes—will not maintain such iniquity, they will give her head to the axe even as her sister's. But with the help of the witch Ftatateeta she hath cast a spell on the Roman Julius Caesar to make him uphold her false pretence to rule in Egypt. Take notice then that I will not suffer—that I will not suffer—[*pettishly, to Pothinus*]—What is it that I will not suffer?

POTHINUS. [*suddenly exploding with all the force and emphasis of political passion.*] The King will not suffer a foreigner to take from him the throne of our Egypt. [*A shout of applause.*] Tell the King, Achillas, how many soldiers and horsemen follow the Roman?

THEODOTUS. Let the King's general speak!

ACHILLAS. But two Roman legions, O King. Three thousand soldiers and scarce a thousand horsemen.

[*The court breaks into derisive laughter; and a great chattering begins, amid which Rufio, a Roman officer, appears in the loggia. He is a burly, black-bearded man of middle age, very*

*blunt, prompt and rough, with small clear eyes, and plump nose and cheeks, which, however, like the rest of his flesh, are in ironhard condition.*]

RUFIO. [*from the steps.*] Peace, ho! [*The laughter and chatter cease abruptly.*] Caesar approaches.

THEODOTUS. [*with much presence of mind.*] The King permits the Roman commander to enter!

[*Caesar, plainly dressed, but, wearing an oak wreath to conceal his baldness, enters from, the loggia, attended by Britannus, his secretary, a Briton, about forty, tall, solemn, and already slightly bald, with a heavy, drooping, hazel-colored moustache trained so as to lose its ends in a pair of trim whiskers. He is carefully dressed in blue, with portfolio, inkhorn, and reed pen at his girdle. His serious air and sense of the importance of the business in hand is in marked contrast to the kindly interest of Caesar, who looks at the scene, which is new to him, with the frank curiosity of a child, and then turns to the King's chair: Britannus and Rufio posting themselves near the steps at the other side.*]

CAESAR. [*looking at Pothinus and Ptolemy.*] Which is the King? The man or the boy?

POTHINUS. I am Pothinus, the guardian of my lord the King.

CAESAR. [*patting Ptolemy kindly on the shoulder.*] So you are the King. Dull work at your age, eh? [*To Pothinus*] your servant, Pothinus. [*He turns away unconcernedly and comes slowly along the middle of the hall, looking from side to side at the courtiers until he reaches Achillas.*] And this gentleman?

THEODOTUS. Achillas, the King's general.

CAESAR. [*to Achillas, very friendly.*] A general, eh? I am a general myself. But I began too old, too old. Health and many victories, Achillas!

ACHILLAS. As the gods will, Caesar.

CAESAR. [*turning to Theodotus.*] And you, sir, are—?

THEODOTUS. Theodotus, the King's tutor.

CAESAR. You teach men how to be kings, Theodotus. That is very clever of you. [*Looking at the gods on the walls as he turns away from Theodotus and goes up again to Pothinus.*] And this place?

POTHINUS. The council chamber of the chancellors of the King's treasury, Caesar.

CAESAR. Ah! That reminds me. I want some money.

POTHINUS. The King's treasury is poor, Caesar.

CAESAR. Yes: I notice that there is but one chair in it.

RUFIO. [*shouting gruffly.*] Bring a chair there, some of you, for Caesar.

PTOLEMY. [*rising shyly to offer his chair.*] Caesar—

CAESAR. [*kindly.*] No, no, my boy: that is your chair of state. Sit down.

[*He makes Ptolemy sit down again. Meanwhile Rufio, looking about him, sees in the nearest corner an image of the god Ra, represented as a seated man with the head of a hawk. Before the image is a bronze tripod, about as large as a three-legged stool, with a stick of incense burning on it. Rufio, with Roman resourcefulness and indifference to foreign superstitions, promptly seizes the tripod; shakes off the incense; blows away the ash; and dumps it down behind Caesar, nearly in the middle of the hall.*]

RUFIO. Sit on that, Caesar.

[*A shiver runs through the court, followed by a hissing whisper of Sacrilege!*]

CAESAR. [*seating himself.*] Now, Pothinus, to business. I am badly in want of money.

BRITANNUS. [*disapproving of these informal expressions.*] My master would say that there is a lawful debt due to Rome by Egypt, contracted by the King's deceased father to the Triumvirate; and that it is Caesar's duty to his country to require immediate payment.

CAESAR. [*blandly.*] Ah, I forgot. I have not made my companions known here. Pothinus: this is Britannus, my secretary. He is an islander from the western end of the world, a day's voyage from Gaul. [*Britannus bows stiffly.*] This gentleman is Rufio, my comrade in arms. [*Rufio nods.*] Pothinus: I want 1,600 talents.

[*The courtiers, appalled, murmur loudly, and Theodotus and Achillas appeal mutely to one another against so monstrous a demand.*]

POTHINUS. [*aghast.*] Forty million sesterces! Impossible. There is not so much money in the King's treasury.

CAESAR. [*encouragingly.*] Only sixteen hundred talents, Pothinus. Why count it in sesterces? A sestertius is only worth a loaf of bread.

POTHINUS. And a talent is worth a racehorse. I say it is impossible. We have been at strife here, because the King's sister Cleopatra falsely claims his throne. The King's taxes have not been collected for a whole year.

CAESAR. Yes they have, Pothinus. My officers have been collecting them all the morning. [*Renewed whisper and sensation, not without some stifled laughter, among the courtiers.*]

RUFIO. [*bluntly.*] You must pay, Pothinus. Why waste words? You are getting off cheaply enough.

POTHINUS. [*bitterly.*] Is it possible that Caesar, the conqueror of the world, has time to occupy himself with such a trifle as our taxes?

CAESAR. My friend: taxes are the chief business of a conqueror of the world.

POTHINUS. Then take warning, Caesar. This day, the treasures of the temples and the gold of the King's treasury will be sent to the mint to be melted down for our ransom in the sight of the people. They shall see us sitting under bare walls and drinking from wooden cups. And their wrath be on your head, Caesar, if you force us to this sacrilege!

CAESAR. Do not fear, Pothinus: the people know how well wine tastes in wooden cups. In return for your bounty, I will settle this dispute about the throne for you, if you will. What say you?

POTHINUS. If I say no, will that hinder you?

RUFIO. [*defiantly.*] No.

CAESAR. You say the matter has been at issue for a year, Pothinus. May I have ten minutes at it?

POTHINUS. You will do your pleasure, doubtless.

CAESAR. Good! But first, let us have Cleopatra here.

THEODOTUS. She is not in Alexandria: she is fled into Syria.

CAESAR. I think not. [*To Rufio*] Call Totateeta.

RUFIO. [*calling.*] Ho there, Teetatota.

[*Ftatateeta enters the loggia, and stands arrogantly at the top of the steps.*]

FTATATEETA. Who pronounces the name of Ftatateeta, the Queen's chief nurse?

CAESAR. Nobody can pronounce it, Tota, except yourself. Where is your mistress?

[*Cleopatra, who is hiding behind Ftafateeta, peeps out at them, laughing. Caesar rises.*]

CAESAR. Will the Queen favor us with her presence for a moment?
CLEOPATRA. [*pushing Ftatateeta aside and standing haughtily on the brink of the steps.*] Am I to behave like a Queen?
CAESAR. Yes.

[*Cleopatra immediately comes down to the chair of state; seizes Ptolemy and drags him out of his seat; then takes his place in the chair. Ftatateeta seats herself on the step of the loggia, and sits there, watching the scene with sybilline intensity.*]

PTOLEMY. [*mortified, and struggling with his tears.*] Caesar: this is how she treats me always. If I am a King why is she allowed to take everything from me?
CLEOPATRA. You are not to be King, you little cry-baby. You are to be eaten by the Romans.
CAESAR. [*touched by Ptolemy's distress.*] Come here, my boy, and stand by me.

[*Ptolemy goes over to Caesar, who, resuming his seat on the tripod, takes the boy's hand to encourage him. Cleopatra, furiously jealous, rises and glares at them.*]

CLEOPATRA. [*with flaming cheeks.*] Take your throne: I don't want it. [*She flings away from the chair, and approaches Ptolemy, who shrinks from her.*] Go this instant and sit down in your place.
CAESAR. Go, Ptolemy. Always take a throne when it is offered to you.
RUFIO. I hope you will have the good sense to follow your own advice when we return to Rome, Caesar.

[*Ptolemy slowly goes back to the throne, giving Cleopatra a wide berth, in evident fear of her hands. She takes his place beside Caesar.*]

CAESAR. Pothinus—
CLEOPATRA. [*interrupting him.*] Are you not going to speak to me?

CAESAR. Be quiet. Open your mouth again before I give you leave; and you shall be eaten.

CLEOPATRA. I am not afraid. A queen must not be afraid. Eat my husband there, if you like: he is afraid.

CAESAR. [*starting.*] Your husband! What do you mean?

CLEOPATRA. [*pointing to Ptolemy.*] That little thing.

[*The two Romans and the Briton stare at one another in amazement.*]

THEODOTUS. Caesar: you are a stranger here, and not conversant with our laws. The kings and queens of Egypt may not marry except with their own royal blood. Ptolemy and Cleopatra are born king and consort just as they are born brother and sister.

BRITANNUS. [*shocked.*] Caesar: this is not proper.

THEODOTUS. [*outraged.*] How!

CAESAR. [*recovering his self-possession.*] Pardon him. Theodotus: he is a barbarian, and thinks that the customs of his tribe and island are the laws of nature.

BRITANNUS. On the contrary, Caesar, it is these Egyptians who are barbarians; and you do wrong to encourage them. I say it is a scandal.

CAESAR. Scandal or not, my friend, it opens the gate of peace. [*He rises and addresses Pothinus seriously.*] Pothinus: hear what I propose.

RUFIO. Hear Caesar there.

CAESAR. Ptolemy and Cleopatra shall reign jointly in Egypt.

ACHILLAS. What of the King's younger brother and Cleopatra's younger sister?

RUFIO. [*explaining.*] There is another little Ptolemy, Caesar: so they tell me.

CAESAR. Well, the little Ptolemy can marry the other sister; and we will make them both a present of Cyprus.

POTHINUS. [*impatiently.*] Cyprus is of no use to anybody.

CAESAR. No matter: you shall have it for the sake of peace.

BRITANNUS. [*unconsciously anticipating a later statesman.*] Peace with honor, Pothinus.

POTHINUS. [*mutinously.*] Caesar: be honest. The money you demand is the price of our freedom. Take it; and leave us to settle our own affairs.

THE BOLDER COURTIERS [*encouraged by Pothinus's tone and Caesar's quietness.*] Yes, yes. Egypt for the Egyptians!

[*The conference now becomes an altercation, the Egyptians becoming more and more heated. Caesar remains unruffled; but Rufio grows fiercer and doggeder, and Britannus haughtily indignant.*]

RUFIO. [*contemptuously.*] Egypt for the Egyptians! Do you forget that there is a Roman army of occupation here, left by Aulus Gabinius when he set up your toy king for you?

ACHILLAS. [*suddenly asserting himself.*] And now under my command. I am the Roman general here, Caesar.

CAESAR. [*tickled by the humor of the situation.*] And also the Egyptian general, eh?

POTHINUS. [*triumphantly.*] That is so, Caesar.

CAESAR. [*to Achillas.*] So you can make war on the Egyptians in the name of Rome and on the Romans—on me, if necessary—in the name of Egypt?

ACHILLAS. That is so, Caesar.

CAESAR. And which side are you on at present, if I may presume to ask, general?

ACHILLAS. On the side of the right and of the gods.

CAESAR. Hm! How many men have you?

ACHILLAS. That will appear when I take the field.

RUFIO. [*truculently.*] Are your men Romans? If not, it matters not how many there are, provided you are no stronger than 500 to ten.

POTHINUS. It is useless to try to bluff us, Rufio. Caesar has been defeated before and may be defeated again. A few weeks ago Caesar was flying for his life before Pompey: a few months hence he may be flying for his life before Cato and Juba of Numidia, the African King.

ACHILLAS. [*following up Pothinus's speech menacingly.*] What can you do with 4,000 men?

THEODOTUS. [*following up Achillas's speech with a raucous squeak.*] And without money? Away with you.

ALL THE COURTIERS [*shouting fiercely and crowding towards Caesar.*] Away with you. Egypt for the Egyptians! Begone.

[*Rufio bites his beard, too angry to speak. Caesar sits on comfortably as if he were at breakfast, and the cat were clamoring for a piece of Finnan-haddie.*]

CLEOPATRA. Why do you let them talk to you like that Caesar? Are you afraid?

CAESAR. Why, my dear, what they say is quite true.

CLEOPATRA. But if you go away, I shall not be Queen.

CAESAR. I shall not go away until you are Queen.

POTHINUS. Achillas: if you are not a fool, you will take that girl whilst she is under your hand.

RUFIO. [*daring them.*] Why not take Caesar as well, Achillas?

POTHINUS. [*retorting the defiance with interest.*] Well said, Rufio. Why not?

RUFIO. Try, Achillas. [*Calling*] Guard there.

[*The loggia immediately fills with Caesar's soldiers, who stand, sword in hand, at the top of the steps, waiting the word to charge from their centurion, who carries a cudgel. For a moment the Egyptians face them proudly: then they retire sullenly to their former places.*]

BRITANNUS. You are Caesar's prisoners, all of you.

CAESAR. [*benevolently.*] Oh no, no, no. By no means. Caesar's guests, gentlemen.

CLEOPATRA. Won't you cut their heads off?

CAESAR. What! Cut off your brother's head?

CLEOPATRA. Why not? He would cut off mine, if he got the chance. Wouldn't you, Ptolemy?

PTOLEMY. [*pale and obstinate.*] I would. I will, too, when I grow up.

[*Cleopatra is rent by a struggle between her newly-acquired dignity as a queen, and a strong impulse to put out her tongue at him. She takes no part in the scene which follows, but watches it with curiosity and wonder, fidgeting with the restlessness of a child, and sitting down on Caesar's tripod when he rises.*]

POTHINUS. Caesar: if you attempt to detain us—

RUFIO. He will succeed, Egyptian: make up your mind to that. We hold the palace, the beach, and the eastern harbor. The road to Rome is open; and you shall travel it if Caesar chooses.

CAESAR. [*courteously.*] I could do no less, Pothinus, to secure the retreat of my own soldiers. I am accountable for every life among them. But you are free to go. So are all here, and in the palace.

RUFIO. [*aghast at this clemency.*] What! Renegades and all?

CAESAR. [*softening the expression.*] Roman army of occupation and all, Rufio.

POTHINUS. [*desperately.*] Then I make a last appeal to Caesar's justice. I shall call a witness to prove that but for us, the Roman army of occupation, led by the greatest soldier in the world, would now have Caesar at its mercy. [*Calling through the loggia*] Ho, there, Lucius Septimius [*Caesar starts, deeply moved*]: if my voice can reach you, come forth and testify before Caesar.

CAESAR. [*shrinking.*] No, no.

THEODOTUS. Yes, I say. Let the military tribune bear witness.

[*Lucius Septimius, a clean shaven, trim athlete of about 40, with symmetrical features, resolute mouth, and handsome, thin Roman nose, in the dress of a Roman officer, comes in through the loggia and confronts Caesar, who hides his face with his robe for a moment; then, mastering himself, drops it, and confronts the tribune with dignity.*]

POTHINUS. Bear witness, Lucius Septimius. Caesar came hither in pursuit of his foe. Did we shelter his foe?

LUCIUS. As Pompey's foot touched the Egyptian shore, his head fell by the stroke of my sword.

THEODOTUS. [*with viperish relish.*] Under the eyes of his wife and child! Remember that, Caesar! They saw it from the ship he had just left. We have given you a full and sweet measure of vengeance.

CAESAR. [*with horror.*] Vengeance!

POTHINUS. Our first gift to you, as your galley came into the roadstead, was the head of your rival for the empire of the world. Bear witness, Lucius Septimius: is it not so?

LUCIUS. It is so. With this hand, that slew Pompey, I placed his head at the feet of Caesar.

CAESAR. Murderer! So would you have slain Caesar, had Pompey been victorious at Pharsalia.

LUCIUS. Woe to the vanquished, Caesar! When I served Pompey, I slew as good men as he, only because he conquered them. His turn came at last.

THEODOTUS. [*flatteringly.*] The deed was not yours, Caesar, but ours—nay, mine; for it was done by my counsel. Thanks to us, you keep your reputation for clemency, and have your vengeance too.

CAESAR. Vengeance! Vengeance!! Oh, if I could stoop to vengeance, what would I not exact from you as the price of this murdered

man's blood. [*They shrink back, appalled and disconcerted.*] Was he not my son-in-law, my ancient friend, for 20 years the master of great Rome, for 30 years the compeller of victory? Did not I, as a Roman, share his glory? Was the Fate that forced us to fight for the mastery of the world, of our making? Am I Julius Caesar, or am I a wolf, that you fling to me the grey head of the old soldier, the laurelled conqueror, the mighty Roman, treacherously struck down by this callous ruffian, and then claim my gratitude for it! [*To Lucius Septimius*] Begone: you fill me with horror.

LUCIUS. [*cold and undaunted.*] Pshaw! You have seen severed heads before, Caesar, and severed right hands too, I think; some thousands of them, in Gaul, after you vanquished Vercingetorix. Did you spare him, with all your clemency? Was that vengeance?

CAESAR. No, by the gods! Would that it had been! Vengeance at least is human. No, I say: those severed right hands, and the brave Vercingetorix basely strangled in a vault beneath the Capitol, were [*with shuddering satire*] a wise severity, a necessary protection to the commonwealth, a duty of statesmanship—follies and fictions ten times bloodier than honest vengeance! What a fool was I then! To think that men's lives should be at the mercy of such fools! [*Humbly*] Lucius Septimius, pardon me: why should the slayer of Vercingetorix rebuke the slayer of Pompey? You are free to go with the rest. Or stay if you will: I will find a place for you in my service.

LUCIUS. The odds are against you, Caesar. I go. [*He turns to go out through the loggia.*]

RUFIO. [*full of wrath at seeing his prey escaping.*] That means that he is a Republican.

LUCIUS. [*turning defiantly on the loggia steps.*] And what are you?

RUFIO. A Caesarian, like all Caesar's soldiers.

CAESAR. [*courteously.*] Lucius: believe me, Caesar is no Caesarian. Were Rome a true republic, then were Caesar the first of Republicans. But you have made your choice. Farewell.

LUCIUS. Farewell. Come, Achillas, whilst there is yet time.

[*Caesar, seeing that Rufio's temper threatens to get the worse of him, puts his hand on his shoulder and brings him down the hall out of harm's way, Britannus accompanying them and posting himself on Caesar's right hand. This movement brings the three in a little group to the place occupied by Achillas, who moves haughtily away and joins Theodotus on the other side. Lucius Septimius goes out through the soldiers in the*

*loggia. Pothinus, Theodotus and Achillas follow him with the courtiers, very mistrustful of the soldiers, who close up in their rear and go out after them, keeping them moving without much ceremony. The King is left in his chair, piteous, obstinate, with twitching face and fingers. During these movements Rufio maintains an energetic grumbling, as follows:—*]

RUFIO. [*as Lucius departs.*] Do you suppose he would let us go if he had our heads in his hands?

CAESAR. I have no right to suppose that his ways are any baser than mine.

RUFIO. Psha!

CAESAR. Rufio: if I take Lucius Septimius for my model, and become exactly like him, ceasing to be Caesar, will you serve me still?

BRITANNUS. Caesar: this is not good sense. Your duty to Rome demands that her enemies should be prevented from doing further mischief. [*Caesar, whose delight in the moral eye-to-business of his British secretary is inexhaustible, smiles intelligently.*]

RUFIO. It is no use talking to him, Britannus: you may save your breath to cool your porridge. But mark this, Caesar. Clemency is very well for you; but what is it for your soldiers, who have to fight tomorrow the men you spared yesterday? You may give what orders you please; but I tell you that your next victory will be a massacre, thanks to your clemency. I, for one, will take no prisoners. I will kill my enemies in the field; and then you can preach as much clemency as you please: I shall never have to fight them again. And now, with your leave, I will see these gentry off the premises. [*He turns to go.*]

CAESAR. [*turning also and seeing Ptolemy.*] What! Have they left the boy alone! Oh shame, shame!

RUFIO. [*taking Ptolemy's hand and making him rise.*] Come, your majesty!

PTOLEMY. [*to Caesar, drawing away his hand from Rufio.*] Is he turning me out of my palace?

RUFIO. [*grimly.*] You are welcome to stay if you wish.

CAESAR. [*kindly.*] Go, my boy. I will not harm you; but you will be safer away, among your friends. Here you are in the lion's mouth.

PTOLEMY. [*turning to go.*] It is not the lion I fear, but [*looking at Rufio*] the jackal. [*He goes out through the loggia.*]

CAESAR. [*laughing approvingly.*] Brave boy!

CLEOPATRA. [*jealous of Caesar's approbation, calling after Ptolemy.*] Little silly. You think that very clever.

CAESAR. Britannus: Attend the King. Give him in charge to that Pothinus fellow. [*Britannus goes out after Ptolemy.*]

RUFIO. [*pointing to Cleopatra.*] And this piece of goods? What is to be done with her? However, I suppose I may leave that to you. [*He goes out through the loggia.*]

CLEOPATRA. [*flushing suddenly and turning on Caesar.*] Did you mean me to go with the rest?

CAESAR. [*a little preoccupied, goes with a sigh to Ptolemy's chair, whilst she waits for his answer with red cheeks and clenched fists.*] You are free to do just as you please, Cleopatra.

CLEOPATRA. Then you do not care whether I stay or not?

CAESAR. [*smiling.*] Of course I had rather you stayed.

CLEOPATRA. Much, much rather?

CAESAR. [*nodding.*] Much, much rather.

CLEOPATRA. Then I consent to stay, because I am asked. But I do not want to, mind.

CAESAR. That is quite understood. [*Calling*] Totateeta.

[*Ftatateeta, still seated, turns her eyes on him with a sinister expression, but does not move.*]

CLEOPATRA. [*with a splutter of laughter.*] Her name is not Totateeta: it is Ftatateeta. [*Calling*] Ftatateeta. [*Ftatateeta instantly rises and comes to Cleopatra.*]

CAESAR. [*stumbling over the name.*] Ftatafeeta will forgive the erring tongue of a Roman. Tota: the Queen will hold her state here in Alexandria. Engage women to attend upon her; and do all that is needful.

FTATATEETA. Am I then the mistress of the Queen's household?

CLEOPATRA. [*sharply.*] No: I am the mistress of the Queen's household. Go and do as you are told, or I will have you thrown into the Nile this very afternoon, to poison the poor crocodiles.

CAESAR. [*shocked.*] Oh no, no.

CLEOPATRA. Oh yes, yes. You are very sentimental, Caesar; but you are clever; and if you do as I tell you, you will soon learn to govern.

[*Caesar, quite dumbfounded by this impertinence, turns in his chair and stares at her.*]

[*Ftatateeta, smiling grimly, and showing a splendid set of teeth, goes, leaving them alone together.*]

CAESAR. Cleopatra: I really think I must eat you, after all.

CLEOPATRA. [*kneeling beside him and looking at him with eager interest, half real, half affected to show how intelligent she is.*] You must not talk to me now as if I were a child.

CAESAR. You have been growing up since the Sphinx introduced us the other night; and you think you know more than I do already.

CLFOPATRA [*taken down, and anxious to justify herself.*] No: that would be very silly of me: of course I know that. But, [*suddenly*] are you angry with me?

CAESAR. No.

CLEOPATRA. [*only half believing him.*] Then why are you so thoughtful?

CAESAR. [*rising.*] I have work to do, Cleopatra.

CLEOPATRA. [*drawing back.*] Work! [*Offended*] You are tired of talking to me; and that is your excuse to get away from me.

CAESAR. [*sitting down again to appease her.*] Well, well: another minute. But then—work!

CLFOPATRA. Work! What nonsense! You must remember that you are a King now: I have made you one. Kings don't work.

CAESAR. Oh! Who told you that, little kitten? Eh?

CLEOPATRA. My father was King of Egypt; and he never worked. But he was a great King, and cut off my sister's head because she rebelled against him and took the throne from him.

CAESAR. Well; and how did he get his throne back again?

CLEOPATRA. [*eagerly, her eyes lighting up.*] I will tell you. A beautiful young man, with strong round arms, came over the desert with many horsemen, and slew my sister's husband and gave my father back his throne. [*Wistfully*] I was only twelve then. Oh, I wish he would come again, now that I am a Queen. I would make him my husband.

CAESAR. It might be managed, perhaps; for it was I who sent that beautiful young man to help your father.

CLEOPATRA. [*enraptured.*] You know him!

CAESAR. [*nodding.*] I do.

CLEOPATRA. Has he come with you? [*Caesar shakes his head: she is cruelly disappointed.*] Oh, I wish he had, I wish he had. If only I were a little older; so that he might not think me a mere kitten, as you do! But perhaps that is because you are old. He is many, many years younger than you, is he not?

CAESAR. [*as if swallowing a pill.*] He is somewhat younger.

CLEOPATRA. Would he be my husband, do you think, if I asked him?

CAESAR. Very likely.

CLEOPATRA. But I should not like to ask him. Could you not persuade him to ask me—without knowing that I wanted him to?

CAESAR. [*touched by her innocence of the beautiful young man's character.*] My poor child!

CLEOPATRA. Why do you say that as if you were sorry for me? Does he love anyone else?

CAESAR. I am afraid so.

CLEOPATRA. [*tearfully.*] Then I shall not be his first love.

CAESAR. Not quite the first. He is greatly admired by women.

CLEOPATRA. I wish I could be the first. But if he loves me, I will make him kill all the rest. Tell me: is he still beautiful? Do his strong round arms shine in the sun like marble?

CAESAR. He is in excellent condition—considering how much he eats and drinks.

CLEOPATRA. Oh, you must not say common, earthly things about him; for I love him. He is a god.

CAESAR. He is a great captain of horsemen, and swifter of foot than any other Roman.

CLEOPATRA. What is his real name?

CAESAR. [*puzzled.*] His REAL name?

CLEOPATRA. Yes. I always call him Horus, because Horus is the most beautiful of our gods. But I want to know his real name.

CAESAR. His name is Mark Antony.

CLEOPATRA. [*musically.*] Mark Antony, Mark Antony, Mark Antony! What a beautiful name! [*She throws her arms round Caesar's neck.*] Oh, how I love you for sending him to help my father! Did you love my father very much?

CAESAR. No, my child; but your father, as you say, never worked. I always work. So when he lost his crown he had to promise me 16,000 talents to get it back for him.

CLEOPATRA. Did he ever pay you?

CAESAR. Not in full.

CLEOPATRA. He was quite right: it was too dear. The whole world is not worth 16,000 talents.

CAESAR. That is perhaps true, Cleopatra. Those Egyptians who work paid as much of it as he could drag from them. The rest is still due. But as I most likely shall not get it, I must go back to my work. So you must run away for a little and send my secretary to me.

CLEOPATRA. [*coaxing.*] No: I want to stay and hear you talk about Mark Antony.

CAESAR. But if I do not get to work, Pothinus and the rest of them will cut us off from the harbor; and then the way from Rome will be blocked.

CLEOPATRA. No matter: I don't want you to go back to Rome.

CAESAR. But you want Mark Antony to come from it.

CLEOPATRA. [*springing up.*] Oh yes, yes, yes: I forgot. Go quickly and work, Caesar; and keep the way over the sea open for my Mark Antony. [*She runs out through the loggia, kissing her hand to Mark Antony across the sea.*]

CAESAR. [*going briskly up the middle of the hall to the loggia steps.*] Ho, Britannus. [*He is startled by the entry of a wounded Roman soldier, who confronts him from the upper step.*] What now?

SOLDIER. [*pointing to his bandaged head.*] This, Caesar; and two of my comrades killed in the market place.

CAESAR. [*quiet but attending.*] Ay. Why?

SOLDIER. There is an army come to Alexandria, calling itself the Roman army.

CAESAR. The Roman army of occupation. Ay?

SOLDIER. Commanded by one Achillas.

CAESAR. Well?

SOLDIER. The citizens rose against us when the army entered the gates. I was with two others in the market place when the news came. They set upon us. I cut my way out; and here I am.

CAESAR. Good. I am glad to see you alive. [*Rufio enters the loggia hastily, passing behind the soldier to look out through one of the arches at the quay beneath.*] Rufio, we are besieged.

RUFIO. What! Already?

CAESAR. Now or tomorrow: what does it matter? We shall be besieged.

[*Britannus runs in.*]

BRITANNUS. Caesar—

CAESAR. [*anticipating him.*] Yes: I know. [*Rufio and Britannus come down the hall from the loggia at opposite sides, past Caesar, who waits for a moment near the step to say to the soldier.*] Comrade: give the word to turn out on the beach and stand by the boats. Get your wound attended to. Go. [*The soldier hurries out. Caesar comes down the hall between Rufio and Britannus*] Rufio: we have some ships in the west harbor. Burn them.

RUFIO. [*staring.*] Burn them!!

CAESAR. Take every boat we have in the east harbor, and seize the Pharos—that island with the lighthouse. Leave half our men behind to hold the beach and the quay outside this palace: that is the way home.

RUFIO. [*disapproving strongly.*] Are we to give up the city?

CAESAR. We have not got it, Rufio. This palace we have; and—what is that building next door?

RUFIO. The theatre.

CAESAR. We will have that too: it commands the strand, for the rest, Egypt for the Egyptians!

RUFIO. Well, you know best, I suppose. Is that all?

CAESAR. That is all. Are those ships burnt yet?

RUFIO. Be easy: I shall waste no more time. [*He runs out.*]

BRITANNUS. Caesar: Pothinus demands speech of you. It's my opinion he needs a lesson. His manner is most insolent.

CAESAR. Where is he?

BRITANNUS. He waits without.

CAESAR. Ho there! Admit Pothinus.

[*Pothinus appears in the loggia, and comes down the hall very haughtily to Caesar's left hand.*]

CAESAR. Well, Pothinus?

POTHINUS. I have brought you our ultimatum, Caesar.

CAESAR. Ultimatum! The door was open: you should have gone out through it before you declared war. You are my prisoner now. [*He goes to the chair and loosens his toga.*]

POTHINUS. [*scornfully.*] I your prisoner! Do you know that you are in Alexandria, and that King Ptolemy, with an army outnumbering your little troop a hundred to one, is in possession of Alexandria?

CAESAR. [*unconcernedly taking off his toga and throwing it on the chair.*] Well, my friend, get out if you can. And tell your friends not to kill any more Romans in the market place. Otherwise my soldiers, who do not share my celebrated clemency, will probably kill you. Britannus: Pass the word to the guard; and fetch my armor. [*Britannus runs out. Rufio returns.*] Well?

RUFIO. [*pointing from the loggia to a cloud of smoke drifting over the harbor.*] See there! [*Pothinus runs eagerly up the steps to look out.*]

CAESAR. What, ablaze already! Impossible!

RUFIO. Yes, five good ships, and a barge laden with oil grappled to each. But it is not my doing: the Egyptians have saved me the trouble. They have captured the west harbor.

CAESAR. [*anxiously.*] And the east harbor? The lighthouse, Rufio?

RUFIO. [*with a sudden splutter of raging ill usage, coming down to Caesar and scolding him.*] Can I embark a legion in five minutes? The first cohort is already on the beach. We can do no more. If you want faster work, come and do it yourself?

CAESAR. [*soothing him.*] Good, good. Patience, Rufio, patience.

RUFIO. Patience! Who is impatient here, you or I? Would I be here, if I could not oversee them from that balcony?

CAESAR. Forgive me, Rufio; and [anxiously] hurry them as much as—

[*He is interrupted by an outcry as of an old man in the extremity of misfortune. It draws near rapidly; and Theodotus rushes in, tearing his hair, and squeaking the most lamentable exclamations. Rufio steps back to stare at him, amazed at his frantic condition. Pothinus turns to listen.*]

THEODOTUS. [*on the steps, with uplifted arms.*] Horror unspeakable! Woe, alas! Help!

RUFIO. What now?

CAESAR. [*frowning.*] Who is slain?

THEODOTUS. Slain! Oh, worse than the death of ten thousand men! Loss irreparable to mankind!

RUFIO. What has happened, man?

THEODOTUS. [*rushing down the hall between them.*] The fire has spread from your ships. The first of the seven wonders of the world perishes. The library of Alexandria is in flames.

RUFIO. Psha! [*Quite relieved, he goes up to the loggia and watches the preparations of the troops on the beach.*]

CAESAR. Is that all?

THEODOTUS. [*unable to believe his senses.*] All! Caesar: will you go down to posterity as a barbarous soldier too ignorant to know the value of books?

CAESAR. Theodotus: I am an author myself; and I tell you it is better that the Egyptians should live their lives than dream them away with the help of books.

THEODOTUS. [*kneeling, with genuine literary emotion: the passion of the pedant.*] Caesar: once in ten generations of men, the world gains an immortal book.

CAESAR. [*inflexible.*] If it did not flatter mankind, the common executioner would burn it.

THEODOTUS. Without history, death would lay you beside your meanest soldier.

CAESAR. Death will do that in any case. I ask no better grave.

THEODOTUS. What is burning there is the memory of mankind.

CAESAR. A shameful memory. Let it burn.

THEODOTUS. [*wildly.*] Will you destroy the past?

CAESAR. Ay, and build the future with its ruins. [*Theodotus, in despair, strikes himself on the temples with his fists.*] But harken, Theodotus, teacher of kings: you who valued Pompey's head no more than a shepherd values an onion, and who now kneel to me, with tears in your old eyes, to plead for a few sheepskins scrawled with errors. I cannot spare you a man or a bucket of water just now; but you shall pass freely out of the palace. Now, away with you to Achillas; and borrow his legions to put out the fire. [*He hurries him to the steps.*]

POTHINUS. [*significantly.*] You understand, Theodotus: I remain a prisoner.

THEODOTUS. A prisoner!

CAESAR. Will you stay to talk whilst the memory of mankind is burning? [*Calling through the loggia*] Ho there! Pass Theodotus out. [*To Theodotus*] Away with you.

THEODOTUS. [*to Pothinus.*] I must go to save the library. [*He hurries out.*]

CAESAR. Follow him to the gate, Pothinus. Bid him urge your people to kill no more of my soldiers, for your sake.

POTHINUS. My life will cost you dear if you take it, Caesar. [*He goes out after Theodotus.*]

[*Rufio, absorbed in watching the embarkation, does not notice the departure of the two Egyptians.*]

RUFIO. [*shouting from the loggia to the beach.*] All ready, there?

A CENTURION. [*from below.*] All ready. We wait for Caesar.

CAESAR. Tell them Caesar is coming—the rogues! [*Calling*] Britannicus. [*This magniloquent version of his secretary's name is one of Caesar's jokes. In later years it would have meant, quite seriously and officially, Conqueror of Britain.*]

RUFIO. [*calling down.*] Push off, all except the longboat. Stand by it to embark, Caesar's guard there. [*He leaves the balcony and comes*

*down into the hall.*] Where are those Egyptians? Is this more clemency? Have you let them go?

CAESAR. [*chuckling.*] I have let Theodotus go to save the library. We must respect literature, Rufio.

RUFIO. [*raging.*] Folly on folly's head! I believe if you could bring back all the dead of Spain, Gaul and Thessaly to life, you would do it that we might have the trouble of fighting them over again.

CAESAR. Might not the gods destroy the world if their only thought were to be at peace next year? [*Rufio, out of all patience, turns away in anger. Caesar suddenly grips his sleeve, and adds slyly in his ear.*] Besides, my friend: every Egyptian we imprison means imprisoning two Roman soldiers to guard him. Eh?

RUFIO. Agh! I might have known there was some fox's trick behind your fine talking. [*He gets away from Caesar with an ill-humored shrug, and goes to the balcony for another look at the preparations; finally goes out.*]

CAESAR. Is Britannus asleep? I sent him for my armor an hour ago. [*Calling*] Britannicus, thou British islander. Britannicus!

[*Cleopatra, runs in through the loggia with Caesar's helmet and sword, snatched from Britannus, who follows her with a cuirass and greaves. They come down to Caesar, she to his left hand, Britannus to his right.*]

CLEOPATRA. I am going to dress you, Caesar. Sit down. [*He obeys.*] These Roman helmets are so becoming! [*She takes off his wreath.*] Oh! [*She bursts out laughing at him.*]

CAESAR. What are you laughing at?

CLEOPATRA. You're bald [*beginning with a big B, and ending with a splutter.*]

CAESAR. [*almost annoyed.*] Cleopatra! [*He rises, for the convenience of Britannus, who puts the cuirass on him.*]

CLEOPATRA. So that is why you wear the wreath—to hide it.

BRITANNUS. Peace, Egyptian: they are the bays of the conqueror. [*He buckles the cuirass.*]

CLEOPATRA. Peace, thou: islander! [*To Caesar*] You should rub your head with strong spirits of sugar, Caesar. That will make it grow.

CAESAR. [*with a wry face.*] Cleopatra: do you like to be reminded that you are very young?

CLEOPATRA. [*pouting.*] No.

CAESAR. [*sitting down again, and setting out his leg for Britannus, who kneels to put on his greaves.*] Neither do I like to be reminded

that I am—middle aged. Let me give you ten of my superfluous years. That will make you 26 and leave me only—no matter. Is it a bargain?

CLEOPATRA. Agreed. 26, mind. [*She puts the helmet on him.*] Oh! How nice! You look only about 50 in it!

BRITANNUS. [*Looking up severely at Cleopatra.*] You must not speak in this manner to Caesar.

CLEOPATRA. Is it true that when Caesar caught you on that island, you were painted all over blue?

BRITANNUS. Blue is the color worn by all Britons of good standing. In war we stain our bodies blue; so that though our enemies may strip us of our clothes and our lives, they cannot strip us of our respectability. [*He rises.*]

CLEOPATRA. [*with Caesar's sword.*] Let me hang this on. Now you look splendid. Have they made any statues of you in Rome?

CAESAR. Yes, many statues.

CLEOPATRA. You must send for one and give it to me.

RUFIO. [*coming back into the loggia, more impatient than ever.*] Now Caesar: have you done talking? The moment your foot is aboard there will be no holding our men back: the boats will race one another for the lighthouse.

CAESAR. [*drawing his sword and trying the edge.*] Is this well set to-day, Britannicus? At Pharsalia it was as blunt as a barrel-hoop.

BRITANNUS. It will split one of the Egyptian's hairs to-day, Caesar. I have set it myself.

CLEOPATRA. [*suddenly throwing her arms in terror round Caesar.*] Oh, you are not really going into battle to be killed?

CAESAR. No, Cleopatra. No man goes to battle to be killed.

CLEOPATRA. But they do get killed. My sister's husband was killed in battle. You must not go. Let him go [pointing to Rufio. They all laugh at her.] Oh please, please don't go. What will happen to me if you never come back?

CAESAR. [*gravely.*] Are you afraid?

CLEOPATRA. [*shrinking.*] No.

CAESAR. [*with quiet authority.*] Go to the balcony; and you shall see us take the Pharos. You must learn to look on battles. Go. [*She goes, downcast, and looks out from the balcony.*] That is well. Now, Rufio. March.

CLEOPATRA. [*suddenly clapping her hands.*] Oh, you will not be able to go!

CAESAR. Why? What now?

CLEOPATRA. They are drying up the harbor with buckets—a multitude of soldiers—over there [*pointing out across the sea to her left*]—they are dipping up the water.

RUFIO. [*hastening to look.*] It is true. The Egyptian army! Crawling over the edge of the west harbor like locusts. [*With sudden anger he strides down to Caesar.*] This is your accursed clemency, Caesar. Theodotus has brought them.

CAESAR. [*delighted at his own cleverness.*] I meant him to, Rufio. They have come to put out the fire. The library will keep them busy whilst we seize the lighthouse. Eh? [*He rushes out buoyantly through the loggia, followed by Britannus.*]

RUFIO. [*disgustedly.*] More foxing! Agh! [*He rushes off. A shout from the soldiers announces the appearance of Caesar below.*]

CENTURION. [*below.*] All aboard. Give way there. [*Another shout.*]

CLEOPATRA. [*waving her scarf through the loggia arch.*] Goodbye, goodbye, dear Caesar. Come back safe. Goodbye!

## ACT III

*The edge of the quay in front of the palace, looking out west over the east harbor of Alexandria to Pharos island, just off the end of which, and connected with it by a narrow mole, is the famous lighthouse, a gigantic square tower of white marble diminishing in size storey by storey to the top, on which stands a cresset beacon. The island is joined to the main land by the Heptastadium, a great mole or causeway five miles long bounding the harbor on the south.*

*In the middle of the quay a Roman sentinel stands on guard, pilum in hand, looking out to the lighthouse with strained attention, his left hand shading his eyes. The pilum is a stout wooden shaft 41 feet long, with an iron spit about three feet long fixed in it. The sentinel is so absorbed that he does not notice the approach from the north end of the quay of four Egyptian market porters carrying rolls of carpet, preceded by Ftatateeta and Apollodorus the Sicilian. Apollodorus is a dashing young man of about 24, handsome and debonair, dressed with deliberate aestheticism in the most delicate purples and dove greys, with ornaments of bronze, oxydized silver, and stones of jade and agate. His sword, designed as carefully as a medieval cross, has a blued blade showing through an openwork scabbard of purple leather and filagree. The porters, conducted by Ftatateeta, pass along the quay behind the sentinel to the steps of the palace, where they put down their bales and squat on the ground. Apollodorus does not pass along with them: he halts, amused by the preoccupation of the sentinel.*

APOLLODORUS. [*calling to the sentinel.*] Who goes there, eh?

SENTINEL [*starting violently and turning with his pilum at the charge, revealing himself as a small, wiry, sandy-haired, conscientious young man with an elderly face.*] What's this? Stand. Who are you?

APOLLODORUS. I am Apollodorus the Sicilian. Why, man, what are you dreaming of? Since I came through the lines beyond the theatre there, I have brought my caravan past three sentinels, all so busy staring at the lighthouse that not one of them challenged me. Is this Roman discipline?

SENTINEL. We are not here to watch the land but the water. Caesar has just landed on the Pharos. [*Looking at Ftatateeta*] What have you here? Who is this piece of Egyptian crockery?

FTATATEETA. Apollodorus: rebuke this Roman dog; and bid him bridle his tongue in the presence of Ftatateeta, the mistress of the Queen's household.

APOLLODORUS. My friend: this is a great lady, who stands high with Caesar.

SENTINEL [*not at all impressed, pointing to the carpets.*] And what is all this truck?

APOLLODORUS. Carpets for the furnishing of the Queen's apartments in the palace. I have picked them from the best carpets in the world; and the Queen shall choose the best of my choosing.

SENTINEL. So you are the carpet merchant?

APOLLODORUS. [*hurt.*] My friend: I am a patrician.

SENTINEL. A patrician! A patrician keeping a shop instead of following arms!

APOLLODORUS. I do not keep a shop. Mine is a temple of the arts. I am a worshipper of beauty. My calling is to choose beautiful things for beautiful Queens. My motto is Art for Art's sake.

SENTINEL. That is not the password.

APOLLODORUS. It is a universal password.

SENTINEL. I know nothing about universal passwords. Either give me the password for the day or get back to your shop.

[*Ftatateeta, roused by his hostile tone, steals towards the edge of the quay with the step of a panther, and gets behind him.*]

APOLLODORUS. How if I do neither?

SENTINEL. Then I will drive this pilum through you.

APOLLODORUS. At your service, my friend. [*He draws his sword, and springs to his guard with unruffled grace.*]

FTATATEETA. [*suddenly seizing the sentinel's arms from behind.*] Thrust your knife into the dog's throat, Apollodorus. [*The chivalrous Apollodorus laughingly shakes his head; breaks ground away from the sentinel towards the palace; and lowers his point.*]

SENTINEL [*struggling vainly.*] Curse on you! Let me go. Help ho!

FTATATEETA. [*lifting him from the ground.*] Stab the little Roman reptile. Spit him on your sword.

[*A couple of Roman soldiers, with a centurion, come running along the edge of the quay from the north end. They rescue their comrade, and throw off Ftatateeta, who is sent reeling away on the left hand of the sentinel.*]

CENTURION. [*an unattractive man of fifty, short in his speech and manners, with a vine wood cudgel in his hand.*] How now? What is all this?

FTATATEETA. [*to Apollodorus.*] Why did you not stab him? There was time!

APOLLODORUS. Centurion: I am here by order of the Queen to—

CENTURION. [*interrupting him.*] The Queen! Yes, yes: [*to the sentinel*] pass him in. Pass all these bazaar people in to the Queen, with their goods. But mind you pass no one out that you have not passed in—not even the Queen herself.

SENTINEL. This old woman is dangerous: she is as strong as three men. She wanted the merchant to stab me.

APOLLODORUS. Centurion: I am not a merchant. I am a patrician and a votary of art.

CENTURION. Is the woman your wife?

APOLLODORUS. [*horrified.*] No, no! [*Correcting himself politely*] Not that the lady is not a striking figure in her own way. But [*emphatically*] she is not my wife.

FTATATEETA. [*to the Centurion.*] Roman: I am Ftatateeta, the mistress of the Queen's household.

CENTURION. Keep your hands off our men, mistress; or I will have you pitched into the harbor, though you were as strong as ten men. [*To his men*] To your posts: march! [*He returns with his men the way they came.*]

FTATATEETA. [*looking malignantly after him.*] We shall see whom Isis loves best: her servant Ftatateeta or a dog of a Roman.

SENTINEL [*to Apollodorus, with a wave of his pilum towards the palace.*] Pass in there; and keep your distance. [*Turning to Ftatateeta*] Come within a yard of me, you old crocodile; and I will give you this [*the pilum*] in your jaws.

CLEOPATRA. [*calling from the palace.*] Ftatateeta, Ftatateeta.

FTATATEETA. [*Looking up, scandalized.*] Go from the window, go from the window. There are men here.

CLEOPATRA. I am coming down.

FTATATEETA. [*distracted.*] No, no. What are you dreaming of? O ye gods, ye gods! Apollodorus: bid your men pick up your bales; and in with me quickly.

APOLLODORUS. Obey the mistress of the Queen's household.

FTATATEETA. [*impatiently, as the porters stoop to lift the bales.*] Quick, quick: she will be out upon us. [*Cleopatra comes from the palace and runs across the quay to Ftatateeta.*] Oh that ever I was born!

CLEOPATRA. [*eagerly.*] Ftatateeta: I have thought of something. I want a boat—at once.

FTATATEETA. A boat! No, no: you cannot. Apollodorus: speak to the Queen.

APOLLODORUS. [*gallantly.*] Beautiful Queen: I am Apollodorus the Sicilian, your servant, from the bazaar. I have brought you the three most beautiful Persian carpets in the world to choose from.

CLEOPATRA. I have no time for carpets today. Get me a boat.

FTATATEETA. What whim is this? You cannot go on the water except in the royal barge.

APOLLODORUS. Royalty, Ftatateeta, lies not in the barge but in the Queen. [*To Cleopatra*] The touch of your majesty's foot on the gunwale of the meanest boat in the harbor will make it royal. [*He turns to the harbor and calls seaward*] Ho there, boatman! Pull in to the steps.

CLEOPATRA. Apollodorus: you are my perfect knight; and I will always buy my carpets through you. [*Apollodorus bows joyously. An oar appears above the quay; and the boatman, a bullet-headed, vivacious, grinning fellow, burnt almost black by the sun, comes up a flight of steps from the water on the sentinel's right, oar in hand, and waits at the top.*] Can you row, Apollodorus?

APOLLODORUS. My oars shall be your majesty's wings. Whither shall I row my Queen? To the lighthouse. Come. [*She makes for the steps.*]

SENTINEL [*opposing her with his pilum at the charge.*] Stand. You cannot pass.

CLEOPATRA. [*flushing angrily.*] How dare you? Do you know that I am the Queen?

SENTINEL. I have my orders. You cannot pass.

CLEOPATRA. I will make Caesar have you killed if you do not obey me.

SENTINEL. He will do worse to me if I disobey my officer. Stand back.

CLEOPATRA. Ftatateeta: strangle him.

SENTINEL [*alarmed—looking apprehensively at Ftatateeta, and brandishing his pilum.*] Keep off there.

CLEOPATRA. [*running to Apollodorus.*] Apollodorus: make your slaves help us.

APOLLODORUS. I shall not need their help, lady. [*He draws his sword.*] Now soldier: choose which weapon you will defend yourself with. Shall it be sword against pilum, or sword against sword?

SENTINEL. Roman against Sicilian, curse you. Take that. [*He hurls his pilum at Apollodorus, who drops expertly on one knee. The pilum passes whizzing over his head and falls harmless. Apollodorus, with a cry of triumph, springs up and attacks the sentinel, who draws his sword and defends himself, crying*] Ho there, guard. Help!

[*Cleopatra, half frightened, half delighted, takes refuge near the palace, where the porters are squatting among the bales. The boatman, alarmed, hurries down the steps out of harm's way, but stops, with his head just visible above the edge of the quay, to watch the fight. The sentinel is handicapped by his fear of an attack in the rear from Ftatateeta. His swordsmanship, which is of a rough and ready sort, is heavily taxed, as he has occasionally to strike at her to keep her off between a blow and a guard with Apollodorus. The Centurion returns with several soldiers. Apollodorus springs back towards Cleopatra as this reinforcement confronts him.*]

CENTURION. [*coming to the sentinel's right hand.*] What is this? What now?

SENTINEL [*panting.*] I could do well enough for myself if it weren't for the old woman. Keep her off me: that is all the help I need.

CENTURION. Make your report, soldier. What has happened?

FTATATEETA. Centurion: he would have slain the Queen.

SENTINEL [*bluntly.*] I would, sooner than let her pass. She wanted to take boat, and go—so she said—to the lighthouse. I stopped her, as I was ordered to; and she set this fellow on me. [*He goes to pick up his pilum and returns to his place with it.*]

CENTURION. [*turning to Cleopatra.*] Cleopatra: I am loath to offend you; but without Caesar's express order we dare not let you pass beyond the Roman lines.

APOLLODORUS. Well, Centurion; and has not the lighthouse been within the Roman lines since Caesar landed there?

CLEOPATRA. Yes, yes. Answer that, if you can.

CENTURION. [*to Apollodorus.*] As for you, Apollodorus, you may thank the gods that you are not nailed to the palace door with a pilum for your meddling.

APOLLODORUS. [*urbanely.*] My military friend, I was not born to be slain by so ugly a weapon. When I fall, it will be [*holding up his sword*] by this white queen of arms, the only weapon fit for an artist. And now that you are convinced that we do not want to go

beyond the lines, let me finish killing your sentinel and depart with the Queen.

CENTURION. [*as the sentinel makes an angry demonstration.*] Peace there. Cleopatra. I must abide by my orders, and not by the subtleties of this Sicilian. You must withdraw into the palace and examine your carpets there.

CLEOPATRA. [*pouting.*] I will not: I am the Queen. Caesar does not speak to me as you do. Have Caesar's centurions changed manners with his scullions?

CENTURION. [*sulkily.*] I do my duty. That is enough for me.

APOLLODORUS. Majesty: when a stupid man is doing something he is ashamed of, he always declares that it is his duty.

CENTURION. [*angry.*] Apollodorus—

APOLLODORUS. [*interrupting him with defiant elegance.*] I will make amends for that insult with my sword at fitting time and place. Who says artist, says duelist. [*To Cleopatra*] Hear my counsel, star of the east. Until word comes to these soldiers from Caesar himself, you are a prisoner. Let me go to him with a message from you, and a present; and before the sun has stooped half way to the arms of the sea, I will bring you back Caesar's order of release.

CENTURION. [*sneering at him*], And you will sell the Queen the present, no doubt.

APOLLODORUS. Centurion: the Queen shall have from me, without payment, as the unforced tribute of Sicilian taste to Egyptian beauty, the richest of these carpets for her present to Caesar.

CLEOPATRA. [*exultantly, to the Centurion.*] Now you see what an ignorant common creature you are!

CENTURION. [*curtly.*] Well, a fool and his wares are soon parted [*He turns to his men.*] Two more men to this post here; and see that no one leaves the palace but this man and his merchandize. If he draws his sword again inside the lines, kill him. To your posts. March.

[*He goes out, leaving two auxiliary sentinels with the other.*]

APOLLODORUS. [*with polite goodfellowship.*] My friends: will you not enter the palace and bury our quarrel in a bowl of wine? [*He takes out his purse, jingling the coins in it.*] The Queen has presents for you all.

SENTINEL [*very sulky.*] You heard our orders. Get about your business.

FIRST AUXILIARY. Yes: you ought to know better. Off with you.

SECOND AUXILIARY. [*looking longingly at the purse—this sentinel is a hooknosed man, unlike his comrade, who is squab faced.*] Do not tantalize a poor man.

APOLLODORUS. [*to Cleopatra.*] Pearl of Queens: the Centurion is at hand; and the Roman soldier is incorruptible when his officer is looking. I must carry your word to Caesar.

CLEOPATRA. [*who has been meditating among the carpets.*] Are these carpets very heavy?

APOLLODORUS. It matters not how heavy. There are plenty of porters.

CLEOPATRA. How do they put the carpets into boats? Do they throw them down?

APOLLODORUS. Not into small boats, majesty. It would sink them.

CLEOPATRA. Not into that man's boat, for instance? [*Pointing to the boatman.*]

APOLLODORUS. No. Too small.

CLEOPATRA. But you can take a carpet to Caesar in it if I send one?

APOLLODORUS. Assuredly.

CLEOPATRA. And you will have it carried gently down the steps and take great care of it?

APOLLODORUS. Depend on me.

CLEOPATRA. Great, great care?

APOLLODORUS. More than of my own body.

CLEOPATRA. You will promise me not to let the porters drop it or throw it about?

APOLLODORUS. Place the most delicate glass goblet in the palace in the heart of the roll, Queen; and if it be broken, my head shall pay for it.

CLEOPATRA. Good. Come, Ftatateeta. [*Ftatateeta comes to her. Apollodorus offers to squire them into the palace.*] No, Apollodorus, you must not come. I will choose a carpet for myself. You must wait here. [*She runs into the palace.*]

APOLLODORUS. [*to the porters.*] Follow this lady [*indicating Ftatateeta*]; and obey her.

The porters rise and take up their bales.

FTATATEETA. [*addressing the porters as if they were vermin.*] This way. And take your shoes off before you put your feet on those stairs.

[*She goes in, followed by the porters with the carpets. Meanwhile Apollodorus goes to the edge of the quay and looks out over the harbor. The sentinels keep their eyes on him malignantly.*]

APOLLODORUS. [*addressing the sentinel.*] My friend—

SENTINEL [*rudely.*] Silence there.

FIRST AUXILIARY. Shut your muzzle, you.

SECOND AUXILIARY. [*in a half whisper, glancing apprehensively towards the north end of the quay.*] Can't you wait a bit?

APOLLODORUS. Patience, worthy three-headed donkey. [*They mutter ferociously; but he is not at all intimidated.*] Listen: were you set here to watch me, or to watch the Egyptians?

SENTINEL. We know our duty.

APOLLODORUS. Then why don't you do it? There's something going on over there. [*Pointing southwestward to the mole.*]

SENTINEL [*sulkily.*] I do not need to be told what to do by the like of you.

APOLLODORUS. Blockhead. [*He begins shouting*] Ho there, Centurion. Hoiho!

SENTINEL. Curse your meddling. [*Shouting*] Hoiho! Alarm! Alarm!

FIRST AND SECOND AUXILIARIES. Alarm! alarm! Hoiho!

[*The Centurion comes running in with his guard.*]

CENTURION. What now? Has the old woman attacked you again? [*Seeing Apollodorus*] Are you here still?

APOLLODORUS. [*pointing as before.*] See there. The Egyptians are moving. They are going to recapture the Pharos. They will attack by sea and land: by land along the great mole; by sea from the west harbor. Stir yourselves, my military friends: the hunt is up. [*A clangor of trumpets from several points along the quay.*] Aha! I told you so.

CENTURION. [*quickly.*] The two extra men pass the alarm to the south posts. One man keep guard here. The rest with me—quick.

[*The two auxiliary sentinels run off to the south. The Centurion and his guard run of northward; and immediately afterwards the bucina sounds. The four porters come from the palace carrying a carpet, followed by Ftatateeta.*]

SENTINEL [*handling his pilum apprehensively.*] You again! [*The porters stop.*]

FTATATEETA. Peace, Roman fellow: you are now single-handed. Apollodorus: this carpet is Cleopatra's present to Caesar. It has rolled up in it ten precious goblets of the thinnest Iberian crystal, and a hundred eggs of the sacred blue pigeon. On your honor, let not one of them be broken.

APOLLODORUS. On my head be it. [*To the porters*] Into the boat with them carefully.

[*The porters carry the carpet to the steps.*]

FIRST PORTER. [*looking down at the boat.*] Beware what you do, sir. Those eggs of which the lady speaks must weigh more than a pound apiece. This boat is too small for such a load.

BOATMAN [*excitedly rushing up the steps.*] Oh thou injurious porter! Oh thou unnatural son of a she-camel! [*To Apollodorus*] My boat, sir, hath often carried five men. Shall it not carry your lordship and a bale of pigeons' eggs? [*To the porter*] Thou mangey dromedary, the gods shall punish thee for this envious wickedness.

FIRST PORTER. [*stolidly.*] I cannot quit this bale now to beat thee; but another day I will lie in wait for thee.

APPOLODORUS [*going between them.*] Peace there. If the boat were but a single plank, I would get to Caesar on it.

FTATATEETA. [*anxiously.*] In the name of the gods, Apollodorus, run no risks with that bale.

APOLLODORUS. Fear not, thou venerable grotesque: I guess its great worth. [*To the porters*] Down with it, I say; and gently; or ye shall eat nothing but stick for ten days.

The boatman goes down the steps, followed by the porters with the bale: [*Ftatateeta and Apollodorus watching from the edge.*]

APOLLODORUS. Gently, my sons, my children—[*with sudden alarm*] gently, ye dogs. Lay it level in the stern—so—'tis well.

FTATATEETA. [*screaming down at one of the porters.*] Do not step on it, do not step on it. Oh thou brute beast!

FIRST PORTER. [*ascending.*] Be not excited, mistress: all is well.

FTATATEETA. [*panting.*] All well! Oh, thou hast given my heart a turn! [*She clutches her side, gasping.*]

[*The four porters have now come up and are waiting at the stairhead to be paid.*]

APOLLODORUS. Here, ye hungry ones. [*He gives money to the first porter, who holds it in his hand to show to the others. They crowd*

*greedily to see how much it is, quite prepared, after the Eastern fashion, to protest to heaven against their patron's stinginess. But his liberality overpowers them.*]

FIRST PORTER. O bounteous prince!

SECOND PORTER. O lord of the bazaar!

THIRD PORTER. O favored of the gods!

FOURTH PORTER. O father to all the porters of the market!

SENTINEL [*enviously, threatening them fiercely with his pilum.*] Hence, dogs: off. Out of this. [*They fly before him northward along the quay.*]

APOLLODORUS. Farewell, Ftatateeta. I shall be at the lighthouse before the Egyptians. [*He descends the steps.*]

FTATATEETA. The gods speed thee and protect my nursling!

[*The sentry returns from chasing the porters and looks down at the boat, standing near the stairhead lest Ftatateeta should attempt to escape.*]

APOLLODORUS. [*from beneath, as the boat moves off.*] Farewell, valiant pilum pitcher.

SENTINEL. Farewell shopkeeper.

APOLLODORUS. Ha, ha! Pull, thou brave boatman, pull. So Ho-o-o-o-o! [*He begins to sing in barcarolle measure to the rhythm of the oars*] My heart, my heart, spread out thy wings: Shake off thy heavy load of love— Give me the oars, O son of a snail.

SENTINEL [*threatening Ftatateeta.*] Now mistress: back to your henhouse. In with you.

FTATATEETA. [*falling on her knees and stretching her hands over the waters.*] Gods of the seas, bear her safely to the shore!

SENTINEL. Bear who safely? What do you mean?

FTATATEETA. [*looking darkly at him.*] Gods of Egypt and of Vengeance, let this Roman fool be beaten like a dog by his captain for suffering her to be taken over the waters.

SENTINEL. Accursed one: is she then in the boat? [*He calls over the sea*] Hoiho, there, boatman! Hoiho!

APOLLODORUS. [*singing in the distance.*] My heart, my heart, be whole and free: Love is thine only enemy.

[*Meanwhile Rufio, the morning's fighting done, sits munching dates on a faggot of brushwood outside the door of the lighthouse, which towers gigantic to the clouds on his left. His helmet, full of dates, is between his knees; and a leathern*

[*bottle of wine is by his side. Behind him the great stone pedestal of the lighthouse is shut in from the open sea by a low stone parapet, with a couple of steps in the middle to the broad coping. A huge chain with a hook hangs down from the lighthouse crane above his head. Faggots like the one he sits on lie beneath it ready to be drawn up to feed the beacon.*]

[*Caesar is standing on the step at the parapet looking out anxiously, evidently ill at ease. Britannus comes out of the lighthouse door.*]

RUFIO. Well, my British islander. Have you been up to the top?

BRITANNUS. I have. I reckon it at 200 feet high.

RUFIO. Anybody up there?

BRITANNUS. One elderly Tyrian to work the crane; and his son, a well conducted youth of 14.

RUFIO. [*looking at the chain.*] What! An old man and a boy work that! Twenty men, you mean.

BRITANNUS. Two only, I assure you. They have counterweights, and a machine with boiling water in it which I do not understand: it is not of British design. They use it to haul up barrels of oil and faggots to burn in the brazier on the roof.

RUFIO. But—

BRITANNUS. Excuse me: I came down because there are messengers coming along the mole to us from the island. I must see what their business is. [*He hurries out past the lighthouse.*]

CAESAR. [*coming away from the parapet, shivering and out of sorts.*] Rufio: this has been a mad expedition. We shall be beaten. I wish I knew how our men are getting on with that barricade across the great mole.

RUFIO. [*angrily.*] Must I leave my food and go starving to bring you a report?

CAESAR. [*soothing him nervously.*] No, Rufio, no. Eat, my son. Eat. [*He takes another turn, Rufio chewing dates meanwhile.*] The Egyptians cannot be such fools as not to storm the barricade and swoop down on us here before it is finished. It is the first time I have ever run an avoidable risk. I should not have come to Egypt.

RUFIO. An hour ago you were all for victory.

CAESAR. [*apologetically.*] Yes: I was a fool—rash, Rufio—boyish.

RUFIO. Boyish! Not a bit of it. Here. [*Offering him a handful of dates.*]

CAESAR. What are these for?

RUFIO. To eat. That's what's the matter with you. When a man comes to your age, he runs down before his midday meal. Eat and drink; and then have another look at our chances.

CAESAR. [*taking the dates.*] My age! [*He shakes his head and bites a date.*] Yes, Rufio: I am an old man—worn out now—true, quite true. [*He gives way to melancholy contemplation, and eats another date.*] Achillas is still in his prime: Ptolemy is a boy. [*He eats another date, and plucks up a little.*] Well, every dog has his day; and I have had mine: I cannot complain. [*With sudden cheerfulness*] These dates are not bad, Rufio. [*Britannus returns, greatly excited, with a leathern bag. Caesar is himself again in a moment.*] What now?

BRITANNUS. [*triumphantly.*] Our brave Rhodian mariners have captured a treasure. There! [*He throws the bag down at Caesar's feet.*] Our enemies are delivered into our hands.

CAESAR. In that bag?

BRITANNUS. Wait till you hear, Caesar. This bag contains all the letters which have passed between Pompey's party and the army of occupation here.

CAESAR. Well?

BRITANNUS. [*impatient of Caesar's slowness to grasp the situation.*] Well, we shall now know who your foes are. The name of every man who has plotted against you since you crossed the Rubicon may be in these papers, for all we know.

CAESAR. Put them in the fire.

BRITANNUS. Put them—[*he gasps*]!!!!

CAESAR. In the fire. Would you have me waste the next three years of my life in proscribing and condemning men who will be my friends when I have proved that my friendship is worth more than Pompey's was—than Cato's is. O incorrigible British islander: am I a bull dog, to seek quarrels merely to show how stubborn my jaws are?

BRITANNUS. But your honor—the honor of Rome—

CAESAR. I do not make human sacrifices to my honor, as your Druids do. Since you will not burn these, at least I can drown them. [*He picks up the bag and throws it over the parapet into the sea.*]

BRITANNUS. Caesar: this is mere eccentricity. Are traitors to be allowed to go free for the sake of a paradox?

RUFIO. [*rising.*] Caesar: when the islander has finished preaching, call me again. I am going to have a look at the boiling water machine. [*He goes into the lighthouse.*]

BRITANNUS. [*with genuine feeling.*] O Caesar, my great master, if I could but persuade you to regard life seriously, as men do in my country!

CAESAR. Do they truly do so, Britannus?

BRITANNUS. Have you not been there? Have you not seen them? What Briton speaks as you do in your moments of levity? What Briton neglects to attend the services at the sacred grove? What Briton wears clothes of many colors as you do, instead of plain blue, as all solid, well esteemed men should? These are moral questions with us.

CAESAR. Well, well, my friend: some day I shall settle down and have a blue toga, perhaps. Meanwhile, I must get on as best I can in my flippant Roman way. [*Apollodorus comes past the lighthouse.*] What now?

BRITANNUS. [*turning quickly, and challenging the stranger with official haughtiness.*] What is this? Who are you? How did you come here?

APOLLODORUS. Calm yourself, my friend: I am not going to eat you. I have come by boat, from Alexandria, with precious gifts for Caesar.

CAESAR. From Alexandria!

BRITANNUS. [*severely.*] That is Caesar, sir.

RUFIO. [*appearing at the lighthouse door.*] What's the matter now?

APOLLODORUS. Hail, great Caesar! I am Apollodorus the Sicilian, an artist.

BRITANNUS. An artist! Why have they admitted this vagabond?

CAESAR. Peace, man. Apollodorus is a famous patrician amateur.

BRITANNUS. [*disconcerted.*] I crave the gentleman's pardon. [*To Caesar*] I understood him to say that he was a professional. [*Somewhat out of countenance, he allows Apollodorus to approach Caesar, changing places with him. Rufio, after looking Apollodorus up and down with marked disparagement, goes to the other side of the platform.*]

CAESAR. You are welcome, Apollodorus. What is your business?

APOLLODORUS. First, to deliver to you a present from the Queen of Queens.

CAESAR. Who is that?

APOLLODORUS. Cleopatra of Egypt.

CAESAR. [*taking him into his confidence in his most winning manner.*] Apollodorus: this is no time for playing with presents. Pray you, go back to the Queen, and tell her that if all goes well I shall return to the palace this evening.

APOLLODORUS. Caesar: I cannot return. As I approached the lighthouse, some fool threw a great leathern bag into the sea. It broke the nose of my boat; and I had hardly time to get myself and my charge to the shore before the poor little cockleshell sank.

CAESAR. I am sorry, Apollodorus. The fool shall be rebuked. Well, well: what have you brought me? The Queen will be hurt if I do not look at it.

RUFIO. Have we time to waste on this trumpery? The Queen is only a child.

CAESAR. Just so: that is why we must not disappoint her. What is the present, Apollodorus?

APOLLODORUS. Caesar: it is a Persian carpet—a beauty! And in it are—so I am told—pigeons' eggs and crystal goblets and fragile precious things. I dare not for my head have it carried up that narrow ladder from the causeway.

RUFIO. Swing it up by the crane, then. We will send the eggs to the cook; drink our wine from the goblets; and the carpet will make a bed for Caesar.

APOLLODORUS. The crane! Caesar: I have sworn to tender this bale of carpet as I tender my own life.

CAESAR. [*cheerfully.*] Then let them swing you up at the same time; and if the chain breaks, you and the pigeons' eggs will perish together. [*He goes to the chairs and looks up along it, examining it curiously.*]

APOLLODORUS. [*to Britannus.*] Is Caesar serious?

BRITANNUS. His manner is frivolous because he is an Italian; but he means what he says.

APOLLODORUS. Serious or not, he spoke well. Give me a squad of soldiers to work the crane.

BRITANNUS. Leave the crane to me. Go and await the descent of the chain.

APOLLODORUS. Good. You will presently see me there [*turning to them all and pointing with an eloquent gesture to the sky above the parapet*] rising like the sun with my treasure.

[*He goes back the way he came. Britannus goes into the lighthouse.*]

RUFIO. [*ill-humoredly.*] Are you really going to wait here for this foolery, Caesar?

CAESAR. [*backing away from the crane as it gives signs of working.*] Why not?

RUFIO. The Egyptians will let you know why not if they have the sense to make a rush from the shore end of the mole before our barricade is finished. And here we are waiting like children to see a carpet full of pigeons' eggs.

[*The chain rattles, and is drawn up high enough to clear the parapet. It then swings round out of sight behind the lighthouse.*]

CAESAR. Fear not, my son Rufio. When the first Egyptian takes his first step along the mole, the alarm will sound; and we two will reach the barricade from our end before the Egyptians reach it from their end—we two, Rufio: I, the old man, and you, his biggest boy. And the old man will be there first. So peace; and give me some more dates.

APOLLODORUS. [*from the causeway below.*] So-ho, haul away. So-ho-o-o-o! [*The chain is drawn up and comes round again from behind the lighthouse. Apollodorus is swinging in the air with his bale of carpet at the end of it. He breaks into song as he soars above the parapet.*]
Aloft, aloft, behold the blue
That never shone in woman's eyes
Easy there: stop her. [*He ceases to rise.*] Further round! [*The chain comes forward above the platform.*]

RUFIO. [*calling up.*] Lower away there. [*The chain and its load begin to descend.*]

APOLLODORUS. [*calling up.*] Gently—slowly—mind the eggs.

RUFIO. [*calling up.*] Easy there—slowly—slowly.

[*Apollodorus and the bale are deposited safely on the flags in the middle of the platform. Rufio and Caesar help Apollodorus to cast off the chain from the bale.*]

RUFIO. Haul up.

[*The chain rises clear of their heads with a rattle. Britannus comes from the lighthouse and helps them to uncord the carpet.*]

APOLLODORUS. [*when the cords are loose.*] Stand off, my friends: let Caesar see. [*He throws the carpet open.*]

RUFIO. Nothing but a heap of shawls. Where are the pigeons' eggs?

APOLLODORUS. Approach, Caesar; and search for them among the shawls.

RUFIO. [*drawing his sword.*] Ha, treachery! Keep back, Caesar: I saw the shawl move: there is something alive there.

BRITANNUS. [*drawing his sword.*] It is a serpent.

APOLLODORUS. Dares Caesar thrust his hand into the sack where the serpent moves?

RUFIO. [*turning on him.*] Treacherous dog—

CAESAR. Peace. Put up your swords. Apollodorus: your serpent seems to breathe very regularly. [*He thrusts his hand under the shawls and draws out a bare arm.*] This is a pretty little snake.

RUFIO. [*drawing out the other arm.*] Let us have the rest of you.

[*They pull Cleopatra up by the wrists into a sitting position. Britannus, scandalized, sheathes his sword with a drive of protest.*]

CLEOPATRA. [*gasping.*] Oh, I'm smothered. Oh, Caesar; a man stood on me in the boat; and a great sack of something fell upon me out of the sky; and then the boat sank, and then I was swung up into the air and bumped down.

CAESAR. [*petting her as she rises and takes refuge on his breast.*] Well, never mind: here you are safe and sound at last.

RUFIO. Ay; and now that she is here, what are we to do with her?

BRITANNUS. She cannot stay here, Caesar, without the companionship of some matron.

CLEOPATRA. [*jealously, to Caesar, who is obviously perplexed.*] Aren't you glad to see me?

CAESAR. Yes, yes; I am very glad. But Rufio is very angry; and Britannus is shocked.

CLEOPATRA. [*contemptuously.*] You can have their heads cut off, can you not?

CAESAR. They would not be so useful with their heads cut off as they are now, my sea bird.

RUFIO. [*to Cleopatra.*] We shall have to go away presently and cut some of your Egyptians' heads off. How will you like being left here with the chance of being captured by that little brother of yours if we are beaten?

CLEOPATRA. But you mustn't leave me alone. Caesar you will not leave me alone, will you?

RUFIO. What! Not when the trumpet sounds and all our lives depend on Caesar's being at the barricade before the Egyptians reach it? Eh?

CLEOPATRA. Let them lose their lives: they are only soldiers.

CAESAR. [*gravely.*] Cleopatra: when that trumpet sounds, we must take every man his life in his hand, and throw it in the face of Death. And of my soldiers who have trusted me there is not one whose hand I shall not hold more sacred than your head. [*Cleopatra is overwhelmed. Her eyes fill with tears.*] Apollodorus: you must take her back to the palace.

APOLLODORUS. Am I a dolphin, Caesar, to cross the seas with young ladies on my back? My boat is sunk: all yours are either at the barricade or have returned to the city. I will hail one if I can: that is all I can do. [*He goes back to the causeway.*]

CLEOPATRA. [*struggling with her tears.*] It does not matter. I will not go back. Nobody cares for me.

CAESAR. Cleopatra—

CLEOPATRA. You want me to be killed.

CAESAR. [*still more gravely.*] My poor child: your life matters little here to anyone but yourself. [*She gives way altogether at this, casting herself down on the faggots weeping. Suddenly a great tumult is heard in the distance, bucinas and trumpets sounding through a storm of shouting. Britannus rushes to the parapet and looks along the mole. Caesar and Rufio turn to one another with quick intelligence.*]

CAESAR. Come, Rufio.

CLEOPATRA. [*scrambling to her knees and clinging to him.*] No, no. Do not leave me, Caesar. [*He snatches his skirt from her clutch.*] Oh!

BRITANNUS. [*from the parapet.*] Caesar: we are cut off. The Egyptians have landed from the west harbor between us and the barricade!!!

RUFIO. [*running to see.*] Curses! It is true. We are caught like rats in a trap.

CAESAR. [*ruthfully.*] Rufio, Rufio: my men at the barricade are between the sea party and the shore party. I have murdered them.

RUFIO. [*coming back from the parapet to Caesar's right hand.*] Ay: that comes of fooling with this girl here.

APOLLODORUS. [*coming up quickly from the causeway.*] Look over the parapet, Caesar.

CAESAR. We have looked, my friend. We must defend ourselves here.

APOLLODORUS. I have thrown the ladder into the sea. They cannot get in without it.

RUFIO. Ay; and we cannot get out. Have you thought of that?

APOLLODORUS. Not get out! Why not? You have ships in the east harbor.

BRITANNUS. [*hopefully, at the parapet.*] The Rhodian galleys are standing in towards us already. [*Caesar quickly joins Britannus at the parapet.*]

RUFIO. [*to Apollodorus, impatiently.*] And by what road are we to walk to the galleys, pray?

APOLLODORUS. [*with gay, defiant rhetoric.*] By the road that leads everywhere—the diamond path of the sun and moon. Have you never seen the child's shadow play of The Broken Bridge? "Ducks and geese with ease get over"—eh? [*He throws away his cloak and cap, and binds his sword on his back.*]

RUFIO. What are you talking about?

APOLLODORUS. I will show you. [*Calling to Britannus*] How far off is the nearest galley?

BRITANNUS. Fifty fathom.

CAESAR. No, no: they are further off than they seem in this clear air to your British eyes. Nearly quarter of a mile, Apollodorus.

APOLLODORUS. Good. Defend yourselves here until I send you a boat from that galley.

RUFIO. Have you wings, perhaps?

APOLLODORUS. Water wings, soldier. Behold!

[*He runs up the steps between Caesar and Britannus to the coping of the parapet; springs into the air; and plunges head foremost into the sea.*]

CAESAR. [like a schoolboy—wildly excited.] Bravo, bravo! [Throwing off his cloak] By Jupiter, I will do that too.

RUFIO. [*seizing him.*] You are mad. You shall not.

CAESAR. Why not? Can I not swim as well as he?

RUFIO. [*frantic.*] Can an old fool dive and swim like a young one? He is twenty-five and you are fifty.

CAESAR. [*breaking loose from Rufio.*] Old!!!

BRITANNUS. [*shocked.*] Rufio: you forget yourself.

CAESAR. I will race you to the galley for a week's pay, father Rufio.

CLEOPATRA. But me! Me!! Me!!! What is to become of me?

CAESAR. I will carry you on my back to the galley like a dolphin. Rufio: when you see me rise to the surface, throw her in: I will answer for her. And then in with you after her, both of you.

CLEOPATRA. No, no, no. I shall be drowned.

BRITANNUS. Caesar: I am a man and a Briton, not a fish. I must have a boat. I cannot swim.

CLEOPATRA. Neither can I.

CAESAR. [*to Britannus.*] Stay here, then, alone, until I recapture the lighthouse: I will not forget you. Now, Rufio.

RUFIO. You have made up your mind to this folly?

CAESAR. The Egyptians have made it up for me. What else is there to do? And mind where you jump: I do not want to get your fourteen stone in the small of my back as I come up. [*He runs up the steps and stands on the coping.*]

BRITANNUS. [*anxiously.*] One last word, Caesar. Do not let yourself be seen in the fashionable part of Alexandria until you have changed your clothes.

CAESAR. [*calling over the sea.*] Ho, Apollodorus: [*he points skyward and quotes the barcarolle*]

The white upon the blue above—

APOLLODORUS. [*swimming in the distance*]

Is purple on the green below—

CAESAR. [*exultantly.*] Aha! [*He plunges into the sea.*]

CLEOPATRA. [*running excitedly to the steps.*] Oh, let me see. He will be drowned. [*Rufio seizes her.*] Ah—ah—ah—ah! [*He pitches her screaming into the sea. Rufio and Britannus roar with laughter.*]

RUFIO. [*looking down after her.*] He has got her. [*To Britannus*] Hold the fort, Briton. Caesar will not forget you. [*He springs off.*]

BRITANNUS. [*running to the steps to watch them as they swim.*] All safe, Rufio?

RUFIO. [*swimming.*] All safe.

CAESAR. [*swimming further of.*] Take refuge up there by the beacon; and pile the fuel on the trap door, Britannus.

BRITANNUS. [*calling in reply.*] I will first do so, and then commend myself to my country's gods. [*A sound of cheering from the sea. Britannus gives full vent to his excitement*] The boat has reached him: Hip, hip, hip, hurrah!

# ACT IV

*Cleopatra's sousing in the east harbor of Alexandria was in October 48 B. C. In March 47 she is passing the afternoon in her boudoir in the palace, among a bevy of her ladies, listening to a slave girl who is playing the harp in the middle of the room. The harpist's master, an old musician, with a lined face, prominent brows, white beard, moustache and eyebrows twisted and horned at the ends, and a consciously keen and pretentious expression, is squatting on the floor close to her on her right, watching her performance. Ftatateeta is in attendance near the door, in front of a group of female slaves. Except the harp player all are seated: Cleopatra in a chair opposite the door on the other side of the room; the rest on the ground. Cleopatra's ladies are all young, the most conspicuous being Charmian and Iras, her favorites. Charmian is a hatchet faced, terra cotta colored little goblin, swift in her movements, and neatly finished at the hands and feet. Iras is a plump, goodnatured creature, rather fatuous, with a profusion of red hair, and a tendency to giggle on the slightest provocation.*

CLEOPATRA. Can I—

FTATATEETA. [*insolently, to the player.*] Peace, thou! The Queen speaks. [*The player stops.*]

CLEOPATRA. [*to the old musician.*] I want to learn to play the harp with my own hands. Caesar loves music. Can you teach me?

MUSICIAN. Assuredly I and no one else can teach the Queen. Have I not discovered the lost method of the ancient Egyptians, who could make a pyramid tremble by touching a bass string? All the other teachers are quacks: I have exposed them repeatedly.

CLEOPATRA. Good: you shall teach me. How long will it take?

MUSICIAN. Not very long: only four years. Your Majesty must first become proficient in the philosophy of Pythagoras.

CLEOPATRA. Has she [*indicating the slave*] become proficient in the philosophy of Pythagoras?

MUSICIAN. Oh, she is but a slave. She learns as a dog learns.

CLEOPATRA. Well, then, I will learn as a dog learns; for she plays better than you. You shall give me a lesson every day for a fortnight. [*The musician hastily scrambles to his feet and bows profoundly.*] After that, whenever I strike a false note you shall be flogged; and if I strike so many that there is not time to flog you, you shall be thrown into the Nile to feed the crocodiles. Give the girl a piece of gold; and send them away.

MUSICIAN. [*much taken aback*.] But true art will not be thus forced.

FTATATEETA. [*pushing him out*.] What is this? Answering the Queen, forsooth. Out with you.

[*He is pushed out by Ftatateeta, the girl following with her harp, amid the laughter of the ladies and slaves*.]

CLEOPATRA. Now, can any of you amuse me? Have you any stories or any news?

IRAS. Ftatateeta—

CLEOPATRA. Oh, Ftatateeta, Ftatateeta, always Ftatateeta. Some new tale to set me against her.

IRAS. No: this time Ftatateeta has been virtuous. [*All the ladies laugh—not the slaves*.] Pothinus has been trying to bribe her to let him speak with you.

CLEOPATRA. [*wrathfully*.] Ha! You all sell audiences with me, as if I saw whom you please, and not whom I please. I should like to know how much of her gold piece that harp girl will have to give up before she leaves the palace.

IRAS. We can easily find out that for you.

[*The ladies laugh*.]

CLEOPATRA. [*frowning*.] You laugh; but take care, take care. I will find out some day how to make myself served as Caesar is served.

CHARMIAN. Old hooknose! [*They laugh again*.]

CLEOPATRA. [*revolted*.] Silence. Charmian: do not you be a silly little Egyptian fool. Do you know why I allow you all to chatter impertinently just as you please, instead of treating you as Ftatateeta would treat you if she were Queen?

CHARMIAN. Because you try to imitate Caesar in everything; and he lets everybody say what they please to him.

CLEOPATRA. No; but because I asked him one day why he did so; and he said "Let your women talk; and you will learn something from them." What have I to learn from them? I said. "What they are," said he; and oh! you should have seen his eye as he said it. You would have curled up, you shallow things. [*They laugh. She turns fiercely on Iras*] At whom are you laughing—at me or at Caesar?

IRAS. At Caesar.

CLEOPATRA. If you were not a fool, you would laugh at me; and if you were not a coward you would not be afraid to tell me so.

[*Ftatateeta returns.*] Ftatateeta: they tell me that Pothinus has offered you a bribe to admit him to my presence.

FTATATEETA. [*protesting.*] Now by my father's gods—

CLEOPATRA. [*cutting her short despotically.*] Have I not told you not to deny things? You would spend the day calling your father's gods to witness to your virtues if I let you. Go take the bribe; and bring in Pothinus. [*Ftatateeta is about to reply.*] Don't answer me. Go.

Ftatateeta goes out; and Cleopatra rises and begins to prowl to and fro between her chair and the door, meditating. All rise and stand.

IRAS [*as she reluctantly rises.*] Heigho! I wish Caesar were back in Rome.

CLEOPATRA. [*threateningly.*] It will be a bad day for you all when he goes. Oh, if I were not ashamed to let him see that I am as cruel at heart as my father, I would make you repent that speech! Why do you wish him away?

CHARMIAN. He makes you so terribly prosy and serious and learned and philosophical. It is worse than being religious, at our ages. [*The ladies laugh.*]

CLEOPATRA. Cease that endless cackling, will you. Hold your tongues.

CHARMIAN. [*with mock resignation.*] Well, well: we must try to live up to Caesar.

[*They laugh again. Cleopatra rages silently as she continues to prowl to and fro. Ftatateeta comes back with Pothinus, who halts on the threshold.*]

FTATATEETA. [*at the door.*] Pothinus craves the ear of the—

CLEOPATRA. There, there: that will do: let him come in. [*She resumes her seat. All sit down except Pothinus, who advances to the middle of the room. Ftatateeta takes her former place.*] Well, Pothinus: what is the latest news from your rebel friends?

POTHINUS. [*haughtily.*] I am no friend of rebellion. And a prisoner does not receive news.

CLEOPATRA. You are no more a prisoner than I am—than Caesar is. These six months we have been besieged in this palace by my subjects. You are allowed to walk on the beach among the soldiers. Can I go further myself, or can Caesar?

POTHINUS. You are but a child, Cleopatra, and do not understand these matters.

[*The ladies laugh. Cleopatra looks inscrutably at him.*]

CHARMIAN. I see you do not know the latest news, Pothinus.

POTHINUS. What is that?

CHARMIAN. That Cleopatra is no longer a child. Shall I tell you how to grow much older, and much, much wiser in one day?

POTHINUS. I should prefer to grow wiser without growing older.

CHARMIAN. Well, go up to the top of the lighthouse; and get somebody to take you by the hair and throw you into the sea. [*The ladies laugh.*]

CLEOPATRA. She is right, Pothinus: you will come to the shore with much conceit washed out of you. [*The ladies laugh. Cleopatra rises impatiently.*] Begone, all of you. I will speak with Pothinus alone. Drive them out, Ftatateeta. [*They run out laughing. Ftatateeta shuts the door on them.*] What are you waiting for?

FTATATEETA. It is not meet that the Queen remain alone with—

CLEOPATRA. [*interrupting her.*] Ftatateeta: must I sacrifice you to your father's gods to teach you that I am Queen of Egypt, and not you?

FTATATEETA. [*indignantly.*] You are like the rest of them. You want to be what these Romans call a New Woman. [*She goes out, banging the door.*]

CLEOPATRA. [*sitting down again.*] Now, Pothinus: why did you bribe Ftatateeta to bring you hither?

POTHINUS. [*studying her gravely.*] Cleopatra: what they tell me is true. You are changed.

CLEOPATRA. Do you speak with Caesar every day for six months: and you will be changed.

POTHINUS. It is the common talk that you are infatuated with this old man.

CLEOPATRA. Infatuated? What does that mean? Made foolish, is it not? Oh no: I wish I were.

POTHINUS. You wish you were made foolish! How so?

CLEOPATRA. When I was foolish, I did what I liked, except when Ftatateeta beat me; and even then I cheated her and did it by stealth. Now that Caesar has made me wise, it is no use my liking or disliking; I do what must be done, and have no time to attend to myself. That is not happiness; but it is greatness. If Caesar were gone, I think I could govern the Egyptians; for what Caesar is to me, I am to the fools around me.

POTHINUS. [*looking hard at her.*] Cleopatra: this may be the vanity of youth.

CLEOPATRA. No, no: it is not that I am so clever, but that the others are so stupid.

POTHINUS. [*musingly.*] Truly, that is the great secret.

CLEOPATRA. Well, now tell me what you came to say?

POTHINUS. [*embarrassed.*] I! Nothing.

CLEOPATRA. Nothing!

POTHINUS. At least—to beg for my liberty: that is all.

CLEOPATRA. For that you would have knelt to Caesar. No, Pothinus: you came with some plan that depended on Cleopatra being a little nursery kitten. Now that Cleopatra is a Queen, the plan is upset.

POTHINUS. [*bowing his head submissively.*] It is so.

CLEOPATRA. [*exultant.*] Aha!

POTHINUS. [*raising his eyes keenly to hers.*] Is Cleopatra then indeed a Queen, and no longer Caesar's prisoner and slave?

CLEOPATRA. Pothinus: we are all Caesar's slaves—all we in this land of Egypt—whether we will or no. And she who is wise enough to know this will reign when Caesar departs.

POTHINUS. You harp on Caesar's departure.

CLEOPATRA. What if I do?

POTHINUS. Does he not love you?

CLEOPATRA. Love me! Pothinus: Caesar loves no one. Who are those we love? Only those whom we do not hate: all people are strangers and enemies to us except those we love. But it is not so with Caesar. He has no hatred in him: he makes friends with everyone as he does with dogs and children. His kindness to me is a wonder: neither mother, father, nor nurse have ever taken so much care for me, or thrown open their thoughts to me so freely.

POTHINUS. Well: is not this love?

CLEOPATRA. What! When he will do as much for the first girl he meets on his way back to Rome? Ask his slave, Britannus: he has been just as good to him. Nay, ask his very horse! His kindness is not for anything in me: it is in his own nature.

POTHINUS. But how can you be sure that he does not love you as men love women?

CLEOPATRA. Because I cannot make him jealous. I have tried.

POTHINUS. Hm! Perhaps I should have asked, then, do you love him?

CLEOPATRA. Can one love a god? Besides, I love another Roman: one whom I saw long before Caesar—no god, but a man—one who can love and hate—one whom I can hurt and who would hurt me.

POTHINUS. Does Caesar know this?

CLEOPATRA. Yes

POTHINUS. And he is not angry.

CLEOPATRA. He promises to send him to Egypt to please me!

POTHINUS. I do not understand this man?

CLEOPATRA. [*with superb contempt.*] you understand Caesar! How could you? [*Proudly*] I do—by instinct.

POTHINUS. [*deferentially, after a moment's thought.*] Your Majesty caused me to be admitted to-day. What message has the Queen for me?

CLEOPATRA. This. You think that by making my brother king, you will rule in Egypt, because you are his guardian and he is a little silly.

POTHINUB. The Queen is pleased to say so.

CLEOPATRA. The Queen is pleased to say this also. That Caesar will eat up you, and Achillas, and my brother, as a cat eats up mice; and that he will put on this land of Egypt as a shepherd puts on his garment. And when he has done that, he will return to Rome, and leave Cleopatra here as his viceroy.

POTHINUS. [*breaking out wrathfully.*] That he will never do. We have a thousand men to his ten; and we will drive him and his beggarly legions into the sea.

CLEOPATRA. [*with scorn, getting up to go.*] You rant like any common fellow. Go, then, and marshal your thousands; and make haste; for Mithridates of Pergamos is at hand with reinforcements for Caesar. Caesar has held you at bay with two legions: we shall see what he will do with twenty.

POTHINUS. Cleopatra—

CLEOPATRA. Enough, enough: Caesar has spoiled me for talking to weak things like you. [*She goes out. Pothinus, with a gesture of rage, is following, when Ftatateeta enters and stops him.*]

POTHINUS. Let me go forth from this hateful place.

FTATATEETA. What angers you?

POTHINUS. The curse of all the gods of Egypt be upon her! She has sold her country to the Roman, that she may buy it back from him with her kisses.

FTATATEETA. Fool: did she not tell you that she would have Caesar gone?

POTHINUS. You listened?

FTATATEETA. I took care that some honest woman should be at hand whilst you were with her.

POTHINUS. Now by the gods—

FTATATEETA. Enough of your gods! Caesar's gods are all powerful here. It is no use YOU coming to Cleopatra: you are only an

Egyptian. She will not listen to any of her own race: she treats us all as children.

POTHINUS. May she perish for it!

FTATATEETA. [*balefully*.] May your tongue wither for that wish! Go! send for Lucius Septimius, the slayer of Pompey. He is a Roman: may be she will listen to him. Begone!

POTHINUS. [*darkly*.] I know to whom I must go now.

FTATATEETA. [*suspiciously*.] To whom, then?

POTHINUS. To a greater Roman than Lucius. And mark this, mistress. You thought, before Caesar came, that Egypt should presently be ruled by you and your crew in the name of Cleopatra. I set myself against it.

FTATATEETA. [*interrupting him—wrangling*.] Ay; that it might be ruled by you and YOUR crew in the name of Ptolemy.

POTHINUS. Better me, or even you, than a woman with a Roman heart; and that is what Cleopatra is now become. Whilst I live, she shall never rule. So guide yourself accordingly. [*He goes out*.]

[*It is by this time drawing on to dinner time. The table is laid on the roof of the palace; and thither Rufio is now climbing, ushered by a majestic palace official, wand of office in hand, and followed by a slave carrying an inlaid stool. After many stairs they emerge at last into a massive colonnade on the roof. Light curtains are drawn between the columns on the north and east to soften the westering sun. The official leads Rufio to one of these shaded sections. A cord for pulling the curtains apart hangs down between the pillars.*]

THE OFFICIAL. [*bowing*.] The Roman commander will await Caesar here.

[*The slave sets down the stool near the southernmost column, and slips out through the curtains.*]

RUFIO. [*sitting down, a little blown*.] Pouf! That was a climb. How high have we come?

THE OFFICIAL. We are on the palace roof, O Beloved of Victory!

RUFIO. Good! the Beloved of Victory has no more stairs to get up.

A second official enters from the opposite end, walking backwards.

THE SECOND OFFICIAL. Caesar approaches.

[*Caesar, fresh from the bath, clad in a new tunic of purple silk, comes in, beaming and festive, followed by two slaves carrying a light couch, which is hardly more than an elaborately designed bench. They place it near the northmost of the two curtained columns. When this is done they slip out through the curtains; and the two officials, formally bowing, follow them. Rufio rises to receive Caesar.*]

CAESAR. [*coming over to him.*] Why, Rufio! [*Surveying his dress with an air of admiring astonishment*] A new baldrick! A new golden pommel to your sword! And you have had your hair cut! But not your beard—? Impossible! [*He sniffs at Rufio's beard.*] Yes, perfumed, by Jupiter Olympus!

RUFIO. [*growling.*] Well: is it to please myself?

CAESAR. [*affectionately.*] No, my son Rufio, but to please me—to celebrate my birthday.

RUFIO. [*contemptuously.*] Your birthday! You always have a birthday when there is a pretty girl to be flattered or an ambassador to be conciliated. We had seven of them in ten months last year.

CAESAR. [*contritely.*] It is true, Rufio! I shall never break myself of these petty deceits.

RUFIO. Who is to dine with us—besides Cleopatra?

CAESAR. Apollodorus the Sicilian.

RUFIO. That popinjay!

CAESAR. Come! the popinjay is an amusing dog—tells a story; sings a song; and saves us the trouble of flattering the Queen. What does she care for old politicians and campfed bears like us? No: Apollodorus is good company, Rufio, good company.

RUFIO. Well, he can swim a bit and fence a bit: he might be worse, if he only knew how to hold his tongue.

CAESAR. The gods forbid he should ever learn! Oh, this military life! this tedious, brutal life of action! That is the worst of us Romans: we are mere doers and drudgers: a swarm of bees turned into men. Give me a good talker—one with wit and imagination enough to live without continually doing something!

RUFIO. Ay! a nice time he would have of it with you when dinner was over! Have you noticed that I am before my time?

CAESAR. Aha! I thought that meant something. What is it?

RUFIO. Can we be overheard here?

CAESAR. Our privacy invites eavesdropping. I can remedy that. [*He claps his hands twice. The curtains are drawn, revealing the roof garden with a banqueting table set across in the middle for four*

*persons, one at each end, and two side by side. The side next Caesar and Rufio is blocked with golden wine vessels and basins. A gorgeous major-domo is superintending the laying of the table by a staff of slaves. The colonnade goes round the garden at both sides to the further end, where a gap in it, like a great gateway, leaves the view open to the sky beyond the western edge of the roof, except in the middle, where a life size image of Ra, seated on a huge plinth, towers up, with hawk head and crown of asp and disk. His altar, which stands at his feet, is a single white stone.] Now everybody can see us, nobody will think of listening to us. [He sits down on the bench left by the two slaves.]*

RUFIO. [*sitting down on his stool.*] Pothinus wants to speak to you. I advise you to see him: there is some plotting going on here among the women.

CAESAR. Who is Pothinus?

RUFIO. The fellow with hair like squirrel's fur—the little King's bear leader, whom you kept prisoner.

CAESAR. [*annoyed.*] And has he not escaped?

RUFIO. No.

CAESAR. [*rising imperiously.*] Why not? You have been guarding this man instead of watching the enemy. Have I not told you always to let prisoners escape unless there are special orders to the contrary? Are there not enough mouths to be fed without him?

RUFIO. Yes; and if you would have a little sense and let me cut his throat, you would save his rations. Anyhow, he won't escape. Three sentries have told him they would put a pilum through him if they saw him again. What more can they do? He prefers to stay and spy on us. So would I if I had to do with generals subject to fits of clemency.

CAESAR. [*resuming his seat, argued down.*] Hm! And so he wants to see me.

RUFIO. Ay. I have brought him with me. He is waiting there [*jerking his thumb over his shoulder*] under guard.

CAESAR. And you want me to see him?

RUFIO. [*obstinately.*] I don't want anything. I daresay you will do what you like. Don't put it on to me.

CAESAR. [*with an air of doing it expressly to indulge Rufio.*] Well, well: let us have him.

RUFIO. [*calling.*] Ho there, guard! Release your man and send him up. [*Beckoning*] Come along!

*Pothinus enters and stops mistrustfully between the two, looking from one to the other.*

CAESAR. [*graciously.*] Ah, Pothinus! You are welcome. And what is the news this afternoon?

POTHINUS. Caesar: I come to warn you of a danger, and to make you an offer.

CAESAR. Never mind the danger. Make the offer.

RUFIO. Never mind the offer. What's the danger?

POTHINUS. Caesar: you think that Cleopatra is devoted to you.

CAESAR. [*gravely.*] My friend: I already know what I think. Come to your offer.

POTHINUS. I will deal plainly. I know not by what strange gods you have been enabled to defend a palace and a few yards of beach against a city and an army. Since we cut you off from Lake Mareotis, and you dug wells in the salt sea sand and brought up buckets of fresh water from them, we have known that your gods are irresistible, and that you are a worker of miracles. I no longer threaten you.

RUFIO. [*sarcastically.*] Very handsome of you, indeed.

POTHINUS. So be it: you are the master. Our gods sent the north west winds to keep you in our hands; but you have been too strong for them.

CAESAR. [*gently urging him to come to the point.*] Yes, yes, my friend. But what then?

RUFIO. Spit it out, man. What have you to say?

POTHINUS. I have to say that you have a traitress in your camp. Cleopatra.

THE MAJOR-DOMO. [*at the table, announcing.*] The Queen! [*Caesar and Rufio rise.*]

RUFIO. [*aside to Pothinus.*] You should have spat it out sooner, you fool. Now it is too late.

[*Cleopatra, in gorgeous raiment, enters in state through the gap in the colonnade, and comes down past the image of Ra and past the table to Caesar. Her retinue, headed by Ftatateeta, joins the staff at the table. Caesar gives Cleopatra his seat, which she takes.*]

CLEOPATRA. [*quickly, seeing Pothinus.*] What is he doing here?

CAESAR. [*seating himself beside her, in the most amiable of tempers.*] Just going to tell me something about you. You shall hear it. Proceed, Pothinus.

POTHINUS. [*disconcerted.*] Caesar— [He stammers.]

CAESAR. Well, out with it.

POTHINUS. What I have to say is for your ear, not for the Queen's.

CLEOPATRA. [*with subdued ferocity.*] There are means of making you speak. Take care.

POTHINUS. [*defiantly.*] Caesar does not employ those means.

CAESAR. My friend: when a man has anything to tell in this world, the difficulty is not to make him tell it, but to prevent him from telling it too often. Let me celebrate my birthday by setting you free. Farewell: we'll not meet again.

CLEOPATRA. [*angrily.*] Caesar: this mercy is foolish.

POTHINUS. [*to Caesar.*] Will you not give me a private audience? Your life may depend on it. [*Caesar rises loftily.*]

RUFIO. [*aside to Pothinus.*] Ass! Now we shall have some heroics.

CAESAR. [*oratorically.*] Pothinus—

RUFIO. [*interrupting him.*] Caesar: the dinner will spoil if you begin preaching your favourite sermon about life and death.

CLEOPATRA. [*priggishly.*] Peace, Rufio. I desire to hear Caesar.

RUFIO. [*bluntly.*] Your Majesty has heard it before. You repeated it to Apollodorus last week; and he thought it was all your own. [*Caesar's dignity collapses. Much tickled, he sits down again and looks roguishly at Cleopatra, who is furious. Rufio calls as before*] Ho there, guard! Pass the prisoner out. He is released. [*To Pothinus*] Now off with you. You have lost your chance.

POTHINUS. [*his temper overcoming his prudence.*] I will speak.

CAESAR. [*to Cleopatra.*] You see. Torture would not have wrung a word from him.

POTHINUS. Caesar: you have taught Cleopatra the arts by which the Romans govern the world.

CAESAR. Alas! They cannot even govern themselves. What then?

POTHINUS. What then? Are you so besotted with her beauty that you do not see that she is impatient to reign in Egypt alone, and that her heart is set on your departure?

CLEOPATRA. [*rising.*] Liar!

CAESAR. [*shocked.*] What! Protestations! Contradictions!

CLEOPATRA. [*ashamed, but trembling with suppressed rage.*] No. I do not deign to contradict. Let him talk. [*She sits down again.*]

POTHINUS. From her own lips I have heard it. You are to be her catspaw: you are to tear the crown from her brother's head and set it on her own, delivering us all into her hand—delivering yourself also. And then Caesar can return to Rome, or depart through the gate of death, which is nearer and surer.

CAESAR. [*calmly.*] Well, my friend; and is not this very natural?

POTHINUS. [*astonished.*] Natural! Then you do not resent treachery?

CAESAR. Resent! O thou foolish Egyptian, what have I to do with resentment? Do I resent the wind when it chills me, or the night when it makes me stumble in the darkness? Shall I resent youth when it turns from age, and ambition when it turns from servitude? To tell me such a story as this is but to tell me that the sun will rise tomorrow.

CLEOPATRA. [*unable to contain herself.*] But it is false—false. I swear it.

CAESAR. It is true, though you swore it a thousand times, and believed all you swore. [*She is convulsed with emotion. To screen her, he rises and takes Pothinus to Rufio, saying*] Come, Rufio: let us see Pothinus past the guard. I have a word to say to him. [*Aside to them*] We must give the Queen a moment to recover herself. [*Aloud*] Come. [*He takes Pothinus and Rufio out with him, conversing with them meanwhile.*] Tell your friends, Pothinus, that they must not think I am opposed to a reasonable settlement of the country's affairs—[*They pass out of hearing.*]

CLEOPATRA. [*in a stifled whisper.*] Ftatateeta, Ftatateeta.

FTATATEETA. [*hurrying to her from the table and petting her.*] Peace, child: be comforted—

CLEOPATRA. [*interrupting her.*] Can they hear us?

FTATATEETA. No, dear heart, no.

CLEOPATRA. Listen to me. If he leaves the Palace alive, never see my face again.

FTATATEETA. He? Poth—

CLEOPATRA. [*striking her on the mouth.*] Strike his life out as I strike his name from your lips. Dash him down from the wall. Break him on the stones. Kill, kill, kill him.

FTATATEETA. [*showing all her teeth.*] The dog shall perish.

CLEOPATRA. Fail in this, and you go out from before me forever.

FTATATEETA. [*resolutely.*] So be it. You shall not see my face until his eyes are darkened.

[*Caesar comes back, with Apollodorus, exquisitely dressed, and Rufio.*]

CLEOPATRA. [*to Ftatateeta.*] Come soon—soon. [*Ftatateeta turns her meaning eyes for a moment on her mistress; then goes grimly away past Ra and out. Cleopatra runs like a gazelle to Caesar.*] So you have come back to me, Caesar. [*Caressingly*] I thought you were angry. Welcome, Apollodorus. [*She gives him her hand to kiss, with her other arm about Caesar.*]

APOLLODORUS. Cleopatra grows more womanly beautiful from week to week.

CLEOPATRA. Truth, Apollodorus?

APOLLODORUS. Far, far short of the truth! Friend Rufio threw a pearl into the sea: Caesar fished up a diamond.

CAESAR. Caesar fished up a touch of rheumatism, my friend. Come: to dinner! To dinner! [*They move towards the table.*]

CLEOPATRA. [*skipping like a young fawn.*] Yes, to dinner. I have ordered such a dinner for you, Caesar!

CAESAR. Ay? What are we to have?

CLEOPATRA. Peacocks' brains.

CAESAR. [*as if his mouth watered.*] Peacocks' brains, Apollodorus!

APOLLODORUS. Not for me. I prefer nightingales' tongues. [*He goes to one of the two covers set side by side.*]

CLEOPATRA. Roast boar, Rufio!

RUFIO. [*gluttonously.*] Good! [*He goes to the seat next Apollodorus, on his left.*]

CAESAR. [*looking at his seat, which is at the end of the table, to Ra's left hand.*] What has become of my leathern cushion?

CLEOPATRA. [*at the opposite end.*] I have got new ones for you.

THE MAJOR-DOMO. These cushions, Caesar, are of Maltese gauze, stuffed with rose leaves.

CAESAR. Rose leaves! Am I a caterpillar? [*He throws the cushions away and seats himself on the leather mattress underneath.*]

CLEOPATRA. What a shame! My new cushions!

THE MAJOR-DOMO. [*at Caesar's elbow.*] What shall we serve to whet Caesar's appetite?

CAESAR. What have you got?

THE MAJOR-DOMO. Sea hedgehogs, black and white sea acorns, sea nettles, beccaficoes, purple shellfish—

CAESAR. Any oysters?

THE MAJOR-DOMO. Assuredly.

CAESAR. BRITISH oysters?

THE MAJOR-DOMO. [*assenting.*] British oysters, Caesar.

CAESAR. Oysters, then. [*The Major-Domo signs to a slave at each order; and the slave goes out to execute it.*] I have been in Britain—that western land of romance—the last piece of earth on the edge of the ocean that surrounds the world. I went there in search of its famous pearls. The British pearl was a fable; but in searching for it I found the British oyster.

APOLLODORUS. All posterity will bless you for it. [*To the Major-Domo*] Sea hedgehogs for me.

RUFIO. Is there nothing solid to begin with?

THE MAJOR-DOMO. Fieldfares with asparagus—

CLEOPATRA. [*interrupting.*] Fattened fowls! Have some fattened fowls, Rufio.

RUFIO. Ay, that will do.

CLEOPATRA. [*greedily.*] Fieldfares for me.

THE MAJOR-DOMO. Caesar will deign to choose his wine? Sicilian, Lesbian, Chian—

RUFIO. [*contemptuously.*] All Greek.

APOLLODORUS. Who would drink Roman wine when he could get Greek? Try the Lesbian, Caesar.

CAESAR. Bring me my barley water.

RUFIO. [*with intense disgust.*] Ugh! Bring ME my Falernian. [*The Falernian is presently brought to him.*]

CLEOPATRA. [*pouting.*] It is waste of time giving you dinners, Caesar. My scullions would not condescend to your diet.

CAESAR. [*relenting.*] Well, well: let us try the Lesbian. [*The Major-Domo fills Caesar's goblet; then Cleopatra's and Apollodorus's.*] But when I return to Rome, I will make laws against these extravagances. I will even get the laws carried out.

CLEOPATRA. [*coaxingly.*] Never mind. To-day you are to be like other people: idle, luxurious, and kind. [*She stretches her hand to him along the table.*]

CAESAR. Well, for once I will sacrifice my comfort [*kissing her hand*] there! [*He takes a draught of wine.*] Now are you satisfied?

CLEOPATRA. And you no longer believe that I long for your departure for Rome?

CAESAR. I no longer believe anything. My brains are asleep. Besides, who knows whether I shall return to Rome?

RUFIO. [*alarmed.*] How? Eh? What?

CAESAR. What has Rome to show me that I have not seen already? One year of Rome is like another, except that I grow older, whilst the crowd in the Appian Way is always the same age.

APOLLODORUS. It is no better here in Egypt. The old men, when they are tired of life, say "We have seen everything except the source of the Nile."

CAESAR. [*his imagination catching fire.*] And why not see that? Cleopatra: will you come with me and track the flood to its cradle in the heart of the regions of mystery? Shall we leave Rome behind us—Rome, that has achieved greatness only to learn how greatness destroys nations of men who are not great! Shall I make you a new kingdom, and build you a holy city there in the great unknown?

CLEOPATRA. [*rapturously.*] Yes, Yes. You shall.

RUFIO. Ay: now he will conquer Africa with two legions before we come to the roast boar.

APOLLODORUS. Come: no scoffing, this is a noble scheme: in it Caesar is no longer merely the conquering soldier, but the creative poet-artist. Let us name the holy city, and consecrate it with Lesbian Wine—and Cleopatra shall name it herself.

CLEOPATRA. It shall be called Caesar's Gift to his Beloved.

APOLLODORUS. No, no. Something vaster than that—something universal, like the starry firmament.

CAESAR. [*prosaically.*] Why not simply The Cradle of the Nile?

CLEOPATRA. No: the Nile is my ancestor; and he is a god. Oh! I have thought of something. The Nile shall name it himself. Let us call upon him. [*To the Major-Domo*] Send for him. [*The three men stare at one another; but the Major-Domo goes out as if he had received the most matter-of-fact order.*] And [*to the retinue*] away with you all.

[*The retinue withdraws, making obeisance.*]

[*A priest enters, carrying a miniature sphinx with a tiny tripod before it. A morsel of incense is smoking in the tripod. The priest comes to the table and places the image in the middle of it. The light begins to change to the magenta purple of the Egyptian sunset, as if the god had brought a strange colored shadow with him. The three men are determined not to be impressed; but they feel curious in spite of themselves.*]

CAESAR. What hocus-pocus is this?

CLEOPATRA. You shall see. And it is not hocus-pocus. To do it properly, we should kill something to please him; but perhaps he will answer Caesar without that if we spill some wine to him.

APOLLODORUS. [*turning his head to look up over his shoulder at Ra.*] Why not appeal to our hawkheaded friend here?

CLEOPATRA. [*nervously.*] Sh! He will hear you and be angry.

RUFIO. [*phlegmatically.*] The source of the Nile is out of his district, I expect.

CLEOPATRA. No: I will have my city named by nobody but my dear little sphinx, because it was in its arms that Caesar found me asleep. [*She languishes at Caesar; then turns curtly to the priest.*] Go, I am a priestess, and have power to take your charge from you.

[*The priest makes a reverence and goes out.*] Now let us call on the Nile all together. Perhaps he will rap on the table.

CAESAR. What! Table rapping! Are such superstitions still believed in this year 707 of the Republic?

CLEOPATRA. It is no superstition: our priests learn lots of things from the tables. Is it not so, Apollodorus?

APOLLODORUS. Yes: I profess myself a converted man. When Cleopatra is priestess, Apollodorus is devotee. Propose the conjuration.

CLEOPATRA. You must say with me "Send us thy voice, Father Nile."

ALL FOUR [*holding their glasses together before the idol.*] Send us thy voice, Father Nile.

[*The death cry of a man in mortal terror and agony answers them. Appalled, the men set down their glasses, and listen. Silence. The purple deepens in the sky. Caesar, glancing at Cleopatra, catches her pouring out her wine before the god, with gleaming eyes, and mute assurances of gratitude and worship. Apollodorus springs up and runs to the edge of the roof to peer down and listen.*]

CAESAR. [*looking piercingly at Cleopatra.*] What was that?

CLEOPATRA. [*petulantly.*] Nothing. They are beating some slave.

CAESAR. Nothing!

RUFIO. A man with a knife in him, I'll swear.

CAESAR. [*rising.*] A murder!

APOLLODORUS. [*at the back, waving his hand for silence.*] S-sh! Silence. Did you hear that?

CAESAR. Another cry?

APOLLODORUS. [*returning to the table.*] No, a thud. Something fell on the beach, I think.

RUFIO. [*grimly, as he rises.*] Something with bones in it, eh?

CAESAR. [*shuddering.*] Hush, hush, Rufio. [*He leaves the table and returns to the colonnade: Rufio following at his left elbow, and Apollodorus at the other side.*]

CLEOPATRA. [*still in her place at the table.*] Will you leave me, Caesar? Apollodorus: are you going?

APOLLODORUS. Faith, dearest Queen, my appetite is gone.

CAESAR. Go down to the courtyard, Apollodorus; and find out what has happened.

Apollodorus nods and goes out, making for the staircase by which Rufio ascended.

CLEOPATRA. Your soldiers have killed somebody, perhaps. What does it matter?

[*The murmur of a crowd rises from the beach below. Caesar and Rufio look at one another.*]

CAESAR. This must be seen to. [*He is about to follow Apollodorus when Rufio stops him with a hand on his arm as Ftatateeta comes back by the far end of the roof, with dragging steps, a drowsy satiety in her eyes and in the corners of the bloodhound lips. For a moment Caesar suspects that she is drunk with wine. Not so Rufio: he knows well the red vintage that has inebriated her.*]

RUFIO. [*in a low tone.*] There is some mischief between those two.

FTATATEETA. The Queen looks again on the face of her servant.

[*Cleopatra looks at her for a moment with an exultant reflection of her murderous expression. Then she flings her arms round her; kisses her repeatedly and savagely; and tears off her jewels and heaps them on her. The two men turn from the spectacle to look at one another. Ftatateeta drags herself sleepily to the altar; kneels before Ra; and remains there in prayer. Caesar goes to Cleopatra, leaving Rufio in the colonnade.*]

CAESAR. [*with searching earnestness.*] Cleopatra: what has happened?

CLEOPATRA. [*in mortal dread of him, but with her utmost cajolery.*] Nothing, dearest Caesar. [*With sickly sweetness, her voice almost failing*] Nothing. I am innocent. [*She approaches him affectionately*] Dear Caesar: are you angry with me? Why do you look at me so? I have been here with you all the time. How can I know what has happened?

CAESAR. [*reflectively.*] That is true.

CLEOPATRA. [*greatly relieved, trying to caress him.*] Of course it is true. [*He does not respond to the caress.*] You know it is true, Rufio.

[*The murmur without suddenly swells to a roar and subsides.*]

RUFIO. I shall know presently. [*He makes for the altar in the burly trot that serves him for a stride, and touches Ftatateeta on the shoulder.*] Now, mistress: I shall want you. [*He orders her, with a gesture, to go before him.*]

FTATATEETA. [*rising and glowering at him.*] My place is with the Queen.

CLEOPATRA. She has done no harm, Rufio.

CAESAR. [*to Rufio.*] Let her stay.

RUFIO. [*sitting down on the altar.*] Very well. Then my place is here too; and you can see what is the matter for yourself. The city is in a pretty uproar, it seems.

CAESAR. [*with grave displeasure.*] Rufio: there is a time for obedience.

RUFIO. And there is a time for obstinacy. [*He folds his arms doggedly.*]

CAESAR. [*to Cleopatra.*] Send her away.

CLEOPATRA. [*whining in her eagerness to propitiate him.*] Yes, I will. I will do whatever you ask me, Caesar, always, because I love you. Ftatateeta: go away.

FTATATEETA. The Queen's word is my will. I shall be at hand for the Queen's call. [*She goes out past Ra, as she came.*]

RUFIO. [*following her.*] Remember, Caesar, your bodyguard also is within call. [*He follows her out.*]

[*Cleopatra, presuming upon Caesar's submission to Rufio, leaves the table and sits down on the bench in the colonnade.*]

CLEOPATRA. Why do you allow Rufio to treat you so? You should teach him his place.

CAESAR. Teach him to be my enemy, and to hide his thoughts from me as you are now hiding yours.

CLEOPATRA. [*her fears returning.*] Why do you say that, Caesar? Indeed, indeed, I am not hiding anything. You are wrong to treat me like this. [*She stifles a sob.*] I am only a child; and you turn into stone because you think some one has been killed. I cannot bear it. [*She purposely breaks down and weeps. He looks at her with profound sadness and complete coldness. She looks up to see what effect she is producing. Seeing that he is unmoved, she sits up, pretending to struggle with her emotion and to put it bravely away.*] But there: I know you hate tears: you shall not be troubled with them. I know you are not angry, but only sad; only I am so silly, I cannot help being hurt when you speak coldly. Of course

you are quite right: it is dreadful to think of anyone being killed or even hurt; and I hope nothing really serious has— [*Her voice dies away under his contemptuous penetration.*]

CAESAR. What has frightened you into this? What have you done? [*A trumpet sounds on the beach below.*] Aha! That sounds like the answer.

CLEOPATRA. [*sinking back trembling on the bench and covering her face with her hands.*] I have not betrayed you, Caesar: I swear it.

CAESAR. I know that. I have not trusted you. [*He turns from her, and is about to go out when Apollodorus and Britannus drag in Lucius Septimius to him. Rufio follows. Caesar shudders.*] Again, Pompey's murderer!

RUFIO. The town has gone mad, I think. They are for tearing the palace down and driving us into the sea straight away. We laid hold of this renegade in clearing them out of the courtyard.

CAESAR. Release him. [*They let go his arms.*] What has offended the citizens, Lucius Septimius?

LUCIUS. What did you expect, Caesar? Pothinus was a favorite of theirs.

CAESAR. What has happened to Pothinus? I set him free, here, not half an hour ago. Did they not pass him out?

LUCIUS. Ay, through the gallery arch sixty feet above ground, with three inches of steel in his ribs. He is as dead as Pompey. We are quits now, as to killing—you and I.

CAESAR. [*shocked.*] Assassinated!—our prisoner, our guest! [*He turns reproachfully on Rufio*] Rufio—

RUFIO. [*emphatically—anticipating the question.*] Whoever did it was a wise man and a friend of yours [*Cleopatra is greatly emboldened*]; but none of US had a hand in it. So it is no use to frown at me. [*Caesar turns and looks at Cleopatra.*]

CLEOPATRA. [*violently—rising.*] He was slain by order of the Queen of Egypt. I am not Julius Caesar the dreamer, who allows every slave to insult him. Rufio has said I did well: now the others shall judge me too. [*She turns to the others.*] This Pothinus sought to make me conspire with him to betray Caesar to Achillas and Ptolemy. I refused; and he cursed me and came privily to Caesar to accuse me of his own treachery. I caught him in the act; and he insulted me—me, the Queen! To my face. Caesar would not revenge me: he spoke him fair and set him free. Was I right to avenge myself? Speak, Lucius.

LUCIUS. I do not gainsay it. But you will get little thanks from Caesar for it.

CLEOPATRA. Speak, Apollodorus. Was I wrong?

APOLLODORUS. I have only one word of blame, most beautiful. You should have called upon me, your knight; and in fair duel I should have slain the slanderer.

CLEOPATRA. [*passionately.*] I will be judged by your very slave, Caesar. Britannus: speak. Was I wrong?

BRITANNUS. Were treachery, falsehood, and disloyalty left unpunished, society must become like an arena full of wild beasts, tearing one another to pieces. Caesar is in the wrong.

CAESAR. [*with quiet bitterness.*] And so the verdict is against me, it seems.

CLEOPATRA. [*vehemently.*] Listen to me, Caesar. If one man in all Alexandria can be found to say that I did wrong, I swear to have myself crucified on the door of the palace by my own slaves.

CAESAR. If one man in all the world can be found, now or forever, to know that you did wrong, that man will have either to conquer the world as I have, or be crucified by it. [*The uproar in the streets again reaches them.*] Do you hear? These knockers at your gate are also believers in vengeance and in stabbing. You have slain their leader: it is right that they shall slay you. If you doubt it, ask your four counselors here. And then in the name of that right [*He emphasizes the word with great scorn.*] shall I not slay them for murdering their Queen, and be slain in my turn by their countrymen as the invader of their fatherland? Can Rome do less then than slay these slayers too, to show the world how Rome avenges her sons and her honor? And so, to the end of history, murder shall breed murder, always in the name of right and honor and peace, until the gods are tired of blood and create a race that can understand. [*Fierce uproar. Cleopatra becomes white with terror.*] Hearken, you who must not be insulted. Go near enough to catch their words: you will find them bitterer than the tongue of Pothinus. [*Loftily wrapping himself up in an impenetrable dignity.*] Let the Queen of Egypt now give her orders for vengeance, and take her measures for defense; for she has renounced Caesar. [*He turns to go.*]

CLEOPATRA. [*terrified, running to him and falling on her knees.*] You will not desert me, Caesar. You will defend the palace.

CAESAR. You have taken the powers of life and death upon you. I am only a dreamer.

CLEOPATRA. But they will kill me.

CAESAR. And why not?

CLEOPATRA. In pity—

CAESAR. Pity! What! Has it come to this so suddenly, that nothing can save you now but pity? Did it save Pothinus?

[*She rises, wringing her hands, and goes back to the bench in despair. Apollodorus shows his sympathy with her by quietly posting himself behind the bench. The sky has by this time become the most vivid purple, and soon begins to change to a glowing pale orange, against which the colonnade and the great image show darklier and darklier.*]

RUFIO. Caesar: enough of preaching. The enemy is at the gate.

CAESAR. [*turning on him and giving way to his wrath.*] Ay; and what has held him baffled at the gate all these months? Was it my folly, as you deem it, or your wisdom? In this Egyptian Red Sea of blood, whose hand has held all your heads above the waves? [*Turning on Cleopatra*] And yet, When Caesar says to such an one, "Friend, go free," you, clinging for your little life to my sword, dare steal out and stab him in the back? And you, soldiers and gentlemen, and honest servants as you forget that you are, applaud this assassination, and say "Caesar is in the wrong." By the gods, I am tempted to open my hand and let you all sink into the flood.

CLEOPATRA. [*with a ray of cunning hope.*] But, Caesar, if you do, you will perish yourself.

[*Caesar's eyes blaze.*]

RUFIO. [*greatly alarmed.*] Now, by great Jove, you filthy little Egyptian rat, that is the very word to make him walk out alone into the city and leave us here to be cut to pieces. [*Desperately, to Caesar*] Will you desert us because we are a parcel of fools? I mean no harm by killing: I do it as a dog kills a cat, by instinct. We are all dogs at your heels; but we have served you faithfully.

CAESAR. [*relenting.*] Alas, Rufio, my son, my son: as dogs we are like to perish now in the streets.

APOLLODORUS. [*at his post behind Cleopatra's seat.*] Caesar, what you say has an Olympian ring in it: it must be right; for it is fine art. But I am still on the side of Cleopatra. If we must die, she shall not want the devotion of a man's heart nor the strength of a man's arm.

CLEOPATRA. [*sobbing.*] But I don't want to die.

CAESAR. [*sadly.*] Oh, ignoble, ignoble!

LUCIUS. [*coming forward between Caesar and Cleopatra.*] Hearken to me, Caesar. It may be ignoble; but I also mean to live as long as I can.

CAESAR. Well, my friend, you are likely to outlive Caesar. Is it any magic of mine, think you, that has kept your army and this whole city at bay for so long? Yesterday, what quarrel had they with me that they should risk their lives against me? But to-day we have flung them down their hero, murdered; and now every man of them is set upon clearing out this nest of assassins—for such we are and no more. Take courage then; and sharpen your sword. Pompey's head has fallen; and Caesar's head is ripe.

APOLLODORUS. Does Caesar despair?

CAESAR. [*with infinite pride.*] He who has never hoped can never despair. Caesar, in good or bad fortune, looks his fate in the face.

LUCIUS. Look it in the face, then; and it will smile as it always has on Caesar.

CAESAR. [*with involuntary haughtiness.*] Do you presume to encourage me?

LUCIUS. I offer you my services. I will change sides if you will have me.

CAESAR. [*suddenly coming down to earth again, and looking sharply at him, divining that there is something behind the offer.*] What! At this point?

LUCIUS. [*firmly.*] At this point.

RUFIO. Do you suppose Caesar is mad, to trust you?

LUCIUS. I do not ask him to trust me until he is victorious. I ask for my life, and for a command in Caesar's army. And since Caesar is a fair dealer, I will pay in advance.

CAESAR. Pay! How?

LUCIUS. With a piece of good news for you.

Caesar divines the news in a flash.

RUFIO. What news?

CAESAR. [*with an elate and buoyant energy which makes Cleopatra sit up and stare.*] What news! What news, did you say, my son Rufio? The relief has arrived: what other news remains for us? Is it not so, Lucius Septimius? Mithridates of Pergamos is on the march.

LUCIUS. He has taken Pelusium.

CAESAR. [*delighted.*] Lucius Septimius: you are henceforth my officer. Rufio: the Egyptians must have sent every soldier from the city to prevent Mithridates crossing the Nile. There is nothing in the streets now but mob—mob!

LUCIUS. It is so. Mithridates is marching by the great road to Memphis to cross above the Delta. Achillas will fight him there.

CAESAR. [*all audacity.*] Achillas shall fight Caesar there. See, Rufio. [*He runs to the table; snatches a napkin; and draws a plan on it with his finger dipped in wine, whilst Rufio and Lucius Septimius crowd about him to watch, all looking closely, for the light is now almost gone.*] Here is the palace [*pointing to his plan*]: here is the theatre. You [*to Rufio*] take twenty men and pretend to go by that street [*pointing it out*]; and whilst they are stoning you, out go the cohorts by this and this. My streets are right, are they, Lucius?

LUCIUS. Ay, that is the fig market—

CAESAR. [*too much excited to listen to him.*] I saw them the day we arrived. Good! [*He throws the napkin on the table and comes down again into the colonnade.*] Away, Britannus: tell Petronius that within an hour half our forces must take ship for the western lake. See to my horse and armor. [*Britannus runs out.*] With the rest I shall march round the lake and up the Nile to meet Mithridates. Away, Lucius; and give the word.

[*Lucius hurries out after Britannus.*]

RUFIO. Come: this is something like business.

CAESAR. [*buoyantly.*] Is it not, my only son? [*He claps his hands. The slaves hurry in to the table.*] No more of this mawkish reveling: away with all this stuff: shut it out of my sight and be off with you. [*The slaves begin to remove the table; and the curtains are drawn, shutting in the colonnade.*] You understand about the streets, Rufio?

RUFIO. Ay, I think I do. I will get through them, at all events.

[*The bucina sounds busily in the courtyard beneath.*]

CAESAR. Come, then: we must talk to the troops and hearten them. You down to the beach: I to the courtyard. [*He makes for the staircase.*]

CLEOPATRA. [*rising from her seat, where she has been quite neglected all this time, and stretching out her hands timidly to him.*] Caesar.

CAESAR. [*turning.*] Eh?

CLEOPATRA. Have you forgotten me?

CAESAR. [*indulgently.*] I am busy now, my child, busy. When I return your affairs shall be settled. Farewell; and be good and patient.

[*He goes, preoccupied and quite indifferent. She stands with clenched fists, in speechless rage and humiliation.*]

RUFIO. That game is played and lost, Cleopatra. The woman always gets the worst of it.

CLEOPATRA. [*haughtily.*] Go. Follow your master.

RUFIO. [*in her ear, with rough familiarity.*] A word first. Tell your executioner that if Pothinus had been properly killed—in the throat—he would not have called out. Your man bungled his work.

CLEOPATRA. [*enigmatically.*] How do you know it was a man?

RUFIO. [*startled, and puzzled.*] It was not you: you were with us when it happened. [*She turns her back scornfully on him. He shakes his head, and draws the curtains to go out. It is now a magnificent moonlit night. The table has been removed. Ftatateeta is seen in the light of the moon and stars, again in prayer before the white altar-stone of Ra. Rufio starts; closes the curtains again softly; and says in a low voice to Cleopatra*] Was it she? With her own hand?

CLEOPATRA. [*threateningly.*] Whoever it was, let my enemies beware of her. Look to it, Rufio, you who dare make the Queen of Egypt a fool before Caesar.

RUFIO. [*looking grimly at her.*] I will look to it, Cleopatra. [*He nods in confirmation of the promise, and slips out through the curtains, loosening his sword in its sheath as he goes.*]

ROMAN SOLDIERS [*in the courtyard below.*] Hail, Caesar! Hail, hail!

Cleopatra listens. The bucina sounds again, followed by several trumpets.

CLEOPATRA. [*wringing her hands and calling.*] Ftatateeta. Ftatateeta. It is dark; and I am alone. Come to me. [*Silence.*] Ftatateeta. [*Louder.*] Ftatateeta. [*Silence. In a panic she snatches the cord and pulls the curtains apart.*]

[*Ftatateeta is lying dead on the altar of Ra, with her throat cut. Her blood deluges the white stone.*]

## ACT V

*High noon. Festival and military pageant on the esplanade before the palace. In the east harbor Caesar's galley, so gorgeously decorated that it seems to be rigged with flowers, is along-side the quay, close to the steps Apollodorus descended when he embarked with the carpet. A Roman guard is posted there in charge of a gangway, whence a red floorcloth is laid down the middle of the esplanade, turning off to the north opposite the central gate in the palace front, which shuts in the esplanade on the south side. The broad steps of the gate, crowded with Cleopatra's ladies, all in their gayest attire, are like a flower garden. The facade is lined by her guard, officered by the same gallants to whom Bel Affris announced the coming of Caesar six months before in the old palace on the Syrian border. The north side is lined by Roman soldiers, with the townsfolk on tiptoe behind them, peering over their heads at the cleared esplanade, in which the officers stroll about, chatting. Among these are Belzanor and the Persian; also the Centurion, vinewood cudgel in hand, battle worn, thick-booted, and much outshone, both socially and decoratively, by the Egyptian officers.*

*Apollodorus makes his way through the townsfolk and calls to the officers from behind the Roman line.*

APOLLODORUS. Hullo! May I pass?

CENTURION. Pass Apollodorus the Sicilian there! [*The soldiers let him through.*]

BELZANOR. Is Caesar at hand?

APOLLODORUS. Not yet. He is still in the market place. I could not stand any more of the roaring of the soldiers! After half an hour of the enthusiasm of an army, one feels the need of a little sea air.

PERSIAN. Tell us the news. Hath he slain the priests?

APOLLODORUS. Not he. They met him in the market place with ashes on their heads and their gods in their hands. They placed the gods at his feet. The only one that was worth looking at was Apis: a miracle of gold and ivory work. By my advice he offered the chief priest two talents for it.

BELZANOR. [*appalled.*] Apis the all-knowing for two talents! What said the chief priest?

APOLLODORUS. He invoked the mercy of Apis, and asked for five.

BELZANOR. There will be famine and tempest in the land for this.

PERSIAN. Pooh! Why did not Apis cause Caesar to be vanquished by Achillas? Any fresh news from the war, Apollodorus?

APOLLODORUS. The little King Ptolemy was drowned.

BELZANOR. Drowned! How?

APOLLODORUS. With the rest of them. Caesar attacked them from three sides at once and swept them into the Nile. Ptolemy's barge sank.

BELZANOR. A marvelous man, this Caesar! Will he come soon, think you?

APOLLODORUS. He was settling the Jewish question when I left.

[*A flourish of trumpets from the north, and commotion among the townsfolk, announces the approach of Caesar.*]

PERSIAN. He has made short work of them. Here he comes. [*He hurries to his post in front of the Egyptian lines.*]

BELZANOR. [*following him.*] Ho there! Caesar comes.

[*The soldiers stand at attention, and dress their lines. Apollodorus goes to the Egyptian line.*]

CENTURION. [*hurrying to the gangway guard.*] Attention there! Caesar comes.

[*Caesar arrives in state with Rufio: Britannus following. The soldiers receive him with enthusiastic shouting.*]

RUFIO. [*at his left hand.*] You have not yet appointed a Roman governor for this province.

CAESAR. [*Looking whimsically at him, but speaking with perfect gravity.*] What say you to Mithridates of Pergamos, my reliever and rescuer, the great son of Eupator?

RUFIO. Why, that you will want him elsewhere. Do you forget that you have some three or four armies to conquer on your way home?

CAESAR. Indeed! Well, what say you to yourself?

RUFIO. [*incredulously.*] I! I a governor! What are you dreaming of? Do you not know that I am only the son of a freedman?

CAESAR. [*affectionately.*] Has not Caesar called you his son? [*Calling to the whole assembly*] Peace awhile there; and hear me.

THE ROMAN SOLDIERS. Hear Caesar.

CAESAR. Hear the service, quality, rank and name of the Roman governor. By service, Caesar's shield; by quality, Caesar's friend;

by rank, a Roman soldier. [*The Roman soldiers give a triumphant shout.*] By name, Rufio. [*They shout again.*]

RUFIO. [*kissing Caesar's hand.*] Ay: I am Caesar's shield; but of what use shall I be when I am no longer on Caesar's arm? Well, no matter—[*He becomes husky, and turns away to recover himself.*]

CAESAR. Where is that British Islander of mine?

BRITANNUS. [*coming forward on Caesar's right hand.*] Here, Caesar.

CAESAR. Who bade you, pray, thrust yourself into the battle of the Delta, uttering the barbarous cries of your native land, and affirming yourself a match for any four of the Egyptians, to whom you applied unseemly epithets?

BRITANNUS. Caesar: I ask you to excuse the language that escaped me in the heat of the moment.

CAESAR. And how did you, who cannot swim, cross the canal with us when we stormed the camp?

BRITANNUS. Caesar: I clung to the tail of your horse.

CAESAR. These are not the deeds of a slave, Britannicus, but of a free man.

BRITANNUS. Caesar: I was born free.

CAESAR. But they call you Caesar's slave.

BRITANNUS. Only as Caesar's slave have I found real freedom.

CAESAR. [*moved.*] Well said. Ungrateful that I am, I was about to set you free; but now I will not part from you for a million talents. [*He claps him friendly on the shoulder. Britannus, gratified, but a trifle shamefaced, takes his hand and kisses it sheepishly.*]

BELZANOR. [*to the Persian.*] This Roman knows how to make men serve him.

PERSIAN. Ay: men too humble to become dangerous rivals to him.

BELZANOR. O subtle one! O cynic!

CAESAR. [*seeing Apollodorus in the Egyptian corner and calling to him.*] Apollodorus: I leave the art of Egypt in your charge. Remember: Rome loves art and will encourage it ungrudgingly.

APOLLODORUS. I understand, Caesar. Rome will produce no art itself; but it will buy up and take away whatever the other nations produce.

CAESAR. What! Rome produces no art! Is peace not an art? Is war not an art? Is government not an art? Is civilization not an art? All these we give you in exchange for a few ornaments. You will have the best of the bargain. [*Turning to Rufio*] And now, what else have I to do before I embark? [*Trying to recollect*] There is something I cannot remember: what can it be? Well, well: it must

remain undone: we must not waste this favorable wind. Farewell, Rufio.

RUFIO. Caesar: I am loath to let you go to Rome without your shield. There are too many daggers there.

CAESAR. It matters not: I shall finish my life's work on my way back; and then I shall have lived long enough. Besides: I have always disliked the idea of dying: I had rather be killed. Farewell.

RUFIO. [*with a sigh, raising his hands and giving Caesar up as incorrigible.*] Farewell. [*They shake hands.*]

CAESAR. [*waving his hand to Apollodorus.*] Farewell, Apollodorus, and my friends, all of you. Aboard!

> [*The gangway is run out from the quay to the ship. As Caesar moves towards it, Cleopatra, cold and tragic, cunningly dressed in black, without ornaments or decoration of any kind, and thus making a striking figure among the brilliantly dressed bevy of ladies as she passes through it, comes from the palace and stands on the steps. Caesar does not see her until she speaks.*]

CLEOPATRA. Has Cleopatra no part in this leave taking?

CAESAR. [*enlightened.*] Ah, I knew there was something. [*To Rufio*] How could you let me forget her, Rufio? [*Hastening to her*] Had I gone without seeing you, I should never have forgiven myself. [*He takes her hands, and brings her into the middle of the esplanade. She submits stonily.*] Is this mourning for me?

CLEOPATRA. No.

CAESAR. [*remorsefully.*] Ah, that was thoughtless of me! It is for your brother.

CLEOPATRA. No.

CAESAR. For whom, then?

CLEOPATRA. Ask the Roman governor whom you have left us.

CAESAR. Rufio?

CLEOPATRA. Yes: Rufio. [*She points at him with deadly scorn.*] He who is to rule here in Caesar's name, in Caesar's way, according to Caesar's boasted laws of life.

CAESAR. [*dubiously.*] He is to rule as he can, Cleopatra. He has taken the work upon him, and will do it in his own way.

CLEOPATRA. Not in your way, then?

CAESAR. [*puzzled.*] What do you mean by my way?

CLEOPATRA. Without punishment. Without revenge. Without judgment.

CAESAR. [*approvingly.*] Ay: that is the right way, the great way, the only possible way in the end. [*To Rufio*] Believe it, Rufio, if you can.

RUFIO. Why, I believe it, Caesar. You have convinced me of it long ago. But look you. You are sailing for Numidia to-day. Now tell me: if you meet a hungry lion you will not punish it for wanting to eat you?

CAESAR. [*wondering what he is driving at.*] No.

RUFIO. Nor revenge upon it the blood of those it has already eaten.

CAESAR. No.

RUFIO. Nor judge it for its guiltiness.

CAESAR. No.

RUFIO. What, then, will you do to save your life from it?

CAESAR. [*promptly.*] Kill it, man, without malice, just as it would kill me. What does this parable of the lion mean?

RUFIO. Why, Cleopatra had a tigress that killed men at bidding. I thought she might bid it kill you some day. Well, had I not been Caesar's pupil, what pious things might I not have done to that tigress? I might have punished it. I might have revenged Pothinus on it.

CAESAR. [*interjects.*] Pothinus!

RUFIO. [*continuing.*] I might have judged it. But I put all these follies behind me; and, without malice, only cut its throat. And that is why Cleopatra comes to you in mourning.

CLEOPATRA. [*vehemently.*] He has shed the blood of my servant Ftatateeta. On your head be it as upon his, Caesar, if you hold him free of it.

CAESAR. [*energetically.*] On my head be it, then; for it was well done. Rufio: had you set yourself in the seat of the judge, and with hateful ceremonies and appeals to the gods handed that woman over to some hired executioner to be slain before the people in the name of justice, never again would I have touched your hand without a shudder. But this was natural slaying: I feel no horror at it.

[*Rufio, satisfied, nods at Cleopatra, mutely inviting her to mark that.*]

CLEOPATRA. [*pettish and childish in her impotence.*] No: not when a Roman slays an Egyptian. All the world will now see how unjust and corrupt Caesar is.

CAESAR. [*taking her handy coaxingly.*] Come: do not be angry with me. I am sorry for that poor Totateeta. [*She laughs in spite of herself.*] Aha! You are laughing. Does that mean reconciliation?

CLEOPATRA. [*angry with herself for laughing.*] No, no, no!! But it is so ridiculous to hear you call her Totateeta.

CAESAR. What! As much a child as ever, Cleopatra! Have I not made a woman of you after all?

CLEOPATRA. Oh, it is you, who are a great baby: you make me seem silly because you will not behave seriously. But you have treated me badly; and I do not forgive you.

CAESAR. Bid me farewell.

CLEOPATRA. I will not.

CAESAR. [*coaxing.*] I will send you a beautiful present from Rome.

CLEOPATRA. [*proudly.*] Beauty from Rome to Egypt indeed! What can Rome give me that Egypt cannot give me?

APOLLODORUS. That is true, Caesar. If the present is to be really beautiful, I shall have to buy it for you in Alexandria.

CAESAR. You are forgetting the treasures for which Rome is most famous, my friend. You cannot buy them in Alexandria.

APOLLODORUS. What are they, Caesar?

CAESAR. Her sons. Come, Cleopatra: forgive me and bid me farewell; and I will send you a man, Roman from head to heel and Roman of the noblest; not old and ripe for the knife; not lean in the arms and cold in the heart; not hiding a bald head under his conqueror's laurels; not stooped with the weight of the world on his shoulders; but brisk and fresh, strong and young, hoping in the morning, fighting in the day, and reveling in the evening. Will you take such an one in exchange for Caesar?

CLEOPATRA. [*palpitating.*] His name, his name?

CAESAR. Shall it be Mark Antony? [*She throws herself in his arms.*]

RUFIO. You are a bad hand at a bargain, mistress, if you will swap Caesar for Antony.

CAESAR. So now you are satisfied.

CLEOPATRA. You will not forget.

CAESAR. I will not forget. Farewell: I do not think we shall meet again. Farewell. [*He kisses her on the forehead. She is much affected and begins to sniff. He embarks.*]

THE ROMAN SOLDIERS [*as he sets his foot on the gangway.*] Hail, Caesar; and farewell!

He reaches the ship and returns Rufio's wave of the hand.

APOLLODORUS. [*to Cleopatra.*] No tears, dearest Queen: they stab your servant to the heart. He will return some day.

CLEOPATRA. I hope not. But I can't help crying, all the same. [*She waves her handkerchief to Caesar; and the ship begins to move.*]

THE ROMAN SOLDIERS [*drawing their swords and raising them in the air.*] Hail, Caesar!

THE END

CPSIA information can be obtained
at www.ICGtesting.com
Printed in the USA
BVHW03s2021060818

523557BV00004B/74/P